Rock
&Roll

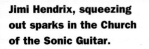

Jimi Hendrix, squeezing out sparks in the Church of the Sonic Guitar.

Rock &Roll

an unruly history

Robert Palmer

Boyle

Harmony Books New York

By the same author:

Deep Blues
A Tale of Two Cities: Memphis Rock and New Orleans Roll
Jerry Lee Lewis Rocks
The Rolling Stones
Baby That Was Rock and Roll: The Legendary Leiber and Stoller

Published by Harmony Books, division of Crown Publishers, 201 East 50th Street, New York, New York 10022. Member of the Crown Publishing Group.

Random House, Inc. New York, Toronto, London, Sydney, Auckland.

Harmony Books and colophon are trademarks of Crown Publishers, Inc.

Manufactured in U.S.A.

Design by Gaye Korbet, Elles Gianocostas, Polly Lockman
WGBH, Boston

Library of Congress Cataloging-in-Publication Data
Palmer, Robert.
      Rock & roll : an unruly history / Robert Palmer
         p.   cm
      Companion book to the PBS television series.
      Discography:
      Includes bibliographical references (p.)
      1. Rock music—History and criticism.   I. Rock & roll
      (Television program) II. Title.
      ML3534.P33   1995
      781.66'09—dc20
      95-13367
      CIP
      MN

ISBN 0-517-70050-6
10 9 8 7 6 5 4 3 2 1
First Edition

This book is dedicated to JoBeth Briton.

Acknowledgments

This unruly history would not have been possible without the resources and the encouragement of a number of people at WGBH-TV in Boston, co-producers with the BBC of the ten-part television history of rock and roll with which the present work is (somewhat loosely) affiliated. I owe them at least two debts: (1) They provided the fruits of their research, including a massive file of interview transcripts; I was able to conduct several of the key interviews myself. All quotes in this volume that are not otherwise attributed are either from WGBH/BBC interviews or from my own archive, which was accumulated during twenty years of writing about music for the *New York Times* and *Rolling Stone*, among other publications; (2) from the beginning, my cohorts at 'GBH encouraged me to write my own book, one that would stand on its own merits. I trust I have fulfilled this brief.

At WGBH, then, I would like to particularly thank Karen Johnson, whose intuition that I was the writer for the job made everything else possible; Elizabeth Deane, Executive Producer for the series and a constant source of inspiration, intelligence, and wit; Nancy Lattanzio, my more than capable and more than patient editor at 'GBH; Gaye Korbet, who is responsible for the book's innovative design and for the visual dimension of what is hopefully its rock and roll "feel," and Debby Paddock, for photo research; Sharon Davis, an associate producer whose passion for the music and willingness to confront the issues it raises played a major role in attracting me to the project; the series producers and writers with whom I worked most closely, sources of information and inspiration all: David Espar, Dan McCabe, Vicky Bippart, Yvonne Smith; and to Rick Brown and Mary Cahill, for keeping the ball rolling. Thanks also to Hugh Thompson and the BBC crew in Bristol; and a special thanks to my editors at Harmony Books, Shaye Areheart and Peter Guzzardi.

Special thanks are due to the many musicians who have shared their thoughts, and sometimes their bandstands, over the years; to my editor at *Rolling Stone*, Anthony DeCurtis, who commissioned an early version of "The Church of the Sonic Guitar" as editor of a special "Rock Culture" issue of the *South Atlantic Quarterly*; to mentors in the academic community who have encouraged my researches over the years, especially Doctors Robert Farris Thompson, H. Wiley Hitchcock, David Evans, and Verna Gillis; to Robbie Norris, my audio engineering partner, for the digital transfers from my tape archive and for all the adventures in Mississippi; to Walter DeVenne, for his generosity with rare original recordings and his incomparable digital transfers; to Mike Lawson of the Gibson Guitar Company; to Mrs. Letitia Nelson; and to my mom, for her lifelong encouragement of my writing.

Funding for the PBS series *Rock & Roll* was provided by the Corporation for Public Broadcasting, the National Endowment for the Arts, and public television viewers.

Extra special thanks to JoBeth Briton, for writing much of the timeline, providing a sound editorial voice on the home front, and helping this book along in all sorts of ways. Truly, JB, I couldn't have done it without you.

Robert Palmer

Thurston Moore, Sonic
Youth guitarist, a modern
master of sustain and
shatter.

Con^{tents}

The joints and dives along the highway straddled the county line, outside town and outside the law, when the author and his saxophone made the Arkansas roadhouse scene, ca. 1960–65.

Intro^{duction}

Central Arkansas, ca. 1960

The strip straddled the county line, outside town and outside the law. Few of the joints and dives strung out along the highway advertised their presence with more than a single dim beer sign, but every weekend the local Billy Bobs—long sideburns, slicked-back hair, pack of Camels rolled up in a T-shirt sleeve—and their bouffant babes flocked to cavernous dance halls like the Club 70 and smaller, darker holes like the Blue Room. So did flyboys stationed at the nearby Jacksonville air force base, most of them Irish- and Italian-rooted inner-city kids from places like Philly and Detroit. Inevitably, a drunken flyer would make eyes at some local's girl, or worse yet, insult the Arkansas Razorbacks, the state's sainted football team. You'd hear glass bottles breaking, chairs would start to fly, and if you were in the band, you'd scurry back behind the stage to the storeroom where they kept the liquor. I read plenty of beer and whiskey labels those nights. If the cops were called, I'd have to remain in hiding until they left; I was underage, fifteen when I started lugging my saxophone out to the strip.

The author in his Blue Room days.

One night in the Blue Room, a sort of elongated shotgun shack in the middle of a field out behind the more commodious Club 70, a wild-eyed Billy Bob approached me during a band break. Peering at him through the smoke, in the minimal blue-tinged lighting that tended to give the joint's regulars a faintly embalmed look, I surmised that he was maximally wired. (The nearby Club 70's parking lot was a trucker's hangout and a widely known connection point for copping speed.) Sure enough, he pulled a pint of sour-mash bourbon and a handful of black beauties out of his jeans as he was sitting down at my table. I eyed him warily; in school, his kind usually meant trouble for kids like me. He downed the pills, chugged the pint in one long gulp, and chased it with a tall Budweiser. Then he asked to see my saxophone. Biceps bulging, veins kicking and throbbing at his temples, eyes glittery and wild, he was a formidable sight. I handed him the sax.

Billy Bob examined the beat-up old Army Band Selmer for a long time, trying to figure out where his fingers would go, how to hold the thing. Finally, he put it to his lips and blew a single, eloquent squawk. Then he handed the horn back and smiled. No words were exchanged; that joyous squawk, and the open, almost childlike, delight in his smile, said everything. Basically a suburban kid, a music freak and a loner, I now felt that I had penetrated some underground cult or secret society, one that somehow thrived in the shadows, out beyond the neat suburban plots and well-lit streets of familiar white-bread reality. Penetrated, but not like an anthropologist braving some primitive backwater. I had been accepted; whatever this new world signified, I was somehow a part of it.

Not long after that—I might have been sixteen—a rumpled old hillbilly approached the Blue Room's tinsel-decked bandstand, peered nervously over his shoulder, and muttered low, "Say, could you boys play me, oh, *any* old Hank Williams tune? It sure would sound good to a man on the run." We played "Your Cheating Heart," giving it all we had. The man broke into another of those unforgettable smiles, gulped a quick beer, and left. Half an hour later, the state troopers arrived. They ignored the almost entirely underage band and questioned everyone at the bar. A man had robbed a bank and they were hot on his trail; they felt sure he must have stopped here. Nope, swore the regulars, ain't seen nobody answering that description all night, not around here. Again, I felt I was *part of something.* I knew I'd never again be able to dismiss Hank's music, and country music in general, from the ironic distance of the suburban hipster manqué. Not when it was so real, and meant so much, for a "man on the run."

These run-ins between the law and the lawless didn't always end happily. When I was seventeen, I played a truly seedy upstairs joint called the South Main Businessmen's Club. Ninth Street, Little Rock's black entertainment strip in those days, was just around the corner, but the club's patrons were white. They were the kind of "businessmen" who wore T-shirts, tattoos, and ducktail haircuts. They were not always entirely happy to see me, the only white musician in a black band led by a middle-aged tenor saxophonist, Mose Reed.

Mose was my first real teacher. He had played bebop in Los Angeles in the wake of Charlie Parker's first mid-forties visit, and later played on r&b sessions for Memphis's Sun Records. When I met him, he was down on his luck, bitter that his teenage rhythm section "don't want to learn their chords, not even their triads." He'd praise my white guitarist friend Fred Tackett and me to the black junior-high-school students in his rhythm section, which added yet another dimension of racial tension to an already volatile situation. Then came the night I showed up early for a gig, sensed something profoundly wrong about the atmosphere in the club, and found myself leaving before I knew what I was doing. I'd paced halfway up the block in puzzlement when a fusillade of shots rang out behind me. The story was in the papers the next day: a table of bank robbers, a table of plainclothes agents, a shootout leaving several bystanders dead or injured. The club closed, Mose Reed disappeared; I never saw him again.

Risky as these scenes were, you wouldn't think they'd be amenable to *musical* risk taking and experimentation. But the way I remember it, the music in those joints did have a freedom about it, a sense of almost limitless possibilities. On the strip, we'd play Hank Williams back-to-back with John Lee Hooker. Every band had its special version of some little-known tune, whether originated by Bobby "Blue" Bland, Fats Waller, or the Valentinos. The top band on the circuit was Ronnie Hawkins's Hawks, later to find fame as Bob Dylan's backup group known only as the Band. The Hawks didn't have to play the latest hits; they had their own ingenious arrangements and were especially admired for their tough takes on the most intense black r&b of the day, from "Shout" to James Brown's "Please Please Please." The Hawks also had a reputation for pill popping, whoring, and brawling that was second to none. That's what made them heroes around the Club 70 (where they often played) and the Blue Room (where my bandmates and I assiduously copied their arrangements).

The Hawks weren't the only musicians on that scene who were going places. Fred Tackett, the school chum who'd taken lessons from black musicians along Ninth Street and took me out on my first gig when I was fifteen, went on to play guitar on hundreds of pop records, toured and recorded with Bob Dylan, and eventually joined Little Feat. That first gig with Tackett

A motel room bacchanal from the Hawks' juke-joint days. Faces in the pileup include Levon Helm (second from top) and Carl Perkins (second from bottom).

3

was also my first intimation of how freely inclusive this thing called "rock and roll" could be.

I'd been waiting for almost an hour, feigning sleep, when my mom glanced into my bedroom, didn't see my horn case under the pillow, and went on to bed herself. The '57 Chevy killed its motor, blinked its taillights, and coasted silently to a stop down the block. Fred and my drummer friend Killer Matthews, fellow outcasts from the high school marching band, waited while I quietly removed the screen from the bedroom window and slipped out. They had a can of Bud open for me and an Old Gold already lit. Killer, who was big and imposing-looking and as mild-mannered as they come, gunned the engine and headed out of town. We took a two-lane asphalt highway, turned onto a rutted local road with packed-dirt shoulders, and followed it through stands of oak and cypress and the occasional field of rice. "This is really the sticks," I noted as I popped open a second beer. "Just wait," said Fred. Killer turned onto a narrow dirt track. We seemed to be plunging into deep woods, but here and there I noticed cars, mostly old and dilapidated, parked in among the trees. The joint was at the end of the lane, a rambling, single-story frame house, built up above the soggy ground on cinder blocks. There was a Jax beer sign; the place had no name.

I'd gravitated to Fred and Killer because they seemed to be the only other kids in our (all-white) high school who bought Ray Charles and Charlie Parker records and subscribed to Cannonball Adderly's dictum (on *The Cannonball Adderly Quintet Live in San Francisco*) that "hipness isn't a state of mind, it's a fact of life." We often went to r&b package shows, where we were usually the only whites in attendance, and we'd organized a jazz band among our schoolmates. Fred and Killer played Buddy Holly songs and early surf music at school dances, and from time to time they subbed with bands in the black clubs along Ninth Street. They were vastly more experienced than I was, and seldom let me forget it.

The two guys who'd hired us were frat men/hustlers at the local community college. They played corny trumpet and trombone by ear, knew a few songs, and were paying us something in the neighborhood of ten dollars apiece to complete their "band," or more accurately, to *be* their band. Killer had filled me in on the drive out: "Last time we played for these guys, they went off and got drunk and left Fred and me there for an hour. We played everything we knew by Duane Eddy, everything by the Ventures, everything by Link Wray—not much else you can do with just guitar and drums. Then they came back in, and one of 'em staggers up to the mike and says, 'And now, Killer Matthews, one of Little Rock's most fantastic young drummers, will play a dynamic drum solo!' And I played a half-hour drum solo and we all went home."

Inside the joint, the jukebox wailed Ferlin Huskey and Sonny James. Couples were dancing in a desultory fashion around the rough plank floor, the hard-faced women in gingham thrift-store dresses, the men in overalls and work shirts, skin ruddy and creased from hard labor and hard drinking. The two frat men, spiffy in their Gant shirts and striped ties, watched silently while the three of us carried in Fred's guitar and amp and Killer's drum kit. We set up in a corner. There was no stage, and a single microphone for announcements and the occasional ill-advised vocal. When we'd huddled and come up with a few songs we thought we all knew, our stay-pressed leaders deferred to Fred, who named a key and counted off the tempo. The bartender sullenly unplugged the jukebox, right in the middle of a Marty Robbins gunslinger ballad. We got a few glares for that, but we were on.

And somehow it worked. The horns would take the lead on old pop and Dixieland tunes; we'd jazz up some Hank Williams and Lefty Frizzell; Fred and Killer would do their minimalist Ventures impersonation; and we'd start the cycle again. Forty minutes on, fifteen minutes off, all night long. Nobody seemed particularly enthusiastic about the evening's entertainment, but then, nobody seemed enthusiastic about much of anything. These folks were either dead drunk or dead on their feet, or both. They danced like the zombies in *Carnival of Souls*. But when Killer did his big drum solo, cribbed for the most part from Gene Krupa's work on "Sing Sing Sing," he actually drew a smattering of applause—the first, and last, of the evening.

"I don't think they liked us much," I mused drunkenly on the way home.

"Aw, they liked us okay," said Fred. "When they *don't* like you, they let you know. Some of these places have to string chicken wire up around the bandstand so that when people start throwing things at you, you can keep right on playing." Tales of knife fights, shootings, and other adventures filled up the time on the drive back into Little Rock. I would have my own tales soon enough. One thing we didn't talk about was what a contemporary music critic might call the astonishing eclecticism of our musical offering. There we were, stirring Dixieland and surf music, rockabilly and r&b, pseudojazz and honky-tonk country and western into a big gumbo. We had no idea we were breaking down barriers and cross-fertilizing genres. In those days, the definitions were not so firmly fixed.

These days, people tend to take musical categories seriously, as if they actually predetermine the shape and form music will assume. In fact, such categories are simply a convenience for nonmusicians, enabling them to discuss musical specifics in a nontechnical manner. Genre catchphrases are rarely coined and seldom used by the musicians themselves, and in any case are only applied after the fact of the music's creation. Today's listeners are likely to get incensed if you play jazz on a blues gig, or, heaven forbid, rock out in a jazz club. If such an attitude had been widespread during rock and roll's formative years, Elvis Presley might never have progressed beyond local talent shows, and Chuck Berry probably would have had to fall back on his skills as a beautician.

When rock and roll was forming, in the 1940s and 1950s, people weren't constantly bombarded with music and entertainment. There weren't televisions droning in every den and living room; radio stations didn't broadcast around the clock. The media provided only a portion of most people's musical nourishment, and these media weren't nationally standardized or programmed from one central source. Local radio stations might carry national network programming during certain hours, but most of their shows were locally generated, and responsive to the tastes of the area. Radio-station program directors were not the powers they later became; disc jockeys played whatever they liked, or whatever their audience wanted to hear. There were local hits, records that sold almost exclusively within a given area, and local artists whose styles—familiar to their fans— might differ considerably from national norms. When a performer or group established a solid regional following, there was often a small record company in the area that would take a chance on them, hoping for national hits but making records that largely reflected local trends. These were the labels that first gave rock and roll a hearing, and later the labels with the first rock and roll hits: Sun in Memphis, Chess in Chicago, King/Federal in Cincinnati, Los Angeles's Imperial and Specialty with their strong New Orleans connections, and so on.

The men who ran these labels, and the singers and musicians who performed on the records, have become visionaries in retrospect. But they were hardly revolutionaries. Even a man as creative and outspoken as Sun's founder, Sam C. Phillips, who gave Elvis, Howling Wolf, Jerry Lee Lewis, B. B. King, Johnny Cash, Carl Perkins, and Ike Turner their first shots at recording, was solidly rooted in the swing-band era of popular music. Phillips's first job in Memphis was engineering network radio broadcasts by nationally known dance bands from the swank roof garden of Memphis's Peabody Hotel. He was an avid follower of the big bands, and once told me that his favorite record of all time was "T. D.'s Boogie Woogie" by the Tommy Dorsey Orchestra. In New Orleans, Dave Bartholomew, who produced all Fats Domino's hits and led the band that played on Little Richard's breakthrough recordings, was a jazz trumpeter by training and inclination, another key creator of rock and roll's first generation whose tastes and values were shaped by the swing era.

For many of these "first-generation rockers," the idea of a separate category of music called rock and roll is itself inherently suspect. "We had rhythm and blues for many, many a year," says Bartholomew, "and here come in a couple of white people and they call it rock and roll, and it was rhythm and blues all the time!" Ike Turner, who was making cutting-edge records like "Rocket '88'" and setting his electric guitar for maximum sonic stun years before he hooked up with Tina, comments wryly, "I don't think that when somebody puts a name on something, that makes it the beginning of it. Fats Waller, Cab Calloway—if you just take the color off of it, man, these guys rocked and rolled way back then. So how could the first rock and roll be when they decided to name it rock and roll? Now, I can sit right here at this piano and play you jazz, I can play you country, I can play you anything you name, and to me it's all the same. How can you say what I play is r&b? If you want to classify it as far as the music is concerned, that's okay. But if you're going to classify it because of my color, well, then I don't know about that."

FIRST TIME IN MEMPHIS!
W.C. HANDY THEATRE
2 DAYS ONLY - SAT. & SUN. APRIL 7-8
ON STAGE! ..... IN PERSON

★ JACKIE BRENSTON ★
The Terrific ROCKET "88" Sensation
★ WITH ★
IKE TURNER
"THE KING OF THE PIANO"
AND
★—"HIS KING OF RHYTHM"—★
JACKIE IS GONNA TEAR THE HOUSE DOWN
ADMISSION_____ 60c Tax. Incl.

Ike Turner, at the piano, and singing saxophonist Jackie Brenston, riding the success of their single "Rocket '88'" into Memphis's W. C. Handy Theatre.

"Rhythm and blues" was a catchall rubric, coined by future Atlantic Records producer Jerry Wexler when he was writing for *Billboard* in the late 1940s to refer to any sort of music that was made by and for black Americans. "Rock and roll" was black slang for having sex when disc jockey Alan Freed seized on it as a marketing ploy, indicating music that was black ("r&b") in style but not necessarily made by black artists or aimed primarily at black audiences. Throughout his reign as King Jock of fifties radio, Freed played black originals rather than white "cover" versions of black records. But somehow the term "rock and roll" came to designate guitar-based music with a "black" beat, primarily played by and for whites. By the sixties, "rock and roll" carried such "white" connotations that writers began referring to the new, rhythm-oriented styles in black popular music first as "soul," then "funk." By the time rap and hip-hop came along, many younger artists took pains to differentiate their music from "rock and roll" altogether. In Britain, since the late seventies, "being in a rock and roll band" has been considered so hopelessly retrograde and unpostmodern in hipster circles that even white musicians in guitar-based bands feel called upon to deny having "rockist tendencies."

Categories and labeling would seem to obscure at least as much as they illuminate. My own mistrust of them stems from my initiation into rock's mysteries, and from later experience playing in bands whose members introduced me to the music of many people, many periods, many lands, without regard for generic distinctions. In a sense, that's what rock and roll is about: not so much a distinctive style as a culture in which musicians have access to an unprecedented heritage of live and recorded music, and the creative freedom to take what they want from it, hopefully while contributing something of their own. But there is more to rock and roll than that. Elusive as a stylistic idiom, it nevertheless surrounds us, pervading our culture. Today's popular music could hardly have evolved out of "Your Hit Parade" and the pre-r&r popular mainstream that show exemplified. Rap, metal, thrash, grunge, have different attitudes toward the organization of sound and rhythm, different ideas concerning the nature of *the song*. Their distance from pre-r&r norms cannot be explained by advances in musical instruments and recording technology alone. Far more than musical hybrids, these sounds proceed from what amounts to a different tradition, different from the old mainstream pop and different right on down to the most basic musical values. Generation after generation, musicians have made artistic *choices,* opting for the values of what we might call the rock and roll tradition over those of the popular tradition that preceded it.

"Pop" music is any music that happens to be popular. But rock and roll is not just what's popular, nor is it simply the sum of its own tradition. Some generic tags are better than others, and "rock and roll" at least tells you something fundamental about the music it describes: *The music wants to rock you.* At its best, rock and roll retains at least something of the insurgent edge and anarchic kick that first propelled it into mass consciousness. Much writing about rock more or less ignores the continuity of the tradition, the better to focus on those indelible moments of inspired insurgency when *the music changed.* Often the search for these moments leads away from the glare of the media mainstream and into subcultural shadows, for rock is often most exciting when it is still defining its stance and fighting for its turf, far from the best-seller charts. Examples include punk, which enjoyed little or no commercial success in America in the seventies and eighties but has informed every important new rock development of the eighties and nineties; and funk, which has provided the rhythmic foundation for contemporary rap and hip-hop (and much rock and pop) by percolating up from the dance floor rather than down from the rarefied heights of the charts.

In fact, rock and roll's relationship to the corporate music business has always been a volatile and uneasy one, despite the music's commercial status as a major cash cow. To put it another way, rock and roll is *in* pop but not necessarily *of* it. Rock often seems to be operating as an ongoing, semi-sanctioned rebellion within the music business, with its own identity and agenda. Corporate execs can always *manufacture* pregroomed stars and manicured bands to jump on the latest trend, sometimes with a degree of success. But there's always something coming from left field—a local scene that suddenly explodes like Seattle; rap from the moonscape of the South Bronx; a home-recorded, do-it-yourself indie-label release with a touch of genius. And no matter how sophisticated their demographics and marketing surveys, the execs are left scrambling. It's the nature of the game.

Sam Phillips once described his own contribution to rock and roll as "the freedom we tried to give the people, black and white, to express their very complex personalities. . . . I just hope I was a part of giving the influence to the people to be free in their expression." That freedom attracted me to rock and roll—that and the early perception that it was important enough to become, in certain instances, a matter of life and death—and it's kept me listening through all the buyouts and sellouts, the media overkill and the terminological confusion. I've played it, studied it, taught college courses on its history, and written reams about it, and that means I've had to fall back on generic categories just like everybody else, though I retain my mistrust of them and still insist that they are not to be confused with musical realities. But in all this time, I haven't found a definition of rock and roll, or an overview of the tradition, that really works for me. Which brings us to this book.

Rock and Roll is a ten-hour television history of the music, produced by WGBH-TV in the U.S. and the BBC in Britain. Although I served as chief consultant to the series, this book is not intended to be a duplication or condensation of it. My major borrowing from the television production is its schematic division of rock and roll history into ten episodes, paralleled here by chapters one through ten. In the series, each episode is a more or less chronological narrative. In my own more unruly telling of the story, I have taken the subject matter of each of the ten episodes as the jumping-off point for an essay that attempts, by various stratagems, to get *inside* its subject. Often this has meant focusing on a character or group of characters who may not be the familiar darlings of popular and critical consensus, but happen to have more interesting and relevant stories to tell. To paraphrase Neil Young, we've had our look at the well-traveled roads, and concluded that some of the more interesting scenery only becomes visible when we take the side roads—or the ditch. In fact, the view from the ditch often proves most attractive—and seductive.

One of the consequences of taking the rougher roads and routes is that we miss some of the more familiar names and faces. In other words, if you're interested enough in rock and roll to have your special favorites, some of them are going to get short shrift or no shrift at all in the chapters that follow. I know, because some of my own stone favorites are among the missing. Artists who have had long, productive careers, explored more than one genre successfully, and avoided becoming identified with any particular period or movement are rare and to be cherished. Shining examples include the aforementioned Neil Young, Sam Cooke, the Kinks, Curtis Mayfield, John Lennon, and arguably, the Rolling Stones—none of whom get anything approaching their due in the present work. The characters we do spend some time with will, however, be amply intriguing, inspiring, or exasperating, and the stories they tell will offer their own rewards. I might also point out that the literature of rock and roll is increasingly compendious, and includes individual studies of most of the major artists we've bypassed here in search of more rarefied epiphanies.

History is never tidy, but rock and roll history is particularly resistant to neatness and order. It's almost as unruly as the music itself, which is saying a lot. It follows that any attempt at a definitive overview is going to be, to some extent, an exercise in wishful thinking—or critical megalomania. In my view, the best histories are often personal histories, informed by the author's own experiences and passions. This is the sort of history I have aspired to here; any attempt to extrapolate an "objective" or "definitive" critical perspective from what follows will be the responsibility—and largely the fantasy—of the individual reader.

Rock and roll has sometimes been described as "dangerous." In the fifties and early sixties, rock and roll artists, especially black artists, often found themselves on the front lines in the battle for desegregation and equal rights; the first racially integrated public functions in many American cities and towns (including Little Rock, where I grew up) were not church services or school board meetings; they were rock and roll concerts. So the music *was* dangerous to racists, demagogues, and the self-appointed moral guardians of the status quo. Today these secular and fundamentalist authoritarians seem at least as ubiquitous and vocal as ever; I'd *like* to think rock and roll is still a danger to them. But after forty-odd years of commodification, the increasing concentration of the music business in the hands of a few giant corporations, and the video revolution's reduction of so much of rock to the electronic equivalent of wallpaper, I can't seriously imagine the music I love being really dangerous to anyone. And when you stop and think about it, asking rock and roll to save us from political repression or social oppression is asking too much of it. We have to undertake those tasks for ourselves.

Nevertheless, I do continue to believe in the transformative power of rock and roll—a power that can only be accessed by the individual listener. It's my contention that this transformative power inheres not so much in the words of songs or the stances of the stars, but in the music itself—in the *sound,* and above all, in the *beat.* Surely that's what Lou Reed is talking about in his song "Rock and Roll," which tells the stories of several individuals who were at war with their environment and their upbringing, uncertain and despairing of the future. Reed tells us what the music did for these people in the plainest possible language: their lives were saved by rock and roll. This is an energizing, inspiring, personally liberating sort of power; I have no problem thinking of it as spiritual power, although for some "spiritual" is a loaded word.

The narrative approach to rock and roll history does not readily lend itself to the sort of in-depth analysis the music's transformative powers demand. That's why I have included three additional essays, "I Put a Spell on You," "Delinquents of Heaven, Hoodlums from Hell," and "The Church of the Sonic Guitar." These are intended to serve as explorations of some of the "bigger" issues, focusing on sources and origins but not tied to any particular time period. Hopefully this arrangement will enable us to enjoy the best of the two primary approaches to rock and roll history—the history of creative flashpoints, and the history of an ongoing tradition. You can read the three longer essays first, follow the narrative history, read straight through, or browse at leisure—any old way you choose it. Have a good time, and keep rocking.

Robert Palmer

Awopbopalubop! Little Richard and his mighty Upsetters slippin', slidin', and shakin' at Los Angeles's Wrigley Field, September 2, 1956.

Whole Lotta Shakin' Goin' On

1

"*My music has a little bit of a spiritual taste, but it's also primitive. I play the guitar as if I was playing drums.*"

Bo Diddley

"*That's different; it just might sell.*"

Leonard Chess, to Bo Diddley

"*When I was singing in church, twelve, thirteen, fourteen years old, the sisters would sit down and clap their hands and just be rocking. And I guess that was there all the time, in the back of my mind. But now, 'Good Rockin' Tonight,' you know what that means. I had my mind on this girl in the bedroom, I'm not going to lie to you. Listen, man, I wrote them kind of songs. I was a dirty cat.*"

Roy Brown, composer of "Good Rockin' Tonight"

"*Back when they wouldn't play my records on the white radio stations, they said, 'This is vulgar.' But that was what people loved, they loved that little sexy sound in it, because it* did *suggest something, no doubt about that. But hell, let's face it, everybody knows about it; that's how all of us got here. I don't know what the world wants to hide from it for.*"

Ray Charles

1928

Clarence "Pinetop" Smith
unleashes "Pinetop's
Boogie Woogie," the first
hit with the boogie beat, an
inspiration for blues/pop/
c&w performers to come.

1938

John Hammond, whose
later discoveries include
Dylan, Aretha Franklin, and
Springsteen, introduces
boogie-woogie, rocking
blues and gospel, and

Count Basie's proto-r&b
to Carnegie Hall at his
first "Spirituals to Swing"
concert.

Rock and roll's coming in the mid-fifties was not so much a single event or series of events as an opening of America's sonic floodgates. Musicians had been rocking out across America for years—there were boogie and blues in the Deep South, jazz-flavored jump blues and western swing in Texas and the Southwest, hard-driving gospel rhythms in the black churches, street-corner vocal groups in the big cities, and myriad forms of boogie-woogie: barrelhouse piano in the logging camps, country boogie for the hillbillies, big-band boogie in the urban dance halls. These currents, and more, were increasingly subsumed under a single rubric: rock and roll.

Mainstream pop music was somnolent and squeaky-clean, despite the occasional watered-down pop-boogie hit. Perry Como crooned for sub-urban snoozers in his V-necked sweaters, Frankie Laine whinnied "I must go where the wild goose goes," and warbling Miss Patti Page wanted to know "How much is that doggie in the window?" Pop enthusiasts like to pretend that their brand of music was "good music," but the heyday of Tin Pan Alley, when songwriters like Irving Berlin, George and Ira Gershwin, and Cole Porter had ruled the roost, was long gone; for the most part, fifties pop was treacle.

The new sounds, deeply rooted in nonmainstream cultures, existed on the margins of the pop-music business—in ghetto taverns and hillbilly roadhouses, on indifferently distributed independent record labels, crack-ling over late-night radio stations on the fringes of the dial. For the most part, these sounds came not from the traditional music-business centers of New York and Los Angeles, but from middle-American cities whose popu-lations still had largely rural roots. Three cities in particular, New Orleans, Memphis, and Chicago, got a head start on the new sounds. Though the music-business centers were quick to emulate their example, it was in New Orleans, Memphis, and Chicago that a new breed of American musicians

1938–42

T-Bone Walker and Charlie Christian write the book on electric blues and jazz guitar.

1945

Delmore Brothers' "Hillbilly Boogie" introduces rocking black rhythm to c&w.

and entrepreneurs found the literal and imaginative space to create something fresh.

These marginal musics might have remained marginal for some time had the post–World War II baby boom, the suburban migrations, and a new standard of economic prosperity not conspired to create an entirely new class of consumers: the American teenager. Sam Phillips, the wild-eyed Memphis visionary who first recorded Elvis Presley, Jerry Lee Lewis, and other early rock and roll icons, has noted that fifties teenagers had no music to speak to and for them. There were adult records and children's records, and nothing in between. Rhythm and blues, as the period's black popular music was called, was not aimed at any particular age group, but teenagers, whatever their racial and socioeconomic background, knew the sound of excitement when they heard it. Compared to Perry Como and Patti Page, even the most formulaic r&b seemed to sizzle. It was more sexually explicit than any mainstream pop, it had a more forceful beat for dancing, and it seemed to mirror more directly the flux and frenzy of the times as seen through a teenager's eyes. America was changing, and change is the essence of the adolescent experience.

The Greek philosopher Plato warned in his *Republic* that changes in the modes and rhythms of popular music inevitably lead to changes in society at large. For Plato, this was an unpleasant prospect, and he suggested that government strictly limit the permissible musical modes. In mid-fifties America, parents and self-appointed authority figures attempted to do just that. "When the white kids would buy my records, they'd have to hide 'em from their parents," says Little Richard. His feral howls first hit the pop charts—and the television screens and phonographs of white America—only weeks before Rosa Parks, taking a seat on a Montgomery, Alabama, bus in the whites-only front section, refused to yield her place to a white man.

Jerry Lee Lewis embraced by a shirtless and wild-eyed Sam Phillips: "Freeing up a man's thoughts can be the catalyst for his creativity in any field, and especially music."

17

1948

Roy Brown and Wynonie
Harris go head to head
with competing versions
of Brown's "Good Rockin'
Tonight," both sizable
r&b hits.

June 1948

Columbia Records
introduces the 33⅓
rpm LP album.

This simple act of human dignity had the effect of rallying individual aspirations into a collective endeavor: the civil rights movement, which was
taking shape just as teenage America was learning to rock. Few rock and roll
records commented overtly on this synchronicity. But the mere fact that
performers as freewheeling, sensual, and *self-assertive* as Little Richard,
Chuck Berry, and Elvis Presley were on television and radio and in the
movies, with Daddy's little girl swooning at their feet, was enough to trig-
ger apoplexy in paternalist circles.

Of necessity, then, rock and roll's original audience was in many
respects a secret audience—teenagers gathering after school, cruising in
their cars, or lying awake under their bedclothes deep in the night, their ears
pressed to tinny little transistor radios. For the medium that spread the new
message of rock and roll was above all the radio—especially the transistor
portable, then a new invention. Searching the margins of the radio dial,
they found disc jockeys dispensing hepcat jive and playing records with an
elemental sense of excitement and adventure: "Have you heard the news?"
shouted Roy Brown—and a few years later, Elvis Presley—"There's good
rockin' tonight." "There's a thrill up on the hill," promised Hank Ballard and
the Midnighters, "Let's go let's go let's go."

A few stations employed black disc jockeys and instituted full-time
black music formats, most notably Memphis's trailblazing WDIA. More
often the disc jockeys were white; some of them employed black "coaches"
to teach them the latest slang. One of the most important forces in the dis-
semination of rhythm and blues across racial barriers was Nashville's
WLAC, which broadcast the grittiest rural blues as well as urban r&b over
a fifty-thousand-watt transmitter. On a clear night, WLAC's decidedly
down-home programming could be heard as far afield as Canada and the
Caribbean. 'LAC disc jockey William "Hoss" Allen recalls being surrounded

**WLAC power jock
William "Hoss" Allen.**

1949

John Lee Hooker advises parents to "Let that boy boogie-woogie/If it's in him, it's got to come out" in his first r&b hit, "Boogie Chillen" (Modern Records).

1949

Goree Carter's "Rock Awhile" introduces a proto–Chuck Berry guitar style and rocks like crazy—is this the first rock and roll record?

by an excited throng on a vacation in Havana when he unthinkingly slipped into his "Hossman" voice in a bar. He says he often received requests from U.S. military personnel stationed in the Mediterranean basin—on a really good night, WLAC's signal reached that far.

"Gene Nobles at WLAC was the first guy anywhere to play black music on a power station," says Allen. "And he got into it quite by accident. One night in 1946, some black GIs who had come back to Nashville to attend Fisk University on the GI Bill showed up at the station. They brought some black records and asked him to play them, which he did, just for kicks. And there was a response: The station started getting mail from all over the South. This led, in late '46, to a black music show with some black sponsors.

"Then Gene met Randy Wood, who would go on to start Dot Records and become successful with Pat Boone. Randy was from Gallatin, Tennessee, near Nashville, and when he got back from the war, he bought a little appliance store. In the store's back room he found three or four thousand old 78 records, and they were all boogie-woogie and blues records. Somehow he met Gene Nobles, and together they came up with the idea of selling these records on the air, five records for a very cheap price plus C.O.D. and handling. At first nothing happened, but on the third Monday they got two sacks of mail, of *orders,* from all over the South and Southwest." Randy's Record Shop became one of Nobles's major sponsors.

Among Hoss Allen's earliest jobs at WLAC was filling in for the wildly popular but frequently absent Nobles. "Gene had a real following, and not just among the black people," Allen notes. "As early as 1952, he was voted the most popular DJ by the students at the University of Mississippi, which of course was all-white. But Gene was a great follower of the horses. Every now and then when his bankroll'd get in good shape, he'd go off to the track, and management didn't really care as long as he came back *sometime.*"

1949

"The Fat Man," a sanitized version of the traditional doper anthem "Junker Blues," is Fats Domino's first record and first r&b hit.

1949

RCA introduces the 45 rpm single.

WLAC's disc jockeys all had to be adept pitchmen, Allen recalls with a chuckle, selling "everything from baby chicks to hair preparations—make it curly or straight—to stimulator tablets for nature problems. It was hard sell, and no spot ran sixty seconds; you'd be talking about this stuff for anywhere from three to ten minutes. Gene Nobles had been a carnival pitchman for thirty years before he got into radio, and he used to talk 'carny' on the air when he was making his pitches—that's kind of like pig latin."

The other 'LAC jocks tended to talk and dress black. "John R. [Richbourg] was from Charleston," says Allen, "and I grew up in a small town, so we could revert back to our childhoods, when we played a lot with black children, remember the colloquialisms, the street talk. That was the thing we used on the air. I never played a white artist on my show; I never played Elvis—not for any particular reason, except that I was into black music, and I didn't see any reason for mixin' the two up. Socially, I didn't mess around with a lot of white people. When I'd get off the air, I'd go down to the New Era, which was a big black club in Nashville, and hang out. In town there, the white people weren't listening to us. But in most southern college towns, you couldn't *get* a lot of radio stations. It was often a choice between listening to country music on WSM, or to our blues, and they'd rather listen to blues than country. We found this to be true at the University of Alabama, LSU, Georgia, Florida, all the colleges, we had them locked up. And out in the country also. White guys growing up in Tennessee, Louisiana, Mississippi, Arkansas, Texas, Alabama, if they were musically inclined, they *played* country music but they *listened* to WLAC, as well as to the Grand Ole Opry on WSM, and it all influenced them. They started trying to hold those guitar chords like the blues guys, play in minor keys and stuff, but it didn't come out like Muddy Waters or Howling Wolf, it came out rockabilly, and from rockabilly came white rock and roll."

1950

Country catches the boogie disease as Tennessee Ernie Ford's "Shotgun Boogie" and Moon Mulligan's "I'll Sail My Ship Alone" top the c&w charts.

1950

Sam Phillips opens Phillips Recording Service at 706 Union Avenue in Memphis, advertising, "We record anything—anywhere—anytime."

The raw blues and hard-edged r&b being broadcast over WLAC and like-minded stations in the early fifties was a revelation, not just for white southerners but for teenagers everywhere. It quickly became the rallying point for an emerging teen subculture that had already begun to embrace media-made role models for rebellion, such as James Dean (*Rebel Without a Cause*) and Marlon Brando (*The Wild One*). If teens didn't make the connection between the manufactured rebellion of these screen icons and the rebellious new music on their radios, Hollywood was ready to explicitly link juvenile delinquency and r&b, beginning in 1955 with the controversial *The Blackboard Jungle* and its featured song, Bill Haley and the Comets' Tin Pan Alley–penned "Rock Around the Clock."

As rock and roll developed, record producers, singers, and musicians perfected their own distinctive hybrids, reflecting the local and regional musics with which they were most familiar as well as their own creative vision. This was especially true in New Orleans. African-based drumming, singing, and dancing, discouraged and repeatedly banned elsewhere in North America, had flourished there since the early eighteenth century. This unique heritage has informed and enlivened New Orleans music ever since, as well as distinguishing it from the rest of American musical culture, making the city an ideal incubator for a nonmainstream music as rhythmically oriented as rock and roll.

New Orleans's *laissez-faire, bon-temps-roulez* social attitudes proved stronger than a more recent but still decades-long tradition of strict racial segregation. In fact, rock and roll played a major role in bringing racial barriers down. Cosimo Matassa, who built and staffed the tiny recording studio where Fats Domino and Little Richard recorded their breakthrough hits, saw these changes coming when he worked for his father's jukebox business as a teenager. He recalls separate rooms and separate jukeboxes for

They called him the Fat man, but Antoine Domino notched up more hits than any other fifties rocker besides Elvis Presley.

Jackie Brenston's "Rocket '88,'" featuring Ike Turner's Kings of Rhythm, puts Sam Phillips's Memphis studio on the map and becomes the year's top r&b hit; later called the first rock and roll record.

Dave Bartholomew, the bandleader, songwriter, and producer behind Fats Domino's hits, plays his Dizzy Gillespie–style "upswept" trumpet for a throng of New Orleans admirers.

blacks and whites in his father's place of business, "but at least the phone booth was integrated." The music increasingly integrated the business as well; white teenagers would cross the barrier to play black records, and black teenagers would play white pop and country records when they had the chance.

Once Matassa, who is white, began making records, usually in the company of black bandleader-producer Dave Bartholomew, he saw the black-white crossover he had first noted in his dad's jukebox business flower in the music itself. Bartholomew believes an important element in Fats Domino's broad appeal was that while he played boogie-woogie and blues, he sang more like a country and western artist. Perhaps this explains the crude hand-lettered sign session man/producer Allen Toussaint recalls noticing on a New Orleans telephone pole sometime in the late fifties: Send All the Niggers Back to Africa—Except for Fats Domino.

New Orleans had an opera company, and a tradition of Sunday slave dances, when New York and Boston were still frontier trading posts. This background, and a long-standing tradition of family and neighborhood music making, bred a different caliber of musicians, men who could handle Dixieland and swing jazz, gutbucket blues, and European notated music with equal aplomb.

The men in Dave Bartholomew's band epitomized the New Orleans brand of musicianship; they were versatile enough to support Fats Domino's big-beat versions of pop, country, folk, and other traditional song forms, then provide socking, full-throated backup for Little Richard, who arrived in 1955 to help spearhead the burgeoning rock revolution. Bartholomew and Matassa learned by study and by trial and error to "mix" the musicians' various parts—by carefully placing each player in relation to the handful of recording microphones. Working in this manner, they were

1951

The Dominoes' "Sixty Minute Man," a #1 r&b hit, sells to whites as well; leaves little doubt as to the original meaning of "rock and roll."

1952

Alan Freed's Moondog Coronation Ball, held at the Cleveland Arena on March 21, is the first r&r stage show; turns into the first rock and roll riot when crowd outside outnumbers arena's capacity.

able to emphasize Earl Palmer's parade-band drum rhythms, and to beef up a record's propulsive bass figure by directing string bass, electric guitar, and sometimes baritone sax to play the part in unison. As the fifties progressed, the bass parts grew ever thicker and more prominent.

New Orleans recordings by Domino, Richard, Lloyd Price (the original "Lawdy Miss Clawdy," 1952), Smiley Lewis ("I Hear You Knocking," 1955), and Shirley and Lee ("Let the Good Times Roll," 1956), among others, furnished a musical blueprint for rock and roll that was influential in recording centers like New York and Los Angeles, and in Memphis and Texas as well. D. J. Fontana, who played drums for Elvis Presley, and Buddy Holly and the Crickets' drummer, Jerry Allison, have both singled out Earl Palmer's work as a primary inspiration. J. M. Van Eaton, Sun session drummer and Jerry Lee Lewis mainstay, has recalled playing Little Richard records backstage to kindle his energy before performances. For years, these drummers, and the general public, knew Palmer only as "the guy on the Little Richard and Fats Domino records." As of this writing, Palmer has yet to receive a nomination to the Rock and Roll Hall of Fame or other appropriate honors; most of his peers among rock and roll session musicians have been similarly passed over.

Memphis's location just to the north of Mississippi and its short, fragmented, often violent social history made it a city where rural populations, and rural traditions, met and mixed in a freewheeling atmosphere, constrained by segregation but not by any long-standing social equilibrium. If New Orleans's first-generation rockers were an urbane lot, their Memphis counterparts were country boys who saw Memphis as the "big city" and as something more—something like the Promised Land. "Once I heard the music on Beale Street," Alabama-born Sam Phillips recalls, his voice still tinged with a kind of awe, "I knew I had to be *here,* in Memphis, Tennessee."

Earl Palmer, the master drummer of first-generation rock and roll, powered hits by Fats Domino, Little Richard, Sam Cooke, Eddie Cochran, Ritchie Valens, Phil Spector—and the beat goes on.

1952

Lloyd Price's "Lawdy, Miss
Clawdy" continues the
trend of r&b picking up
white listeners; white
matrons observed buying
the #1 hit "for the maid."

1952

Sam Phillips debuts the
Sun label, the future
launching pad for Elvis
Presley, Jerry Lee Lewis,
Carl Perkins, Johnny Cash,
and many more.

Like Dave Bartholomew in New Orleans, Phillips came to rock and roll from a background in big-band jazz and swing. And like many of his contemporaries who were attracted to rhythm and blues and other black music of the time, Phillips found early encouragement and support among the white radio personalities then playing black records for a racially mixed listening audience. In Memphis, disc jockey Dewey Phillips (not related to Sam) was such a figure; he consistently helped the fledgling Sun label by giving its releases generous airtime.

"The first thing to remember about Sam Phillips is that he was a great audio man, a radio engineer," says Stan Kesler, who played steel guitar and bass at Sun, wrote songs for Elvis Presley, and later produced records himself, including the epochal "Wooly Bully" by Sam the Sham and the Pharoahs. "And what made Sam great, Sam was not afraid to experiment." In 1950, Phillips built and opened his Memphis Recording Service, hoping to capture the crackling energy of the black music he heard along Beale Street. From the first, his records sounded different, using tape echo, distortion, and a canny command of room acoustics to create big sounds and vivid atmosphere with unusually small groups of musicians. (Elvis Presley's early Sun discs featured only Scotty Moore's electric guitar, Bill Black's stand-up bass, and Presley's own acoustic rhythm guitar.) B. B. King and Howling Wolf made some of their earliest recordings at Phillips's studio, often with the minimal backing of guitar, piano, drums, and sometimes a bass. In 1951, when a teenage Ike Turner arrived at Sun with his Kings of Rhythm and one damaged guitar amp, they were far and away the most well rehearsed band to have passed through Phillips's studio door. Instead of bemoaning the amplifier's burst speaker cone, Phillips cleverly used the distorted guitar sound to create a huge, booming boogie rhythm on "Rocket '88.'"

On hearing Howling Wolf for the first time, Sun Records founder Sam Phillips said, "This is for me! This is where the soul of man never dies."

1953

White Los Angelenos Jerry Leiber and Mike Stoller write "Hound Dog" for the formidable Big Mama Thornton.

1953

Bill Haley's "Crazy Man Crazy" is the first white rock and roll hit.

As the only professional recording facility in Memphis during the early fifties, Phillips's tiny studio (renamed Sun when he started his own record label in 1953) began to attract the attention of a handful of young white musicians who shared Phillips's enthusiasm for the rawer edges of the area's black music. He recorded several blues-inspired white singers, such as the hobo Harmonica Frank Floyd, country-boogie man Malcolm Yelvington, and a gravel-voiced pothead pianist "Smokey" Joe Baugh, who played boogie with an on-the-upbeat accent reminiscent of black Memphis pianist Roscoe Gordon's work, and uncannily similar to the ska style that was about to emerge out of Jamaica. But blues had been a part of country music for years. Phillips was looking for something else, a white singer with a truly contemporary rhythm and blues feel, and he found that singer in Elvis Presley.

When Elvis walked into the Sun studio in 1953, he was painfully timid. "He tried not to show it," says Phillips, "but he felt so *inferior.* He reminded me of a black man in a way; his insecurity was so *markedly* like that of a black person." But there was *something* there, and Phillips was on a kind of crusade. "I tried my best to let people be individuals," he says. "If it took a week or a month to get out of a person what they really, truly had to say, this is what we did. A lot of times you've just got to *unlock* that person. I think freeing up a man's thoughts can be the catalyst for his creativity in any field, and especially music."

So Phillips entrusted his discovery to two local western-swing musicians, guitarist Scotty Moore and bassist Bill Black. After they had done some initial work with Presley (who had no performing experience, except for practicing in front of his bedroom mirror), Moore and Black began rehearsing with him at Sun, under Phillips's watchful eye. Several months later, they produced an initial single with a rhythm and blues tune on one

1953

Elvis Presley walks into
Sun Studio in August to
record a song for his
mother.

1954

Hank Ballard and the
Midnighters appeal to
teens across the color line
with their "Annie" records,
from "Work with Me Annie"

to the inevitable "Annie
Had a Baby"—now Annie
"can't work no more."

**Elvis Presley, guitarist
Scotty Moore, and bassist
Bill Black, rocking out
during an early television
appearance.**

side and a country tune on the other, both performed in a spare but intense style. The blues side, Arthur "Big Boy" Crudup's "That's All Right, Mama," may have been a fluke, the off-the-cuff result of the musicians blowing off steam in the studio. They proceeded from there to Bill Monroe's bluegrass standard "Blue Moon of Kentucky," but this time their revisionist take on the material was the product of sheer hard work. Several takes have survived, and one can follow the Monroe song's step-by-step transformation from a straight country song—though with unconventional instrumentation (no fiddle, no steel guitar)—into a jumping jukebox number, hillbilly with a rocking (but not boogie-woogie) beat.

After some initial confusion, especially at radio stations (was this new singer black or white?), Presley broke through. Phillips sold his contract to RCA and used the money to record and promote new hits by a phalanx of white country boys who seemed to spring up in Presley's wake, ready to rock. Carl Perkins's "Blue Suede Shoes" became the first record ever to top the rhythm and blues, country, and pop charts simultaneously, and even this success was soon eclipsed by a piano-playing fireball from Ferriday, Louisiana, Jerry Lee Lewis. Typically, Phillips recorded Lewis with only one or two backing musicians, usually guitarist Roland Janes and drummer J. M. Van Eaton, using his own audio expertise to enliven and "knit together" the sound. The records that resulted—"Whole Lotta Shakin' Goin' On," "Great Balls of Fire," "Breathless"—were pure primal energy, unencumbered by fancy licks or unnecessary instrumentation. If Dave Bartholomew's New Orleans band set the standards for rock and roll musicianship, Sam Phillips and his crew led the way in showing how to make the rawest sort of records competitive in the pop-music marketplace.

Phillips has taken considerable flak for supposedly abandoning his black artists once he found Elvis Presley. In the case of Rufus Thomas, who gave Sun its first r&b hit with "Bear Cat" and was subsequently shunted to

1954

America shakes, rattles, and rolls, first with Joe Turner, then with Bill Haley and the Comets' "cleaned-up" version of the song.

the side, the complaint carries some weight. "Sam was thinking that blacks and whites couldn't make it working together," says Thomas, "and Stax proved him wrong, so wrong." But Sam's favorite black artists either left of their own accord or were spirited away by competing record companies with better distribution and more money to spend—Howling Wolf, B. B. King, Roscoe Gordon, Big Walter Horton, Ike Turner, and Little Milton all started at Sun but soon left for greener pastures.

Similarly, Elvis Presley stands accused of simply having ripped off black music, without giving anything back. Rufus Thomas and the late Roy Brown have both disagreed with this assessment. "I was the first black jock to play Elvis records," boasts Thomas, who broadcast over all-black-formatted WDIA. "Then later we were doing a WDIA show at Ellis Auditorium, and Elvis was backstage. I took him by the hand and led him onstage, he made that twisting of the leg, and the people, these were all black people now, they stormed that stage trying to get to Elvis. After that, the show was really over. Elvis was doing good music, blues and rhythm and blues, because that was his beginning."

"Elvis used to follow my band, and other black bands," recalled Roy Brown, whose 1947 "Good Rockin' Tonight" was one of the first truly rock-ing r&b hits. "I recall we played Tupelo, his hometown, this one particular time. I went to the High Sheriff's house between shows to change clothes, and to drink some moonshine whiskey with him, because it was a dry county. When I came back, Elvis was on the bandstand, playing his guitar and singing, nobody paying any attention to him. I asked my bandleader from New Orleans, Edgar Blanchard, 'How'd this kid get on the bandstand?' He say, 'To tell the truth, boss man, I didn't think you'd be back so soon. He brought us a little jug . . .' I say, 'Oh, he *bribed* you guys with some corn liquor.' After that, Elvis followed us, from Tupelo to Vicksburg to Hattiesburg, and he just watched us. Later on, when I first saw him on 'The

Roy Brown, blues shouter supreme, came blasting out of New Orleans in 1947 with his band the Mighty, Mighty Men and his original anthem, "Good Rockin' Tonight."

1954
Sun releases first Elvis
Presley disc, "That's All
Right (Mama)"/"Blue
Moon of Kentucky";
Memphis teens love it,
others not so sure.

1955
The big breakthrough:
Presley, Little Richard, Bo
Diddley, and Chuck Berry
debut on the pop charts.

Ed Sullivan Show,' all that wiggling and stuff, man, the blacks had been doing that for years. But there was something about Elvis that was different from the Fabians and them other guys. Elvis could *sing*. And he had a heart.

"Years later, when I started asking questions about my royalties and got in all this trouble with my people, I found out I owed a lot of income tax. I needed sixteen hundred dollars, and I was in Memphis and read in this newspaper where they were giving Elvis a birthday party. I went to the party and they wouldn't let me in, they didn't know who the hell I was. So I gave the doorman a note to give to Elvis, just to say, 'Roy "Good Rockin'" Brown would like to talk to you.' Elvis came out, grabbed me around the waist, took me inside. He didn't drink, but *I* had a drink, and I told him what my problem was. He didn't have his checkbook, so he told the bartender, 'Give me a piece of that brown paper bag.' Elvis wrote his name on it, the account number, the date, and he say, 'Sixteen hundred dollars, is that enough?' I say, 'Yes, that's fine.' And I took it to his bank and they honored it. That's the kind of guy he was. When the sickle-cell anemia telethon would come on, for this disease that blacks get mostly, after they raised whatever money they took in that night, Elvis would double it, I don't care if it was a million dollars; Elvis didn't *have* to do that. The guy was a beautiful human being; he had style, and he had soul."

Sam Phillips, Elvis Presley, and their coconspirators were outsiders in their own culture; Phillips and Presley had grown up among folks who referred to the music they favored as "vulgar animalistic nigger rock and roll bop." Phil and Leonard Chess, whose Chicago-based Chess Records pioneered the recording of electric blues before giving rock and roll Chuck Berry and Bo Diddley, were outsiders par excellence. Born in Poland in a tough Jewish ghetto, they owned and operated a string of businesses on Chicago's mostly black South Side, including a bar and a nightclub called the Mocambo. ("When the bar didn't sell enough whiskey in the early days,

1955

Hollywood's *The Black-board Jungle* boosts "Rock Around the Clock" to the top of the pop charts; identifies r&r with juvenile delinquency in minds of public.

1955

Alan Freed's first Rock 'N' Roll Party stage show in New York draws more than 15,000 to hear Fats Domino, Joe Turner, the Drifters, and others.

they'd be selling reefer out of the register," claimed sometime Chess business associate Teddy Reig. "That wasn't unusual for a black nightclub in those days.") The Mocambo employed up-and-coming jazzmen such as the blues-rooted saxophonist Gene Ammons, son of boogie-woogie pianist Albert Ammons, and it was these involvements that led the Chess brothers into the record business. Their experience has been echoed time and again by other first-generation rock and roll entrepreneurs, producers, and bandleaders; they started with jazz, but jazz didn't sell. The search for what *would* sell led them into vernacular dance music—rhythm and blues, rock and roll.

Chicago was an ideal location for developing an innovative record company catering especially to black Americans. Wartime industrial jobs had drawn so many black migrants from the Deep South that entire musical cultures were transplanted. During and after World War I, the major musical import was New Orleans jazz, with Louis Armstrong, King Oliver, Johnny Dodds, and a host of others settling on Chicago's South Side. World War II brought a brash, amplified version of Mississippi Delta blues; Bo Diddley recalls that Delta-born bluesmen like Muddy Waters, Howling Wolf, Sonny Boy Williamson, and Elmore James "had Chicago all sewed up" by the early fifties, a situation that encouraged younger musicians like Bo to come up with fresh twists of their own. Big-band swing, modern jazz, and sophisticated supper-club floor shows flourished alongside the down-home bluesmen on the mostly black South and West Sides, making for a supremely diverse and highly competitive musical environment. All the sources were at hand for a visionary like Bo Diddley to stir seasonings of Delta blues guitar, street-corner rhythms and verbal games, and the hipster jive of popular bandleaders such as Cab Calloway and Louis Jordan into a gumbo all his own.

Having despaired of making their fortune recording jazz, the Chess brothers began working with Muddy Waters and other Delta-bred blues-

Leonard Chess, who ran Chess Records with his brother Phil, wasn't afraid to put an amplifier in the stairwell or bang on a bass drum if it contributed to the atmosphere of the record.

1955

Presley causes his first rock and roll riot at Jacksonville, Florida, concert, where teens attempt to rip his clothes off.

1955

RCA Victor buys Elvis Presley's recording contract and Sun master recordings for $35,000, a bargain even then.

men. Leonard Chess, who generally supervised recording sessions while Phil took care of other aspects of the business, launched what would become an unparalleled blues catalog by recording Muddy simply, generally with just his own electric slide guitar and a string bass as accompaniment. Muddy was working the South Side clubs with a full band, but Leonard brought additional musicians to the recording sessions one by one, making sure he had achieved a well-meshed ensemble sound and had created an atmosphere you could practically cut with a knife before proceeding to add another instrument to the mix. Leonard took to sonic experimentation in the studio like a duck to water. His company soon acquired a reputation among musicians for their willingness to take chances on idiosyncratic music, and to throw away the rule book when recording it. Leonard's son Marshall Chess recalls both his father and his uncle Phil saying, again and again, "That's different; it just might sell." The result was a string of hits in the mid-fifties that not only defined the times, but later became a key source of inspiration for sixties rockers such as the Rolling Stones and Bob Dylan.

The distinctive but complementary approaches taken by Chess's front-running rock and roll artists, Bo Diddley and Chuck Berry, contrasted with earlier blues styles primarily in terms of subject matter and rhythmic organization. Bo Diddley adapted children's game songs and oral street culture, such as the ritual trading of insults known as the dozens, into brisk, often humorous wordplay, and created a larger-than-life performing persona; most Bo Diddley records, from "Bo Diddley" and "I'm a Man" (1955) to the later "Say Man" and "Who Do You Love," chronicled the adventures of Bo Diddley, superhero. Working with his own street-seasoned rhythm section, he brought traditional African-derived rhythms into rock and roll.

Chuck Berry wrote songs identifying teenage problems and celebrating the emerging teen culture ("School Day," "Sweet Little Sixteen," "Almost Grown"), as well as songs that slyly addressed racial and class issues,

1956

Little Richard, appalled when Pat Boone's covers of his records outsell the originals, sings "Long Tall Sally" extra fast to stymie Mr. White Buck Shoes.

1957

Jerry Lee Lewis, in his national television debut live on the *Steve Allen Show,* throws the piano bench across the stage; Allen throws it back.

such as "Brown Eyed Handsome Man," "No Money Down," "Back in the U.S.A.," and "The Promised Land." The songs tended to feature country-and-western-inflected light-blues melodies, along with plenty of guitar twang. His work with his own St. Louis–based trio, and the augmentation of this group with Chess session musicians for recording, resulted in a deceptively simple-sounding layering of rhythm parts—swing jazz in the bass and drums and boogie-woogie on the piano, all kicked along by Berry's slashing electric-guitar shuffle rhythms. This rhythmic approach would be consciously emulated by sixties groups such as the Rolling Stones, whose guitarist Keith Richards built his own widely influential style on a firm Chuck Berry foundation while Stones bassist Bill Wyman and drummer Charlie Watts worshipped at the shrine of Count Basie's super-swinging "All-American Rhythm Section"—bassist Walter Page, drummer Jo Jones.

Between 1955 and 1958, rock and roll music seemed to explode into public consciousness, propelled by an unprecedented coalition of outsiders: white disc jockeys playing black music, visionary producers and recording engineers, resourceful independent entrepreneurs, and a new generation of creative musicians, singers, and songwriters whose art did not fit into any previously existing categories. In retrospect, the music made by Little Richard and Fats Domino in New Orleans, Elvis Presley and his fellow "hillbilly cats" in Memphis, Chuck Berry and Bo Diddley in Chicago, and the many other musicians who were drawn into their revolution, constituted rock and roll's first Golden Age. And these figures were only the front-runners. As in every subsequent period of rock and roll, the music was partly created, and largely sustained, by performers who never became quite as well known. Some may simply have had fewer hits in them; others were too stable and family-oriented to settle for a life on the road, or too wild and crazy to keep a career going over the long haul. Others lacked some crucial ingredient—songwriting talent, bandleading ability, timing,

Chuck Berry, a brown-eyed, handsome man in the Promised Land, mixed country, blues, boogie, swing, and shuffle into his celebrations of teen culture.

1957

Dick Clark's *American Bandstand* premiers on national TV; first record played is Jerry Lee Lewis's "Whole Lotta Shakin' Goin' On."

luck, determination. Many never recorded at all. But many did, and it's the recordings of these artists (many unfairly categorized as second-string, or second-rate) that make up the greater part of the rock and roll legacy, no matter what period we're talking about.

Looking back at the music's Golden Age, it's hardly surprising that there are so many relatively unsung heroes; as always in rock and roll, the attrition rate was fierce. Among those missing in action, we might mention rockabilly wild men like Billy Lee Riley ("Flying Saucers Rock and Roll") and Charlie Feathers ("One Hand Loose"); blazing r&b duos like Mickey and Sylvia ("Love Is Strange") and Don and Dewey ("Justine"); kid groups like Frankie Lymon and the Teenagers ("Why Do Fools Fall in Love") and rockabilly's Collins Kids ("Rock Away Rock"); grown-up aggregations such as the exquisitely musical Flamingos, the jiving Turbans ("When You Dance") and El Dorados ("At My Front Door"), the smooth-as-silk Moonglows and Harptones, and the rougher Cadillacs ("Speedoo") and Jayhawks ("Stranded in the Jungle"). There were the rock and roll women, ranging from Janis Martin ("the female Elvis") to the country-rooted Wanda Jackson ("Let's Have a Party") to Atlantic's black song stylists LaVern Baker and Ruth Brown. Gifted male singer-songwriters included rockers as disparate as Chuck Willis ("C. C. Rider," "Hang Up My Rock and Roll Shoes"), Eddie Cochran ("Summertime Blues," "C'mon Everybody"), and of course, Buddy Holly and Ritchie Valens, whose careers were cut short in an infamous February 1959 plane crash. And we're still only scratching the surface.

By the end of the fifties, attrition of various sorts seemed to be robbing rock and roll of its biggest stars as well as its more underrecognized talents. Little Richard left the field to sing gospel. Jerry Lee Lewis was derailed when the British press revealed he was married to his teenage cousin. Elvis Presley left for army duty overseas, and Chuck Berry served

Mickey (Baker) and Sylvia (Vanderpool), respectively a top-rated session musician and a slinky, guitar-wielding sex symbol, celebrated the strangeness of love; years later, Sylvia and husband Joe Robinson ran Sugar Hill Records and helped launch hip-hop with hits like "Rapper's Delight."

1959

Buddy Holly, Ritchie
Valens, and the Big
Bopper die in plane crash
on February 3; rockers
mourn, but rock and roll
refuses to die.

1960

U.S. House of Represen-
tatives begins hearings
into record industry
"payola"; Alan Freed
ruined, Dick Clark emerges
as Mr. Clean.

jail time on a Mann Act conviction for having transported an underage prostitute across state lines. The music-industry establishment of corporate record labels and Tin Pan Alley publishing interests, relegated to the side-lines by the mid-fifties explosion of independent labels and independent talent, rushed into the vacuum left by imploding careers and tragedy with a safer, sanitized pop-rock sound and a brace of manufactured teen idols.

For many of the professionals involved in fifties rock, the entire phenomenon had added up to little more than a marketing ploy that selectively allowed some black artists and independently made records access to the electronic mass media, radio and television, which were enjoying their own rapid expansion during this period. "They started calling it rock and roll when the white people started playing it," says Dave Bartholomew, "and it was rhythm and blues all along!" Atlantic Records' Jerry Wexler has a similar perspective, but with a somewhat different emphasis. "One of the psychological and sociological reasons for the development of rock and roll was the exposure of white people to black music," he says. "They began by listening to it. The next thing they did was attempt to play it, quite poorly, but the ones who persisted managed to learn their instruments and soon became perhaps as proficient as their black role models—but maybe not with the same gravamen of authenticity. So it became something else."

And that is a point that bears repeating. The music *became something else*—not just the same old r&b or white approximations of it, but a broader idiom, influenced not only by black originators but by new production styles, new players, and the new context of a potentially wider and more diverse audience. When we speak of rock and roll as a musical idiom, this is precisely what we're talking about; not something warmed over or baldly imitative (though there has always been plenty of that), but a music with a spark of freshness, an attitude of adventure and exploration—a music *with a future*.

33

Be

Producer Phil Spector takes a break from meticulously crafting his "little symphonies for the kids" to have some fun with the Ronettes, including his wife-to-be, the future Ronnie Spector, far right.

My Baby

2

"We didn't write songs; we wrote records."
    Jerry Leiber and Mike Stoller

"Do you love me
* Now that I can dance?*
* WATCH ME NOW!"*
    The Contours

"In the sixties, God was a young black girl who could sing," says pop tune-smith Gerry Goffin. "That was the dominant sound." Al Kooper, who worked in New York's Brill Building songwriting factory before his organ licks on Bob Dylan's "Like a Rolling Stone" made him an in-demand studio musician, concurs: "Every morning . . . I'd come into work and I'd go into this cubicle that had a little upright piano and fake white cork bricks on the wall . . . and a door that locked from the outside. And every day from ten to six we'd go in there and pretend that we were thirteen-year-old girls and write these songs. That was the gig."

    Often dismissed as a dull interregnum between the original fifties rock explosion and the arrival of the "modern pop band" in the person of the Beach Boys and the Beatles, the late fifties/early sixties was in many ways a uniquely rich time for rock and roll, and one that found the music growing in fresh and unexpected directions. This was, among other things, the girl-group era, and not all the music was written and produced by men, the likes of Al Kooper notwithstanding. Brill Building songwriting teams such as Carole King/Gerry Goffin ("Will You Love Me Tomorrow" by the Shirelles, "Up on the Roof" by the Drifters, "One Fine Day" by the Chiffons) and Ellie Greenwich/Jeff Barry ("Leader of the Pack" by the Shangri-Las, written with Shadow Morton, and "Be My Baby"

Carole King and Gerry Goffin wrote songs that helped make New York's Brill Building a bastion of American rock and roll in the face of the British Invasion.

1956

Liverpool skiffle band the Quarrymen, with John Lennon, Paul McCartney, and George Harrison, play their first informal gigs.

1957–59

The Coasters become producers Leiber and Stoller's pop "repertory company," scoring hits with "Searchin'," "Young Blood," "Yakety Yak,"

"Charlie Brown," and "Along Came Jones"; King Curtis does the saxophone honors.

by the Ronettes, written with Phil Spector) took an active role in making the records that would help America hold its own on the pop charts in the face of the 1964 British Invasion.

"We had a kettle-drum guy who was there playing on one of our sessions," recalls the Shirelles' Shirley Owens, "and Carole [King] felt that she could play it better. So she came into the studio and played it." Ellie Greenwich says, "We didn't think in terms of 'girl groups.' We never put a label on it." Considered teen trifles in their day, the records of the pioneering Chantels (with stirring, musicianly lead vocals by Arlene Smith), the Shirelles, and bad-girl groups the Ronettes and Shangri-Las have endured as unassailable three-minute slabs of glory.

But rock and roll was blessed with a multitude of great voices in the late fifties/early sixties, perhaps more than at any time before or since. If you were lucky, you might get to hear and see Sam Cooke, Jackie Wilson, Jesse Belvin, Marv Johnson, the Falcons, and Hank Ballard and the Midnighters on the same package show, a billing chockablock with distinctive, unforgettable stylists. (The Falcons included future soul stars Eddie Floyd and Wilson Pickett and one Sir Mack Rice, author-to-be of "Mustang Sally.") To cut it in this kind of company, you couldn't just be a vocal wizard, you had to *move*. There seemed to be new dance sensations almost weekly, many of them local creations from a particular town, city, or neighborhood; "The Twist" was only the tip of the iceberg. Few rock and roll singles have been as appealingly kinetic, or as amenable to garage-band remakes, as the Contours' "Do You Love Me," the Five Du-Tones' "Shake a Tail Feather," the Rivingtons' "Papa Oom Mow Mow," or the Isley Brothers' "Twist and Shout." And of course there were the Watusi, the Jerk, the Twine, the Georgia Slop, the Bristol Stomp, the Mashed Potato, the Hully Gully, and the rest, each with at least one clarion single to trumpet its charms.

Rock and roll was blessed with a multitude of great voices in the late fifties and early sixties, none greater than the dynamic Jackie Wilson.

1958

Phil Spector makes his r&r debut, singing his song "To Know Him Is to Love Him" on *American Bandstand* with his short-lived group the Teddy Bears.

1959

Leiber and Stoller introduce strings, tympani, and classical borrowings to soul music with "There Goes My Baby," inadvertently creating "sweet soul."

The late fifties/early sixties were also the years in which the record producer, always a major behind-the-scenes player, developed into a self-conscious auteur, a figure comparable to the writer-director in film. "I've always felt each song I wrote or produced in the past was a little film," says Jeff Barry. "I would be as demanding with an artist as a director would be with an actor or actress." Earlier songwriters had been content to sit in their ivory towers, churning out lyrics and sheet music and letting others arrange and produce their creations for recording. Jerry Leiber and Mike Stoller, who exemplified the new breed of independent writer-producers, liked to craft their material with specific artists in mind, from the salty Big Mama Thornton, for whom they originally wrote "Hound Dog," to the Coasters (their favorite "repertory company"), the Drifters, and Ben E. King. They didn't just compose songs for these artists; they arranged the songs, picked the backing musicians, supervised the recording sessions. "We didn't write songs," they said, "we wrote records." Phil Spector, a Leiber and Stoller protégé who became the period's most celebrated producer-auteur, took the lead in transforming the three-minute pop single into a dramatic, richly textured, meticulously crafted work of art; Spector called his records (by the Ronettes, the Crystals, Darlene Love, the Righteous Brothers, and Bob B. Soxx and the Blue Jeans) "little symphonies for the kids."

Spector's example opened the door for even more eccentric auteurs such as the largely self-taught George "Shadow" Morton, who had been a high school classmate of Ellie Greenwich's. Morton explained that his music "was all in my head. I don't play an instrument or anything." If he heard seagull sound effects and jazz licks, or operatic strings and screaming guitars, he used them in his songs and productions for the Shangri-Las. Their "Leader of the Pack," "Remember (Walkin' in the Sand)," the feedback-drenched, protopsychedelic "He Cried," and the gloomy, near-suicidal "I

The Shangri-Las, toughest of the sixties "girl groups," sang "little symphonies" for kids who were perhaps a little twisted, thanks to the unconventional songs and productions of George "Shadow" Morton.

1960

America dances the twist, with Chubby Checker's remake of Hank Ballard's "The Twist"; two years later, Sam Cooke makes "Twistin' the Night Away."

1961

The Beach Boys go "Surfin'," a Southern California hit late in the year, a national hit by spring 1962.

Can Never Go Home Any More" broke all the rules of song structure, arrangement, and formal coherence and were truly "little symphonies," for kids who were perhaps a little twisted. The Shangri-Las could play it innocent, but of all the girl groups, they were the most convincingly tough, with their jailbait looks and authentic street-credibility. "They're getting nutso," Morton complained at one point. "One day they're eating pasta, the next day they're eating chateaubriand, and they don't know how to pronounce it yet." In later years, members of the group were in trouble with the law, reportedly over kidnapping and gun-running charges.

The producer-auteurs of the late fifties/early sixties were all self-styled outsiders: bohemians attracted to black culture, musical polymaths open to a variety of influences. Mike Stoller and Jerry Leiber were both born into working-class East Coast families that moved to Los Angeles when Jerry and Mike were teenagers. They both enjoyed hanging out in the modern-jazz joints along Los Angeles's black entertainment strip, Central Avenue, and both frequently dated black girls. Leiber was into funky back-alley blues; Stoller studied twelve-tone classical composition at UCLA and had one of his atonal, serialist compositions performed by the Los Angeles Symphony, but generally preferred playing knocked-out boogie-woogie piano in a series of Chicano r&b combos. Stoller's most distinctive composing, aside from the songs he wrote with Leiber, was probably the classic saxophone fills he notated on deli takeout napkins for tenor man King Curtis to play on Coasters records.

Jerry Leiber, always an exceptionally literate hipster, had some high-art aspirations of his own. He once only half-jokingly compared some of his rock and roll lyrics to works of fiction by William Styron and William Faulkner. And in fact, the best of the records produced by Leiber and Stoller in their "playlet" style—"Charlie Brown," "Yakety Yak," "Shopping for

Producer-songwriters Mike Stoller, left, and Jerry Leiber.

1961

Dick Dale established as "King of the Surf Guitar" with innovative instrumentals such as "Trippin'" and "Miserlou."

1961

Beatles' first appearance at Liverpool's Cavern Club.

1962

Beatles acquire manager Brian Epstein.

B e   M y   B a b y

Clothes," and many others by the Coasters, as well as the Clovers' "Love Potion No. 9"—were as tightly plotted and paced, and as relentlessly rehearsed, as any evening at the theater. Beneath the surface of teen-oriented lyrics, the songs often bristled with social satire and political irony. Long before Dylan and the Beatles, Leiber and Stoller were making rock and roll records with the most sophisticated and self-conscious artistry.

Meanwhile, in a New York cemetery, a pale young man was contemplating the curiously opaque inscription on his father's tombstone: "To Know Him Was to Love Him." But brooding over his father's suicide wasn't getting him anywhere, so the pale young man, Phil Spector, turned the tombstone inscription into his first hit record—"To Know Him Is to Love Him," by Spector's short-lived group the Teddy Bears. The song's reflective tone, not to mention the circumstances of its composition, betrayed a late-romantic classical sensibility, and Spector's tastes did, in fact, run to Wagner. He was an introspective, sensitive young man, deliberately eccentric as part of a consistent artistic strategy (though the sinister bodyguards, the firearms in the studio, and the "snowy" cocaine Christmas cards would come later, after Spector's abrupt "retirement" in 1966).

The Phil Spector of the early sixties was also a gifted guitarist, good enough to play on numerous sessions and contribute a brief but striking solo to the Drifters' "On Broadway," produced by Leiber and Stoller. And he could be an uncompromising careerist. When "To Know Him Is to Love Him" stalled on its climb up the pop charts, Spector arranged for a favor from Dick Clark, host of the new national television show "American Bandstand." Clark was already a power broker of the first magnitude. After the Teddy Bears appeared on his show, their record peaked at number one on the *Billboard* pop chart. By 1961, Spector was the most talked-about producer in rock and roll—at the age of twenty.

The Coasters, Leiber and Stoller's versatile rock and roll repertory company, doing their "Yakety Yak" stage routine: "If you don't scrub that kitchen floor, you ain't gonna rock and roll no more!"

1962
The Tornados celebrate
the first worldwide TV
broadcast with instrumen-
tal "Telstar"–first British
rock record to reach #1
in the U.S.

1962
American pop charts'
Year of the Woman, with
major hits by the Shirelles,
the Marvelettes, the
Crystals, the Ikettes,
Barbara Lynn, Mary Wells,

Dee Dee Sharp,
Patsy Cline, Barbara
George, Little Eva,
and many others.

Working at Los Angeles's Gold Star studio, an old-fashioned room with high ceilings and a reverberant, acoustically "live" sound, Spector assembled his hand-picked cast of musicians, the Wrecking Crew. The group grew to include multiple guitarists, keyboard players, drummers, percussionists, even multiple bassists, often augmented with horns and strings. Working with engineer Larry Levine, Spector would boil all this instrumentation down into a massive mono mix, a great, grandly textured "wall of sound." The idea was not to hear individual instruments, but to have so many instruments playing a few simple melodic lines and rhythm patterns that the sound was deliberately blurry, atmospheric, and of course *huge:* Wagnerian rock and roll with all the trimmings. Spector wrote and cowrote a succession of flawless teen hits and featured mostly black singers with gospel roots. The best of his lead vocalists, particularly Darlene Love and Spector's wife, Ronnie (née Veronica Bennett), of the Ronettes, stood up to the "wall of sound" with some spectacular but always musicianly emoting. Nevertheless, it was Spector's show. He laid down instrumental tracks before he'd even decided who was going to sing, and the personnel of his vocal groups frequently varied according to his whims. But when the records were as sonically imposing and commercially successful as the Ronettes' "Be My Baby," "Walking in the Rain," and "(The Best Part of) Breakin' Up," the Crystals' "Uptown," "He's a Rebel," and "Da Doo Ron Ron," and the Righteous Brothers' "You've Lost That Lovin' Feelin'," there were few complaints. The "wall of sound" was widely influential, inspiring all sorts of cut-rate imitations and challenging young producers and musicians on both sides of the Atlantic. "I did more than hear it," Beach Boys writer-producer Brian Wilson said of Spector's music, "I envied it."

The Beach Boys' music, like many of the period's myriad dance

Darlene Love of the Crystals, with Spector to the right.

1962

Phil Spector's wall of sound threatens to take over the pop charts with hits like the Crystals' "He's a Rebel" and "Uptown."

1963

Spector finds his ultimate girl group in the Ronettes, featuring the soon-to-be Mrs. Ronnie Spector, hitting first with "Be My Baby."

California surfers flocked to rock and roll shows by one of their own, guitarist Dick Dale (top), and provided inspiration for the mostly nonsurfing Beach Boys (bottom, with chief songwriter-producer Brian Wilson on the right).

crazes, sprang from a local teen subculture. The southern California surfers had a lifestyle, a dress code or "look," a highly developed in-group slang— and their own music. Its major architect, guitarist Dick Dale, was one of their own kind, a fanatical surfer who says he used to come running out of the ocean, strap on his guitar, and hit the stage. Dick Dale and the Del-Tones were regional heroes, drawing more than a thousand kids a night to surfer dances they promoted themselves at the Balboa Ballroom. They were also pioneers of rock's D.I.Y. (Do It Yourself) ethos, making records for their own Deltone label. Dale drew on his Middle Eastern heritage (his family, the Monsours, were Lebanese), adapting the rapid-fire, double-stroke picking he heard his uncle use on the oud to his own Fender Stratocaster. Dale's guitar playing was fast, twangy, and metallic, with long-lined Middle Eastern melodies slithering along atop shimmering Spanish-inflected chording, punctuated by slamming slides up the neck. Dale intended all these effects to mirror specific surfing experiences. Only his aggressive rhythm playing reflected the influence of any earlier rock and roll guitarist; at times, it distantly echoed Chuck Berry.

The Beach Boys simplified this sound, emphasizing the Chuck Berry roots, then topped it with intricate, accomplished vocal harmonies, inspired in part by smooth pre-rock harmony groups like the Four Freshmen. Brian Wilson proved adept at writing songs about surfing, hot rods, and California girls, but he actually hated the ocean. His favorite environment was the recording studio, where he soon took over from the company producer assigned to the group by Capitol Records. There, inspired primarily by Phil Spector (and using Wrecking Crew musicians such as drummer Hal Blaine and bassist Larry Knechtel), Wilson created ever-more-elaborate settings for his sagas of surf and sun. Like Spector, like Leiber and Stoller, he didn't write songs, he wrote records.

1963
Chicago's black-owned Vee Jay Records releases first Beatles disc in U.S., but "Please Please Me" gets a lukewarm response.

1964
February: The Beatles invade the U.S.

1964
RCA releases Sam Cooke's middle-of-the-road-tending *Live at the Copa,* shelves the live album of an incendiary 1963 "Chittlin' Circuit" show.

Hits of 1963

Women rock on with hits such as Jan Bradley's "Mama Didn't Lie," Dee Dee Sharp's "Do the Bird," the Shirelles' "Foolish, Little Girl," Darlene Love's "(Today I Met) the Boy I'm Gonna Marry," the Crystals' "Da Doo Ron Ron," Barbara Lewis's "Hello Stranger," Lesley Gore's "It's My Party," Patsy Cline's "Sweet Dreams (of You)," Doris Troy's "Just One Look," Martha and the Vandellas' "Heat Wave," the Jaynetts' "Sally Go 'Round the Roses," Dionne Warwick's "Anyone Who Had a Heart," and the Singing Nun's "Dominique."

Just as Spector and the Beach Boys were at the height of their powers, a band from Liverpool, England, was looming on the horizon. During their early years, the Beatles were a sweaty, leather-clad bar band, performing frantic, stripped-down covers of American r&b and rockabilly favorites for tavern audiences in Liverpool and Hamburg. John Lennon worked at projecting the black-leather menace of American rockabilly wild man Gene Vincent; Paul McCartney practiced his Little Richard screams. Falling in with a group of bohemian "exi" (existentialist) students in Hamburg, they changed their look; the "Beatle haircut" was born, and the leather was replaced by art-student turtlenecks. When they acquired an ambitious manager, Brian Epstein, they made the transition from bar band to recording group. Encouraged by producer George Martin, they rapidly progressed from cover tunes to original songs. It soon became apparent that Lennon and McCartney were an extraordinary songwriting team, and Martin wisely showcased the songs, keeping the backing simple, essentially re-creating in the studio a more polished version of the group's road-tested live sound.

American rock and roll had caught on rapidly in Britain, and the British continued to buy records and attend shows by many of the more visceral American rockers through the early sixties, when the American pop charts were dominated by manufactured "teen idols." Liverpool alone boasted almost three hundred rock and roll clubs and more than three hundred bands. The Beatles had already risen to the top of the heap locally when they met Brian Epstein in 1961. In retrospect, the group's excitement over Epstein's promise that they would be "bigger than Elvis" seems astonishingly naive; how many young hopefuls had already fallen for this sort of siren song? In 1961, the idea of a British group becoming a major player in rock and roll was laughable. And indeed, American reactions to the Beatles were initially disappointing. Even after Beatlemania began to take hold in

1964

Brill Building songwriting teams lead America's response to the British invasion.

1964

Largely as a result of the British invasion, the year's top 10 has the lowest percentage of records by black artists since 1950.

England, with the Beatles recording for EMI under George Martin's supervision, EMI's American affiliate, Capitol Records, passed on the group. Vee-Jay, a black-owned Chicago label, issued early Beatles discs in the U.S. to lukewarm response. On "American Bandstand," the kids rating records gave "She Loves You" a mediocre response and snickered at the group's haircuts and matching suits. And then the unthinkable happened. Epstein brought the group to the U.S., orchestrated a well-timed publicity campaign, and suddenly the Beatles were not just a British oddity; they were an international sensation.

Rock and roll had been an outsider's music from the beginning, drawing sustenance from oppressed minorities and isolated teen subcultures. The out-of-left-field success of the Beatles caught America's pop-music establishment off guard, in an ironic replay of the original mid-fifties rock and roll explosion. But this time the outsiders were not from Memphis or New Orleans or Chicago; they were from outside America. In a few short years, they would revolutionize the music business, making the self-contained guitar band, writing and singing their own songs and in control of their own creative destinies, a new rock and roll paradigm. Some people would even assert that the Beatles had *saved* rock and roll—but from whom?

The early Beatles, working on their rockabilly body language, with John Lennon (center) as a splay-legged Gene Vincent.

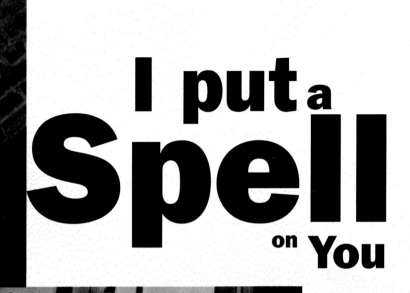

I put a Spell on You

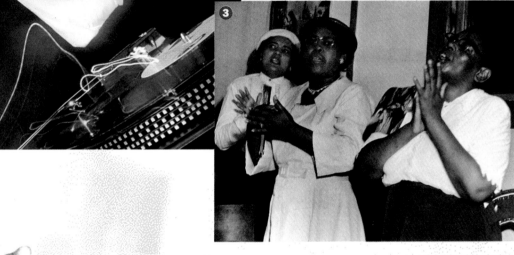

③

④

I Put a Spell on You

"If we seek to discover the foundations of traditional music in Africa, I think we have to look for them . . . in the traditional African's predilection for the esoteric and the occult, in religion and magic."

Fela Sowande, Nigerian musicologist

"You have nearly all the people of this family in your country. They knew too much magic. We sold them because they made too much trouble."

Dahomean village elders, explaining to anthropologist Melville Herskovits why ancestors had sold members of their family into slavery

"The rhythm seems to have some special hypnotic effect."

A Pittsburgh policeman, on behavior at late-fifties rock and roll shows

"Smash the records you possess which present a pagan culture and a pagan way of life."

Newsletter, Minneapolis Catholic Youth Center, 1958, on the subject of rock and roll

"Christians will not attend this show. Ask your preacher about jungle music."

Picket sign outside a 1956 concert by Bill Haley and the Comets in Birmingham, Alabama

"Guys kind of piss me off trying to name what I'm doing. A lot of times I tell people, I don't know what it is, I just play it. But I do know what it is. It's mixed up with spiritual, sanctified rhythms, and the feeling I put into it when I'm playing, I have the feeling of making people shout. I put it right there in the shout mode, and they can't help it, 'cause I got it locked right in there. And that's what you gotta do. If you can't lock them into that mode, they don't move."

Bo Diddley, 1990

Pages 44–45:

❶ Bo Diddley, founding father and rhythmic innovator: "I play the guitar as if I was playing drums."

❷ Grandmaster Flash on the "wheels of steel"— the phonograph turntable, in his hands a virtuoso percussion instrument.

❸ A Church of God in Christ service, prime source for what Lionel Hampton called "that sanctified beat."

❹ *Bata* drums, sacred to the Yoruba people of Nigeria and Cuba: Their push and pull provided a template for the inner rhythms of rock and roll.

"O my Lord
O my Lordy
Well well well
I gotta rock
You gotta rock"

From "Run Old Jeremiah," a traditional shout recorded in Louisiana in 1934 by John and Alan Lomax

Meet Whirling Willie

"Whirling Willie," mused Lionel Hampton, whose mid-1940s big band introduced the heavy backbeat, honking saxophones, and all-out intensity to which the rubrics "rhythm and blues" and "rock and roll" were later attached. "Let me tell you about Whirling Willie."

Hampton grew up in Chicago, along with jazz, blues, boogie-woogie, and the fledgling twentieth century. As a kid, he heard the fabled first wave of New Orleans jazz greats in person — King Oliver, young Louis Armstrong. He attended boisterous tenement rent parties, where pianists rocked the blues and boogie-woogie and contributions were solicited to keep the landlord at bay. "And I was brought up in the Holiness church," he recalled, "where I'd always try to sit by the sister who played the big bass drum. Our church had a whole band, with guitar, trombone, and different drums. That sister on the bass drum would get happy and get up and start dancing up and down the aisles, and I'd get on her drum: boom! boom! I always had that beat in me. That heavy backbeat is pure sanctified, Church of God in Christ." (The C.O.G.I.C., founded in Memphis in the mid-1890s, is a Pentecostal denomination whose members make direct contact with the Holy Spirit. Trance behavior — "getting happy" — is widespread and encouraged, and no musical instrument is considered unworthy of singing God's praises. Sanctified gospel music, which developed at roughly the same time as early blues and jazz, is one of the most important, and perhaps the least well-documented, of the idioms that provided rock and roll's foundations.)

Hampton also learned marching-band drum rudiments in a fife-and-drum corps run by Chicago nuns, and scales and harmony from a black band director who took an interest in him. By 1928, when he left

Chicago for Los Angeles, he was a well-rounded musician, adept on the xylophone as well as drums and percussion. After recording with Louis Armstrong and other leading jazzmen, he happened to meet the white bandleader Benny Goodman, who hired him. It was a controversial move. Hampton and pianist Teddy Wilson were the first black musicians to play with a popular white band, and Goodman's was the most popular swing band in America. Hampton was able to take advantage of the notoriety and form his own band in 1940. At first they played elegant, melodious jazz and Tin Pan Alley pop tunes. The blues, boogie-woogie, the sanctified beat, stayed on the back burner. Then Hampton encountered Whirling Willie.

"I was in Little Rock in the early 1940s," Hamp recalled. "My band had a day off. There was a theater across from the hotel, and I noticed there was going to be a revival that night. I went over to investigate, and everybody was saying, 'Whirlin' Willie! Yeah, Whirlin' Willie comin' tonight. He'll have people lined up all the way down the block, waitin' to be healed.' I decided to look into this.

"I went to the revival. Whirling Willie's band started to play. What a band! First I wanted his trumpet player to join my band; then I wanted to just hire 'em all. They got to swinging, started feeling the Holy Spirit, and man, did they hit a groove. Of course, they wouldn't go out with me. They just wanted to play the Lord's music. And I can't blame 'em, they had the spirit and the power. Well, after they got really going, a door opened in the back, and Whirling Willie came in *whirling,* just whirling around and around, and he didn't stop *once!* The band started groovin' even harder, and the people just started rising up, sick people making their way up to the front, people in wheelchairs. Whirling Willie hit those people like a cyclone! He'd grab 'em, one after another, and *throw 'em out of their wheelchairs,* just kind of barking at 'em: "You're *cured!*" Whap! "*You're* cured!" Whap! Whap! These crippled people would land on the floor in a heap, and then they'd get up with sort of a dazed look on their faces, and just *walk away.* It was one of the most powerful, impressive things I've ever seen.

"When I couldn't hire any of his musicians, well, I started working on my musicians, getting *them* to play with that kind of inspiration. And I think I was the first to bring all that music from the Holiness church — the beat, the hand clapping, the shouting—out into the band business. When rock and roll came in, they took a whole lot of things from us."

In 1942, Hampton took his band into a New York studio to record a tune called "Flying Home," featuring a wild young tenor saxophonist from Houston called Illinois Jacquet. The band rocked while Jacquet screamed and squealed through his horn, honked one note repeatedly, preached as passionately as a sanctified deacon on revival night. When they played the tune onstage, Jacquet would take it further, making moaning, roaring sounds, peeling off his jacket while oscillating one sirenlike high note, and blasting out gruff honks while lying flat on his back. The rest of the band would march out into the audience, playing their horns up in people's faces, encouraging hand clapping, ass shaking, and general mayhem while Hamp egged them on from a precarious perch atop his drum kit. "Jazz had got so cool, we lost the kids who wanted to dance," Hampton remembered. "So we started playing this real gutty jazz, and people called it rhythm and blues." Hampton rode the first r&b wave to fame and (comparative) fortune; Whirling Willie and his rocking sanctified band disappeared into myth.

Conventionally, rock and roll has been seen as a fusion of two musical strains, rhythm and blues and country and western. Lionel Hampton's tales of Whirling Willie suggest another view of rock and roll's lineage: The music is basically an extension of the jazz tradition. Before the 1940s, the argument goes, jazz was art *and* entertainment. The most popular jazz instrumentalists and bandleaders of the pre–World War II era were often de facto pop stars, and no matter how sophisticated the music became in terms of harmonies and arrangements, it was always danceable. But during the mid-1940s—a period poorly documented because of the war, and because of a series of recording bans or strikes called by the American Federation of Musicians—the big river divided. One stream was music for listening, for serious aficionados and not, except perhaps coincidentally, for dancers. This stream became bebop, or modern jazz. The dance-music stream, carrying on the tradition of bluesy, hard-driving "jump" music epitomized by southwestern bands like Count Basie's, evolved into rhythm and blues, which in turn became rock and roll.

Like the r&b/c&w hypothesis, the jazz-offshoot theory is neat, simple, and historically and musically valid—as far as it goes. The trouble with such simplistic thinking is not that it's simple, but that it presupposes an either/or mind-set. The question isn't whether rock and roll is more an outgrowth of r&b/c&w or an outgrowth of jazz. Obviously, it's both of these things, and more. The question is whether the nature and identity of a musical genre as diverse (and slippery) as rock and roll can be adequately understood in terms of other genres. My own feeling is that as long as we confine ourselves to generic comparisons, we are basically talking terminology. How does the music work, and in what ways are the music's inner workings unique to rock and roll? This is a more basic level of discussion, and in *this* music, what could be more basic than rhythm?

It has long been a truism of jazz criticism that every important stylistic innovation begins with a decisive rhythmic shift. It happened before the dawn of recording, when the complex street-beat polyrhythms of much early New Orleans jazz began to be influenced by the emphatic two-beat vamping of ragtime, and then by a steadier, heavier, more evenly four-to-the-bar rhythm, which some New Orleans veterans have referred to as Memphis time. (The interplay of New Orleans's rolling parade-band rhythms and Memphis's steady-rocking blues beat later set up one of the principal rhythmic dynamics of first-generation rock and roll.) During the late 1920s, the tuba began to disappear from indoor jazz bands (as opposed to parade or marching bands), replaced by the more supple upright bass fiddle or "string bass." The drop in rhythm-section volume encouraged drummers like Count Basie's man Jo Jones to lighten up on the heavy artillery, transferring the timekeeping function from the bass drum to the ride cymbal. This was the rhythmic foundation of the jazz style known as swing.

In the forties, the modern jazz or bebop idiom developed an elaborate melodic language based on trickier, more radically syncopated drum patterns. "Even the word 'bebop' is a rhythm pattern," bop innovator Dizzy Gillespie remarked in a mid-1970s interview. "And I always figured that every melody has a specific rhythm. You can embellish on that rhythm, but each melody has a specific rhythmic *feel*. Now, when I want to show guys how to play a phrase, I'll say something like, 'oop bop she oodly bam.' If they can get the syllables they can play the phrase." Bebop proved to be the beginning of jazz music's move out of the dance halls and into the listening clubs and concert halls, a tendency that led inexorably to the free jazz of the sixties, which "freed" the music from the recurrence of a steady beat and regular bar lines.

Rock and roll has crammed a somewhat comparable evolution, from rough dance-hall music to oh-so-serious concert fare, into a much shorter period of time. But rockers have not found it necessary, or desirable, to dispense with a steady beat (except perhaps on the fringes of contemporary art punk and techno). The kids on "American Bandstand" during the 1950s and 1960s had their priorities straight; when rating new rock and roll records, their highest praise was "It's got a good beat; you can dance to it."

Rock and roll's opponents and detractors have confidently expressed their own view of the origins and nature of rock and roll rhythm. "It's the jungle strain that gets 'em all worked up," the manager of Washington, D.C.'s National Guard Armory opined after a June 1956 "riot" at his facility.

"Nothing more than an exhibition of primitive tom-tom thumping," sniffed Sir Malcolm Sargent, conductor of the BBC Symphony Orchestra, after Bill Haley's "Rock Around the Clock" fired up British teens at showings of the film *The Blackboard Jungle.* "Rock and roll," he added, "has been played in the jungle for centuries."

New York's *Daily News* described 1950s rock and roll as "a barrage of primitive jungle-beat rhythm set to lyrics which few adults would care to hear." An essayist in the *Catholic Sun* characterized Elvis Presley's music as a "voodoo of frustration and defiance." If there was any doubt as to where all this talk of jungle primitives and voodoo was leading, a 1956 editorial in the prestigious *Music Journal* spelled it out: Teenagers were "definitely influenced in their lawlessness by this throwback to jungle rhythms. Either it actually stirs them to orgies of sex and violence (as its model did for the savages themselves), or they use it as an excuse for the removal of all inhibitions and the complete disregard of the conventions of decency."

How to combat this menace? A circular distributed by the white supremacist Citizens' Council of Greater New Orleans outlined a plan of attack that many agreed with, though perhaps not everyone expressed it so baldly:

Oddly enough, the ravings of these (let's not mince words) racist swine find echoes of sorts in the words of some African music scholars. The Nigerian musicologist Fela Sowande, for example, notes that traditional views of music and its role in human life differ markedly from the analytical structuralism of Western musicology. In the latter, he writes, there is "an overconcentration on the formal and structural elements to the virtually total neglect of the symbological and psychological elements; the forcing of African culture patterns into Western European musical concepts, such as scale, pitch, etc.; and the use of partial material from one area of Africa to make broad generalizations about what is then termed 'African music' . . . If we seek to discover the foundations of traditional music in Africa, I think we have to look for them . . . in the traditional African's predilection for the esoteric and the occult, in religion and magic."

Drumming in Africa can help mediate social discourse and at the same time express an individual's relationship to the Divine. An example is what the African arts scholar Robert Farris Thompson calls "get-down sequences" in West African village music making: The dancer bends into a crouch and approaches the drummers, sometimes actually touching his or her forehead to the ground in front of the master drummer. Such dance sequences "seem to be frequently correlated in Africa with showing honor and respect, either to a fine drummer, in response to the savor of his phrasing, or to a deity. . . . Getting down encloses a dual expression of salutation and devotion." Thompson feels this African tradition underlies the African-American concept of "getting down" on the dance floor; remember K. C. and the Sunshine Band's 1970s hit "Get Down Tonight?"

The idea that certain rhythm patterns or sequences serve as conduits for spiritual energies, linking individual human consciousness with the gods, is basic to traditional African religions, and to African-derived religions throughout the Americas. And whether we're speaking historically or musicologically, the fundamental riffs, licks, bass figures, and drum rhythms that make rock and roll *rock* can ultimately be traced back to African music of a primarily spiritual or ritual nature. In a sense, rock and roll *is* a kind of "voodoo," rooted in a vigorous tradition of celebrating nature and spirit that's far removed from the sober patriarchal values espoused by the self-appointed guardians of Western culture. Rock and roll's "jungle rhythms"—its rich and sophisticated rhythmic heritage—traveled from specific African cultures to the Caribbean (particularly Cuba) to the black churches of the rural South, from there into the local dance halls, and finally, through recording and broadcast media, into the popular culture at large. This journey, or process, is a central rock and roll paradigm.

Lionel Hampton's tale of Whirling Willie is a perfect illustration of this rock and roll process at work. The whirling motif is reminiscent of an important Yoruba ritual from Nigeria and Dahomey, which Robert Farris Thompson's *African Art in Motion* describes as "the whirling return of the Eternal Kings of Yorubaland." This whirling dance is said to have originated with "a rich and powerful magician-king" who "turns round, round, round, round, round to show he has power." (The Yoruba made up a substantial proportion of Africans brought as slaves to Cuba and the southern United States, and their highly developed urban culture and elaborate religion and metaphysics were influential far beyond their immediate tribal and kinship groups.)

More concretely, one can trace the same fundamental rhythm patterns from Yoruba to Afro-Cuban ritual, to the "ring shouts" of southern backwoods churches, to the "shout" rhythms of sanctified musicians such as Whirling Willie, and on into rhythm and blues, rock and roll, soul, funk, and hip-hop. During the late 1950s, shout rhythms surfaced in a particularly

3

1 Lionel Hampton (at left, with drumsticks) and his orchestra turn up the heat and raise the roof: "I was brought up in the Holiness church... I always had that beat in me."

2 Al Green (left) and producer Willie Mitchell, outside Mitchell's Memphis studio: "The time here isn't so much like a metronome," says Mitchell, "it's more personal."

3 The Isley Brothers, bringing the sanctified "shout" to the pop charts.

4 Count Basie's All-American rhythm section, ca. 1939–40, "the best ever," according to the Rolling Stones' Charlie Watts and Bill Wyman; left to right, Freddie Green, guitar; Walter Page, bass; Jo Jones, drums; Basie, piano.

4

pure form in rock and roll hits such as the Isley Brothers' "Shout" and Ray Charles's "What'd I Say." Before they were records, these songs were onstage improvisations, with performers and listeners "getting down" together in creative call-and-response communal ecstasy.

Far from being a side issue, these processes of rhythmic elaboration and communal creativity are precisely what links early rhythm and blues and rock and roll to the latest developments in dance music and rap. And once we have identified these processes at work, it becomes apparent that rock and roll, in this broader sense, can no longer be considered a strictly made-in-the-U.S.A. phenomenon. In Jamaica, African ritual rhythms also penetrated the urban dance halls, then the media, a process that yielded ska, rock steady, and reggae. Like any other rock and roll, the Jamaican variety was heavily influenced by U.S. r&b and was influential in turn.

In the mid-sixties, for example, the Chicago soul of Curtis Mayfield and the Impressions permeated the Jamaican idiom dubbed rock steady. Within a few years, rock steady and early reggae rhythms were having an audible impact on southern soul music in Memphis, largely because of the interest and the frequent Jamaican vacations of Stax records session drummer and producer Al Jackson Jr. ("Jackson will go to Jamaica or the Bahamas and stay there for three or four days just to pick up on some kind of rhythm," soul singer Al Green reported in 1973. "Then he'll come to the studio and get back there on the drums . . . for hours, just beating the drums with his eyes closed. Willie [Mitchell, producer] will figure the musical changes for this particular rhythm that Al gets in his head.") In the late 1970s, DJ Kool Herc introduced Jamaican-style disc-jockey rapping at block parties in New York's South Bronx, and New Yorkers like Grandmaster Flash and the Furious Five built on this beginning to create rap and hip-hop culture. Hip-hop bounced back to Jamaica, where its influence ushered in the "dancehall" style. And so it goes.

Insofar as rock and roll represents a certain way of processing traditional sources (and all rock and roll comes out of earlier traditions to some degree), the music belongs not so much to "America" as to the African-American diaspora. And in the African traditions at the root of all this, music is never simply "art for art's sake." It has a spiritual dimension, a communications function, an orientation that is participatory right down

Ray Charles, running down an arrangement with soulful alto saxophonist Hank Crawford.

to the fundamentals of musical structure, most notably call-and-response. In traditional Africa, as in rock and roll, people don't just sit and stare at a musical performance, they *get into it.* They *shout.* They *get down.*

Do the Funky Chicken

"Don't use that word 'can't,'" cautioned Sam Phillips, Sun Records founder and rock and roll father figure, slurring his own words ever so slightly and sloshing his drink around in the glass. He was sitting in the comfortable den of his suburban Memphis home, late at night, speaking carefully into the telephone. "I don't believe in that word 'can't.' If *you* can't connect me, then transfer me to somebody who can. This is *Sam C. Phillips* calling, and I am *going* to speak to Fidel."

It was fall 1960, not a good time to be calling Fidel Castro. Hailed as a hero when his revolution toppled Cuba's Mafia-friendly Batista regime, Castro had recently been damned as a devil for his Marxist ideals. He had only recently returned to Havana from New York, where he had addressed the United Nations despite U.S. opposition. Demonstrations and brawls had greeted his arrival in New York. With his entourage and a number of live chickens in tow, he had bypassed the diplomatic watering holes and checked into Harlem's Hotel Theresa, where a constant stream of black jazz bands, blues shouters, and rock and rollers had found a home away from home. The American media had made great sport of these banana-republic bumpkins with their chickens. Castro claimed the chickens were for eating, that he was in danger of being poisoned by the CIA. How absurdly paranoid! Since when had assassinating world leaders been the American way?

Sam Phillips himself had been hailed as a hero and damned as a devil, all for unleashing Elvis Presley and Jerry Lee Lewis and their fellow rock and roll barn burners. And lately, with Elvis gone on to greener pastures—green army uniform, greenbacks from Hollywood and RCA—and Lewis run out of Britain for cradle robbing, rock and roll had been increasingly under siege. Sam was feeling besieged himself.

Phillips was no Commie. He was one hundred percent—*at least* one hundred percent—red-blooded, can-do American. But he also had empathy for all the itinerant bluesmen and hillbilly renegades who'd found their way to his Memphis studio and record company. America, he often said, should have a place for the "little people"—the poor, the undereducated, the disenfranchised. And from what he'd seen, Castro and his cohorts had thrown out a bunch of gangsters, ousted a corrupt and exploitative regime, all on behalf of honest people, working people; wasn't that what *America* was supposed to be about? Yet the American media were giving Castro and company a raw deal, a situation Sam found all too familiar.

So one dark night in Memphis, Sam had a few drinks, gave the matter some thought, and picked up his telephone. The first operator told him calling Havana wasn't possible just now. Sam asked for her supervisor, and when the supervisor was unhelpful, he began working his way up the chain of command. It took most of the night, bouncing from operator to operator, country to country, but Phillips wouldn't take "can't" for an answer. And finally, his deep, magisterial voice patched through singing lines and submerged cables, across the ocean and halfway around the world and back, Sam Phillips got through to Havana.

Fidel, they told him, simply could not be reached; perhaps he was taking briefings on the then-imminent invasion of his country by Cuban exiles and CIA/Mafia goons at the Bay of Pigs. Sam still wouldn't be put off. The Cubans, perhaps out of sheer desperation, finally put him through to Raul Castro, Fidel's brother and right-hand man. Sam realized that this was as far as he was going to get; he might be an idealist, but he was nobody's fool. "Raul," he said, "they just didn't treat you folks *right* up there in New York. You tell Fidel the next time he comes to the United States, he can come to Memphis, Tennessee, and stay with *Sam C. Phillips.* And maybe we can straighten this thing out."

Alas, this potentially golden chapter in Cuban-American relations and rock and roll statesmanship was not to be. The conversation has become a Memphis legend, nothing more. But what a vision to contemplate: Sam and Fidel, getting down in Sam's father-knows-best suburban den, smoking Havana cigars and drinking potent Cuban rum and grooving to some of Sam's Sun 45's, with their yellow labels and crowing-rooster logo—or is it a chicken? Sam puts on an r&b disc with a shave-and-a-haircut/six-bits rhythm pattern. "We have this rhythm in Cuba," says Fidel. "We call it *clave,* and play it on two sticks, like this." He takes a comb out of his pocket and beats out the pattern on a half-empty bottle of rum. "Here," says Sam, "it used to be called the hambone. Now they're calling it the Bo Diddley beat." A puzzled look crosses Fidel's face. "Bo Diddley? Does he stay sometimes at the Hotel Theresa in Harlem? Maybe I met him there. Does he by any chance have a particular fondness for chickens?"

Flights of fancy aside, anyone exploring the musical culture of Cuba and of Sam Phillips's beloved mid-South will find a number of similarities— so many that looking at Cuban traditions in some depth will yield significant information about rhythmic fundamentals of rock and roll. Phillips's success had a great deal to do with his location in Memphis, where they say the Mississippi Delta begins in the lobby of the Peabody Hotel, less than a mile from Sun Records' front door. And musically speaking, Cuba is the Mississippi Delta of the Americas, the root source of rhythms and sounds that have sparked or mediated major transitions in modern popular music: swing into modern jazz, rhythm and blues into rock and roll, soul into funk. Ask the Cubans where their music comes from, and many will point to the mountainous, jungle-lush Oriente province and its capital, Santiago de Cuba, in the far south of Cuba—the heartland of the island's African religious and musical survivals, and the birthplace of Castro's revolution. If Cuba is the Mississippi Delta of the Americas, then Oriente is the Mississippi Delta of Cuba.

Afro-Cuban music and the black music of Mississippi and Louisiana share common ancestry. Early in the nineteenth century, the Haitian revolution sent that island's plantation owners packing. Many managed to escape with their African slaves, whose origins were primarily Yoruba and Fon, from the region of modern Nigeria and Dahomey, with some important Kongo elements. Most of these slaves ended up either in Cuba, where they were concentrated in Oriente province, or in the southern United States, principally in Louisiana but spreading out into Mississippi as well. This common origin is reflected in the respective musical traditions. "In all the Caribbean and Latin America," says musicologist Rene Lopez, "only in Cuban and black American music do you find a heavy emphasis on the backbeat, on 'two' and 'four.' Everything else, from calypso to samba, merengue to reggae, is accented on 'one' and 'three.'" The reorientation of American music toward the "one"—accenting the first beat of every measure—is a recent development, stemming from the funk idiom of the late 1960s and early 1970s.

Certain bass patterns—clipped, telegraphic two-to-four-note phrases called *tumbaos* in Cuba and traditionally known as *rocks* in the southern United States—show up identically in Cuban *son* and American r&b. In Cuba, where African slaves continued to be imported right up to the end of the nineteenth century, African roots played an overt, front-and-center role in the emergence of a distinctively national popular music. Hard-core African rhythms could be heard almost daily in the rituals of the Afro-Cuban religions, and took to the streets every spring at carnival time. During the nineteenth century, African rhythmic structures filtered out of the Oriente countryside and found their way into the popular dance halls of Santiago de Cuba. From there, the new music—African polyrhythms undergirding Spanish guitar styles and stanza forms, all mediated by African-style solo/chorus call-and-response—spread to Havana. They called this music *son.* When asked what *son* means, Cubans tend to laugh. "It doesn't mean anything," people insist. "It's a sound." I once asked a Cuban musician if this *son* business was anything like "a-wop-bop-a-loo-bop-a-lop-bam-boom." "Or like bebop," he countered, then grinned. "Yes, exactly."

By the 1920s, Havana was rocking to *son*'s bass-heavy riffs. The music's most characteristic bass pattern was a three-note figure, harmonically a triad, identical to the bass parts on mid-1950s rock and roll hits such as Lloyd Price's (and later Elvis Presley's) "Lawdy Miss Clawdy" and Fats Domino's "Blueberry Hill" and "Blue Monday," among *many* others. New Orleans producer-bandleader Dave Bartholomew first employed this figure (as a saxophone-section riff) on his own 1949 disc "Country Boy" and subsequently helped make it the most overused rhythmic pattern in 1950s rock and roll. On numerous recordings by Fats Domino, Little Richard, and others, Bartholomew assigned this repeating three-note pattern not just to the string bass, but also to electric guitars and even baritone sax, making for a very heavy bottom. He recalls first hearing the figure—as a bass pattern—on a Cuban disc. He referred to the source recording as a rhumba, but actual Cuban rhumba is a different matter, a heavily African popular idiom for voices and percussion only. With the popularity of heavily diluted rhumba as a U.S. dance craze, danced in Hollywood films by George Raft, among others, record companies began stamping the word *rhumba* on all manner of Latin recordings, many of them actually *son*. The generally accepted term "rhumba-blues," for the New Orleans and Gulf Coast rhythm and blues style popularized by pianists such as Professor Longhair and Lloyd Glenn, is actually a misnomer. "Rhumba-blues" records employ the three-note bass riff (played by the pianist's left hand) and the Bo Diddleyish *clave* rhythm characteristic not of rhumba, but of *son*.

In Cuba, the process of Oriente roots music becoming Havana pop music entailed a certain amount of simplification, especially in the rhythmic sphere. "The syncopated style proved to be too complicated and funky for the taste of the general urban public," writes John Santos in his liner notes to an album of 1920s recordings by Havana's Sexteto Boloña. "As a result, a commercialization of the *son* occurred in which the African elements in the rhythms and vocals were simplified. . . . The role of the *'clave* rhythm' was gradually elevated to major importance when the *son* became established and popular in Havana." Santos might as well be describing the codification of polyrhythms associated with the Deep South ring shout into that American *clave*-rhythm analogue, the Bo Diddley beat.

But in both Cuba and the U.S., the music has shown signs of reversing its direction in recent years. Since James Brown and his fellow funkateers "turned the beat around" in the mid-sixties, rock and roll, especially in its funk and hip-hop guises, has been stripping out the music's more European elements—chord changes, lyrical melodies, stanzaic song forms—and emphasizing the rhythmic interplay of voices and percussion. Melody instruments, such as guitars and horns, have become rhythm instruments. New elements such as turntable scratching, found-sound collage, and various rhythm machines, from basic beat box to sequencing technology, have been put to primarily rhythmic usages as well. Meanwhile, in Cuba, the sacred drums of the Yoruba-derived *Lucumí* religion are no longer heard only in ritual circumstances, as they were for several hundred years. Now the three-drum choirs that rap out the rhythmic tattoos of the various Yoruba gods and goddesses are being heard in jazz and dance bands, and even in the celebrated and highly elaborate floor shows at tourist hotels like the Tropicana in Havana.

These sacred drums, called *bata,* are always played in groups of three, and they come in three different sizes. Each drum has two heads of unequal size, giving the three-drum *bata* ensemble a six-note melodic range. Additional notes can be produced by adept drummers through varying the pressure on the drumheads. The seven principal powers of Yoruba cosmology, their various subpersonalities, and other spiritual presences are each called by a specific rhythmic/melodic formula. When played by a trio of drumming adepts, these formulas unfold into a lucid and stately counterpoint, with the transparent clarity and inner-voiced complexity of a fugue. Among the formulas are rhythms and melodies that have become building blocks for black American musical expression. The *clave* pattern of *son,* and its Bo Diddley analogue, figure in a number of *bata* rhythms, as one rhythmic layer among several. Some *bata* melodies have a familiar ring. A *toque,* or rhythmic formula, sacred to Oyá, for example, is built around a repeated three-note pattern familiar in American pop music as the opening phrase of the Tin Pan Alley favorite "Blues in the Night."

Bata drummers tap out their *toques,* or rhythm patterns, like signals to the realm of the gods, inviting and enticing them to come on down and "mount" or possess their "horses," or devotees. Experienced drummers keep an eye on the crowd, looking for signs that certain members of the congregation known to be devotees of Shango or Oshun or another Yoruba *Orisha* (deity) are on the verge of slipping into an altered state of consciousness—a "trance." The drummers may shift their rhythms to guide a particular dancer into a trance, then shift again, to cajole another dancer with a pattern sacred to a different *Orisha.* The specific drum patterns or *toques* include some riffs and licks basic to the rock and roll vocabulary. In addition to having precise melodic and rhythmic parameters, the *toques* also boast a semantic dimension. Lucumí, the ritual language of the Cuban Yoruba, is a pitch-tone language; each *toque* pattern has verbal content, specifically, praise-formulas and invocations to the gods.

It should be emphasized that the trance rituals of religions such as Cuban *Santeria* and Haitian *vodoun* (voodoo) have nothing to do with hypnosis or "mind control." The ability to respond to a specific trance-rhythm is to some degree a learned, culturally reinforced pattern of behavior, and the process works only when "set and setting" are appropriate. The atmosphere at an Afro-Cuban *bembe,* or ritual service, differs markedly from that of the conventional Christian service. While some participants are in the throes of trance, others circulate, make small talk, or dance just to have a good time. "The success of a *bembé* is not necessarily determined by whether or not the *Orisha* mount participants," writes Robert A. Friedman, an anthropologist who apprenticed himself as a beginning *bata* drummer with an Afro-Cuban congregation in the Bronx. "In the words of one participant, 'If they don't come it's not bad because it's still a party.'" This does not signify a compromised religiosity; it's just that in African tradition, "sacred" and "secular" are not thought of as being mutually exclusive.

The primary responsibility of the *bata* drummers is mediating between the world of men and the world of the *Orisha;* they guide others through trance experiences, but must remain clearheaded themselves. As documented by Friedman, their "shop talk" provides as lucid an analysis of rhythmic praxis in musics of the African diaspora—including rock and roll—as one can find anywhere.

The *bata* drummers Friedman interviewed define the interaction of individual drum parts as rhythmic-melodic "conversation," another example of call-and-response as an African fundamental. When Friedman asked them to break down overall *toques* into their component parts, the drummers' typical response was, "I don't break it down into parts, I break it down in terms of feeling the total picture." Among *bata* drummers, as in rock and roll, this total picture is defined as "the groove"—"that point," according to Friedman and his informants, "at which 'the energy of the music becomes constant and everything clicks.' A groove is constructed at the level of the ensemble rather than the individual . . . and can only be achieved through actual playing." In other words, the give-and-take ("conversation") always aims at creating a *unity:* the groove. And conversely, the groove becomes fully energized only through give-and-take between rhythm patterns and between players and listeners.

Rock and roll is sustained by the same sort of communal groove. When we say a band is *rocking,* we mean they're *in the groove;* together they've reached that point of "forward-propelling directionality" (the phrase is Gunther Schuller's) when "the energy of the music becomes constant and everything clicks." In musicians' slang, "rocking the house," an expression common among blues and barrelhouse players as early as the 1930s, reminds us that the "house" is integral to the total picture—as integral as the musicians themselves. Rock and roll as *recorded* music simply adds another circuit to the feedback loop. Is it any wonder rock and roll listeners often seem to be behaving like entranced devotees, true believers? The music's basic rhythmic structures encourage, even demand, the most committed sort of participation. As in an Afro-Cuban *bembé* celebration, the listener becomes part of the groove. Disapproving parents and self-appointed authority figures are unable to penetrate this charmed circle. They aren't "getting" the groove; it isn't *rocking* them.

In order to function effectively in a ritual context, the *bata* drums are traditionally "baptized," or consecrated. This suggests that the drums are in some sense personalized—given human qualities—and in fact, the three-drum grouping, common throughout West and Central Africa, is traditionally represented as a family. The largest *bata* drum (*iya*) speaks with the deepest voice and is the father. The *itotele,* or middle drum, is the mother. The *okonkolo,* which is the smallest, highest-pitched drum, is the child. This is not simple folklore or fanciful imagery; the symbolism determines each drum's role within the ensemble. As you might expect, the *bata* family is a highly traditional household. Only the largest, deepest drum, the "father," has the authority to initiate conversations, cue changes in rhythm, or improvise. Playing the "father" drum is the prerogative of the ensemble's master drummer. The second-largest drum, the "mother," plays fixed rhythms, except when specifically cued into a "conversation," or series of pattern variations, by the "father." The "child" drum is too young to participate in family discussions as yet; it plays a fixed, repeating pattern throughout each *toque.*

The familial roles of the drums also govern the mechanics of push/pull or rock/roll within the ensemble. According to Friedman, "The individual drummer must . . . be sensitive to how he is supposed to manipulate the tempo of his playing to create rhythmic tension in performance. This is called 'pushing' and 'pulling' the rhythms, or 'playing on top of the beat' and 'laying back.' To 'push' rhythms . . . is to manipulate the tempo of the rhythm so that it sounds as if it is being played slightly ahead of the overall pulse. . . . To 'pull' or 'lay back' is to achieve the opposite performance effect and make the rhythmic pattern appear slightly behind the overall pulse. The art of 'pushing' or 'pulling' the rhythm involves doing so without causing the . . . overall tempo to fluctuate." Family rules dictate that the "child" *okonkolo* always pushes, or plays up on top of the beat, like any eager, active youngster. The parents pull, or exert a subtle "laying back" effect, reflecting their maturity and wisdom.

What does this have to do with rock and roll? Consider a 1950s recording by Little Richard or Fats Domino. Not only do the individual instrumental parts variously push and pull against the beat; listen to who's pushing and who's pulling. The higher-pitched "voices" within the ensemble—the pianist's right-hand triplet figures, the swish and sizzle of the drummer's ride cymbal—play fixed, repetitive parts that "push," or slightly rush the beat, like the high-pitched "child" drum *okonkolo.* The more regular parts in the lower register—bass, bass drum, and tom-toms—tend to "pull," or lay back, like the "parent" drums *iya* and *itotele.*

Earl Palmer, the drummer on 1950s hits by Little Richard and Fats Domino, gives an illuminating demonstration of the way the parts push and pull within a New Orleans rock and roll band on an instructional video, *New Orleans Drumming from R&B to Funk* (DCI Music Video). The various instruments and parts of the drum kit push and pull according to *bata* family rules. Memphis producer and bandleader Willie Mitchell, an active recording musician since the early 1950s but best known for his definitive 1970s production work with Al Green, eloquently outlined a Memphis version of this rock and roll dynamic in 1973: "I used to notice the jazz players here, like George Coleman or Charles Lloyd. Now, they played really *fast,* but still they'd play behind the beat just a little bit. That kind of 'lazy' quality is one thing the jazz players and the r&b players in this town have always had in common. Even when Bill Black hit with 'Smokie' and 'White Silver Sands,' or if you remember Otis Redding's records, they'd be playing behind the tempo just a little bit and all of a sudden everybody would . . . kind of sway. Even the lazy old horns, they'd be half a beat behind where it sounded like they were going to miss it altogether, and all of a sudden they'd sway like that and be right up on the beat. The time here isn't so much like a metronome; it's more personal. Yeah, the horns talk to the bass and the bass talks to the drums, the singer talks to everybody. . . . To me, a record is like people talking, expressing themselves to each other."

With the popularization of funk rhythms in the 1970s and their later absorption into hip-hop grooves, the push-and-pull and call-and-response have moved more and more into the forefront of the music. And it's still a family affair; in hip-hop, those high-pitched syn-drums whack and whoosh, pushing the beat like a hyperactive child. The patriarchal bass has achieved greater freedom of movement and a more prominent level in the mix. Master bassman Doug Wimbish (Grandmaster Flash, Fats Comet, Living Colour) calls it "bass in your face."

The layering of insistent, repetitive rhythm patterns that push and pull in a finely modulated play of tension and release is central to the rock and roll idiom. Coupled with group singing, dancing, and other modes of participation, these rhythmic usages are capable of transforming an audience into participants in communal ecstasy. And why not? The rhythms have been forged and tempered in hundreds of years of religious ritual, from Africa to the Caribbean to the American South. In the U.S., where slaves were generally prohibited from making and playing drums, their hands and feet, and later European instruments, had to take the drums' place. This circumstance, along with the other exigencies of the black experience in the U.S., gave the music here an added urgency. There's even a certain urgency in the name attached to rhythmic music and circle dancing in down-home black churches: the shout.

Shouting "Lost! Lost!"

"It was at night that the most terrible scenes were witnessed, when the campfires blazed in a mighty circle around the vast audience of pioneers."

Is this grabber the beginning of an Old West horror tale? No, it's an account of an 1801 Christian camp meeting and revival held near Lexington, Kentucky, then the American frontier. Compiled from eyewitness accounts, originally published in F. M. Davenport's *Primitive Traits in Religious Revivals,* and unearthed by Marshall Stearns in his groundbreaking roots-music study *The Story of Jazz,* this story recalls a historical moment when Protestant zeal led to mass meetings at which blacks, slave and free, were encouraged to worship alongside whites. The result was a highly contagious religious rapture in which "the volume of song burst all bonds of guidance and control, and broke again and again from the throats of the people, while over all, at intervals, there rang out the shout of ecstasy, the sob and the groan. . . . Men and women shouted aloud . . . running from preacher to preacher if it were whispered that it was 'more lively' at some other point, swarming enthusiastically around a 'fallen' brother, laughing, leaping, sobbing, shouting, swooning. . . . Some, shrieking in agony, bounded about like a live fish out of water. Many lay down and rolled over and over for hours at a time. Others rushed wildly over the stumps and benches, and then plunged, shouting 'Lost! Lost!' into the forest."

With this kind of behavior a camp-meeting norm, it seems incredible that mere *dancing* would cause much of a fuss. But dancing was "sinful," forbidden by Scripture. And dancing was an integral part of the African religious practices that American authorities, secular as well as ecclesiastical, were intent on stamping out. How do you tell a worshipper who's gyrating and jumping, "Lost! Lost!" in trance, to stop that nasty dancing and behave? You don't; you redefine dancing. For the Protestant evangelicals of the early nineteenth century, dancing was a type of physical activity that specifically entailed *crossing the feet*. It seems ludicrous, but think about it. If you're genuinely tranced out, you aren't going to be worrying about your footwork. If you cross your feet, you aren't having a religious experience, you're showing off your moves. At least, that was the theory. What it meant in practice was that the multitude of black dance traditions imported into America gradually became codified into a form of rhythmic song and worship that *looked* a lot like dancing, but wasn't stigmatized as such. This was the shout, or (because it was "danced" in a circle, counterclockwise, like so many traditional West African dances) the *ring shout*—a generative archetype ancestral to all gospel, rock, and soul.

Folklorists John and Alan Lomax recorded an atavistic ring shout in rural Louisiana in 1934. It was eventually issued on LP by the Library of Congress as "Run Old Jeremiah," and it rocks as hard or harder than any music on record. "I gotta rock, you gotta rock," the Jennings, Louisiana, shouters insist, with what is most likely (as in so many spirituals) a double meaning. Jesus is the rock of salvation, a solid rock to cling to in times of trouble. But the shouters are also exhorting each other to rock with the forceful rhythm. A song leader rasps these and other telegraphic phrases, his voice so strained with emotion it frequently forsakes sense for pure sound. A chorus answers in the ubiquitous call-and-response format. The wooden floor of the rural church resonates like a huge drumhead to the inexorable momentum of coordinated foot-stamping rhythms, with hand-clapping patterns providing syncopated cross-rhythms. Again and again in eyewitness accounts of shouting, the observer comments that the feet sound like drumming. They also *function* like drumming, triggering and then guiding or shaping trance experiences. The slaves had found, in the wooden floors of plantation houses and shacks and later in their own churches, the only efficient substitutes for the prohibited drums that were available to them. The floors boomed with deep enough fundamental vibrations and sufficient resonance and frequency range to produce the massive motor and sensory stimulation necessary for triggering and regulating trance experiences.

The ring shout recordings made by the Lomaxes in 1930s Louisiana, and the *Slave Shout Songs* album recorded in the 1980s in Georgia for Folkways, sound as if nothing much has changed since the first published description of the shout in 1845. Art Rosenbaum, who recorded the Folkways album, writes that the shouters "move in a counterclockwise ring, with a compelling hitching shuffle, often stooping or extending their arms in gestures pantomiming the content of the songs being sung." Alan Lomax's description of Louisiana shouters is more vivid: "True to an age-old West African pattern, the dancers shuffle round and round single file, moving in a counterclockwise direction, clapping out the beat in complex counter-rhythms. The floor of the church furnished the drumhead. The lines of the song are partly religious and partly satirical, using as material the groaning delivery of the Negro minister and the shrill screams of the sisters in the throes of religious hysteria." Both accounts suggest that the ring shout preserved something of the West African tendency to mix the secular, the satirical, even the ribald into worship and ritual. (In these traditions, "sacred" and "secular" are not so much integral categories as poles, with most of the action falling somewhere between them.) Thus we have the sensuous, almost erotic, imagery and emotionalism of so much black American gospel music, and the deeply devotional spirituality that informs "secular" celebrations of love and sex such as Smokey Robinson's "Ooo Baby Baby" or Marvin Gaye's "Let's Get It On."

Rhythmically, the action of the ring shout has to do with the syncopation of hand-clapping patterns against the thunderous but steady stamping of feet. With the coming of the sanctified, all-musical-instruments-welcome denominations toward the end of the nineteenth century, the steady-rocking beat of the shouters' feet became the province of "that sister on the bass drum," the bedrock of what Lionel Hampton called the "sanctified beat." The shout's most characteristic hand clapping involved a three-beat accent pattern familiar to any Bo Diddley fan. It's the first half of the Afro-Cuban *clave*/hambone/Bo Diddley beat: "*shave* and-a *hair-cut*" repeated over and over, rather than "*shave* and-a *hair-cut/six bits.*" You can find this three-beat pattern buried in *bata* drum polyrhythms, on recordings of Yoruba music from Nigeria as well as Cuba. Beginning in the late nineteenth century, the same pattern (and related variants) appeared in the notated bass parts of ragtime and early jazz compositions. Sometimes it was identified on the sheet music as a "shout" rhythm (as in James P. Johnson's celebrated piano piece "Carolina Shout"); during the 1920s, it figured in music for dance crazes such as the Charleston and Black Bottom. The three-beat pattern itself was generally referred to as the Habañera, a name that suggests someone was aware of its Cuban (Havana) associations or origins.

One of the curiosities of the shout is the meaning and import of the word itself. Early observers and contemporary scholars agree in their insistence that "The word 'shout' refers specifically to the movement and is only coincidentally the same as the English word meaning a vocal exclamation," wrote Rosenbaum in his notes to *Slave Shout Songs*. In other words, "shouting" describes the counterclockwise circle dance, and not the use of the voice. The meaning persisted in rock and roll usage: the Isley Brothers' hit singles "Shout" and "Twist and Shout" are full of instructions for dancing and say nothing about using the voice: "Shake it shake it baby/Come on and work it on out."

Folklorists working along the coast of Georgia and the Carolinas, the heartland of the shout, have uncovered a number of accounts of trusted house slaves who had learned to read and write in Islamized West Africa.

1. A ring shout from the Georgia Sea Islands, with the shouters demonstrating the body language of this circular "holy dance."

2. Cab Calloway turned conducting his orchestra into a loose-limbed, head-shaking, fluid sort of dancing, creating a gestural vocabulary that later influenced everyone from Bo Diddley to Elvis Presley.

3. James Brown, combining Calloway's precision with the explosive energy and rhythmic mesmerism of the black churches.

3

These slaves were entrusted with the plantation ledger books and kept meticulous records—in Arabic. And one of the oldest forms of traditional Arabic music, spread to Africa through Arab slave trading and Islamic jihad, was the *saut*—pronounced "shout." It involved a deep bass-drum rhythm, syncopated hand clapping, and call-and-response vocal interplay. More: The *saut* is also a kind of holy circle dance, specifically the movement of pilgrims in Mecca circumambulating Islam's most sacred shrine, the *Ka'aba*—always in a counterclockwise direction. These pilgrims would never call their act of worship a dance; dancing is sinful in orthodox Islam no less than among fundamentalist Christians.

The black American ring shout, then, was an institution of decidedly mixed parentage. It was West African, probably Afro-Cuban, possibly Arabic in origin; Yoruba/Lucumí, Christian, and possibly Muslim in terms of religious affiliation. As such, it's a case study in rock and roll genealogy, which is never as linear and clear-cut as the beleaguered student might wish. But this much is clear: Fela Sowande's suggestion that we look for "the foundations of traditional music in Africa . . . in the traditional African's predilection for the esoteric and the occult, in religion and magic," is equally applicable to the African-American foundations of rock and roll. These foundations are primarily spiritual—not "religious" in the sense of Christianity versus "paganism" or "church" versus "cult," but "pertaining to the soul and spirit" and "relating to sacred things," dictionary definitions of the spiritual. Rock and roll aims for liberation and transcendence, eroticizing the spiritual and spiritualizing the erotic, because that is its ecumenical birthright.

So it seems entirely appropriate that Bo Diddley, the man most responsible for putting rock and roll "in the shout mode," got his earliest musical training in church. More surprisingly, his first instrument was the violin; his teacher directed a young people's orchestra that rehearsed at the Ebenezer Baptist Church on Chicago's South Side. In one of those unexpected reversals so characteristic of this music called rock, he then transferred techniques from his classical violin training to the electric guitar. "I call it the muted sound," Diddley elaborated in 1994. "I learned that from playing the classical violin . . . and now they call it funk." What he's referring to is a rhythm style that involves choking the guitar strings. Slashing, choked-string rhythm guitar was heard on Diddley records like "Pretty Thing" almost a decade before it became one of the basics of James Brown's "Brand New Bag," as interpreted by J.B.'s guitarists Jimmy "Chank" Nolen and Alphonso "Country" Kellum.

Bo Diddley's original inspiration on guitar was John Lee Hooker, and especially Hooker's "Boogie Chillen," a hard-rocking stomp with a chant-like melody, no chord changes, heavily amplified electric guitar, and shout-like percussion provided by Hooker's stamping feet. The influence of Hooker's loudly amplified, bass-heavy drones and percussive chording can be heard clearly in Diddley's recordings. But while he was born in Mississippi, Bo Diddley grew up in Chicago, and his other influences were suitably cosmopolitan. These ranged from the down-home electric blues of Chess labelmate Muddy Waters to country and western music to Cab Calloway.

It was Cab who directly inspired Bo's fast line in jive talk and showed him that song subjects were as close at hand as any street corner in the 'hood. Calloway's swing-era hits often recounted the exploits of recogniz-able street-corner characters like "Minnie the Moocher" and the "Reefer Man." Mold a sufficiently clever and memorable tune around these exploits, infuse it with enough energy and flair, and you could score a pop hit, tran-scending the entertainment ghetto with a choice bit of street-corner jive. Calloway in the late 1930s and Louis Jordan in the forties worked variations on this methodology into hit after hit; by 1955 it was Bo Diddley's turn. Adding nursery rhymes, children's games, and down-home traditions of verbal braggadocio and insult competition to his arsenal, he recorded a series of "signifying" singles that found him sparring verbally with his deep-voiced maracas player and alter ego, Jerome Green. The records, ahead-of-their-time rap competitions spoken over churning rhythm jams, included "Say Man," "Hush Your Mouth," "Signifying Blues," and the inevitable "Say Man, Back Again." The insults were choice: "I ran into your girl the other day. I took her home. . . . But that gal was so ugly, she had to sneak up on a glass to get a drink of water." "Aw, I hear you had a job stand-ing in front of a doctor's office makin' people sick!"

Bo was a tireless sonic experimenter who designed and built his own guitars (the flying "V," the square-bodied one, guitars with tail fins, guitars with fur), customized his amp and other equipment, built a series of home studios, and effectively produced many of his own recording sessions. He consistently pushed the envelope in terms of heavy guitar amplification, becoming a pioneer of distortion, sustain, and feedback on bracing discs like the 1956 "Who Do You Love?" His material drew musical inspiration from sources as disparate as gospel quartets and doo-wop ("Diddley Daddy" and "Diddy Wah Diddy" with the Moonglows, "Crackin' Up" with the Carnations) and stone hillbilly music ("Cadillac," "Ride On Josephine"). He was a major first-generation rock and roll artist, far more than a rhythmic one-trick pony. But what he is known for, and probably always will be known for, is one trick: the "Bo Diddley beat." He is not content with this state of affairs. "Guys kind of piss me off trying to name what I'm doing," he said in a 1990 interview. "A lot of people say that's hambone. I'll say that I've always been a lover of African-sounding drums. I play the guitar as if it was a drum. . . . I always just played what I felt."

To young Bo Diddley, growing up in the "Little Mississippi" that was South Side Chicago, what became the "Bo Diddley beat" must have been an environmental presence—booming from Pentecostal storefront churches, popped out with a shoeshine rag, implicit in speech rhythms and in the spring of people's walks. And as John Lee Hooker remarked in Bo's favorite "Boogie Chillen," "It's in him, it's got to come out." At the same time, Bo's claim to have *invented* something, his insistence that he was doing more than simply parroting an already existing beat, has both sincerity and the ring of truth. The very concept of the "Bo Diddley beat" is inadequate; what Bo came up with was a comprehensive theory of rhythmic orchestration. The traditional rhythms he picked up were merely raw materials.

Listen again to "Bo Diddley," "Pretty Thing," "Hush Your Mouth," and "Say Man"—records built around the beat, as opposed to the gospel-ish rave-ups, doo-wop, blues, guitar instrumentals, and tongue-in-cheek hillbilly songs that make up a surprisingly large proportion of the Diddley discography. Neither the exact rhythm patterns nor the way these patterns are parceled out among the various instruments remain constant from song to song. What does remain constant is the method of rhythmic layering. Generally, the drummer is directed to concentrate on his deeper drums, especially the bass drum and tom-toms. There is rarely a cymbal

John Lee Hooker, king of the stompdown boogie: "Let that boy boogie-woogie!"

pattern. Instead, the sort of cross-rhythms carried by hand clapping in the old-time ring shout, and by the ride and sock cymbals in much rock and jazz drumming, are assigned to Jerome Green's maracas. These maracas are always prominent in the mix, with a presence equal in sonic weight to that of the drum kit. Bo's electric guitar, often played through an early tremolo attachment or other effects, takes care of two distinct layers of rhythm all by itself, one in the instrument's bass range, the other in the treble. Having played for years without a bassist, Bo lays down basic bass-range riff patterns on his bottom strings. Simultaneously, vigorous high-end picking is weaving in and out of the maracas' double-time swish. On some records this carefully ordered and dynamically balanced density of polyrhythms is further elaborated by claves (the wooden strikers that sound the *clave* pattern in Cuban music) and other percussion instruments. Sometimes piano, harmonica, or a second guitar add seasoning to the gumbo. The specific balance and deployment of instruments vary from tune to tune, and so does the overall rhythmic resultant, a.k.a. the groove.

With hindsight, and a handful of late-sixties James Brown records, it isn't difficult to divine which way Bo Diddley's music was heading. The tendency is for every instrument to become a rhythm instrument. One song is differentiated from another not so much by melody (which tends to flatten out into a kind of chant) or harmony (which is reduced to one or two chord changes, or none at all) as by the particular character and content of its rhythmic organization and rhythmic wordplay. What this amounts to is a *different kind of song*. According to the old Tin Pan Alley model, still the basis of much pop and rock songcraft and of our antiquated music copyright laws, a song has a lyric, a melody, and a sequence of chords. In a court of law, you can sue and win if someone writes a song that quotes substantially from the words, the tune, or the chord progression of a song you have previously copyrighted. You cannot sue on the basis of a pirated rhythm pattern or beat, which is one of the main reasons rhythmic innovators like Bo Diddley and James Brown are not millionaires many times over. You can churn out songs built around Bo Diddley rhythms or James Brown funk grooves to your heart's content, and according to the law, you won't owe Bo or James one dime. Lesser artists have been doing just that for decades now.

As is so often the case in the tangled history of this music, technological developments have brought this particular issue to the fore. Now that digital sampling is street-level tech, you no longer have to *imitate* a rhythm or a groove; you can snatch a piece of it right off the original record and use *that* as the basis of your song. With the ascendancy of hip-hop, disc jockeys have become sound-collagists, and rappers can deliver an album's worth of messages over elaborately orchestrated backing tracks made entirely from borrowed or sampled sounds and drum-machine beats. There's lots of money to be made by copyright owners whose recordings have been sampled and recycled on popular rap discs. But "sampling" doesn't begin with digital technology; Diddley-beat hits such as Johnny Otis's "Willie and the Hand Jive" and "Crazy Country Hop," Buddy Holly's (and the Rolling Stones') "Not Fade Away," even the Smiths' mid-eighties British hit "How Soon Is Now?" were in effect sampling Bo's work. The difference is that the samplers were human musicians rather than machines.

In traditional West African cultures, a piece of music is held to be satisfying and complete if there is sufficient rhythmic interest; to oversimplify, rhythm is as fundamental to African music as harmony in European tradition and melodic sophistication in the music of India. Indian music has no harmony as such, and nobody complains; much European classical music is rhythmically one-dimensional—one is tempted to say primitive—and you don't hear symphony subscribers complaining about that. But when pop music begins moving away from Tin Pan Alley song forms and musical values and embracing the aesthetics of its African origins, suddenly our culture is seen as adrift, endangered, riven by decadence and decay. Some pundits write books bemoaning "The Loss of Beauty and Meaning in American Popular Music." Others assert that heavy metal, or punk, or gangster rap—whatever the latest pop-music bogeyman happens to be—imperils the very fabric of civilization! ("Others rushed wildly over the stumps and benches, and then plunged, shouting 'Lost! Lost!' into the forest.")

It would help if these gloom-and-doom mongers could see the history of this music as a matter of cycles within cycles, or as a developing idiom that periodically refreshes itself by drinking from its own deepest wellsprings. Rock and roll's earliest American antecedents, such as the shout and the work song, emphasized voices and rhythm—a message with a beat. This was partly a matter of (African) tradition, and partly a matter of necessity; voices, feet to stamp, and hands to clap were often the only means of musical expression available. After emancipation, musical instruments became more readily available, and black culture responded with an astonishing flowering of musical styles and idioms. During the last decade or two of the nineteenth century and the first and second decades of the twentieth, an unprecedented range of new musics emerged—ragtime, blues, jazz, rocking sanctified gospel. A similarly feverish and even briefer creative flowering in the years during and just after World War II brought bebop, which was a concert music quite distinct from the dance-oriented jazz of the swing era; Afro-Cuban jazz and salsa, which introduced the telegraphic bass ostinatos and one-chord vamps of the Cuban *son* into the American musical mainstream; and the many varieties of rhythm and blues, from jazzy band-blues to boogie-woogie to down-home electric blues to variously pop and gospel-oriented vocal groups. Most of these distinct genres and subgenres (which overlap considerably in practice) have periodically paused to drink from the well. Often, the combination of roots and refinements yields a new form, which the young people who support it hear as fresh and novel.

White musicians have long since made the rock and roll idiom their own; white producers have wrought changes great and small; white packagers have presented the music to the world. The fact remains that the music's wellsprings, its governing aesthetic precepts, its "deep structures," are fundamentally African and African-American. Spirit and rhythm, the message and the beat, are the music's ruling principles. At a certain emotional temperature, they fuse: The rhythm is spiritualized and the spirituality has a beat you can dance to. Make you want to *shout!*

R-E-S-P

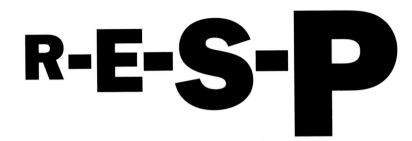

The Wicked Pickett, a panther on the prowl in the midnight hour, a mustang on funky Broadway.

E-C-T

"*Real gospel music has* got *to make a comeback.*"
  Sam Cooke, 1964

"*I'm young, I'm loose, I'm full of juice, I got the goose, so what's the use?*
 We're feeling gay though we ain't got a dollar; Rufus is here, so hoot
 and holler!"
  Rufus Thomas radio rap

"*Now if there's a smile on my face*
 It's only there tryin' to fool the public
 But when it comes down to foolin' you
 Now, honey, that's quite a different subject."
  Smokey Robinson, "The Tears of a Clown"

Wilson Pickett, soul singer supreme and urbane man of the world, couldn't believe his eyes. Here he was, dressed in his black-and-white houndstooth coat and black leather pants, standing on the tarmac of a small southern airport, right in the middle of a *cotton field*. Pickup trucks kicking up the dust along dirt roads, black workers bending low in the cotton patch—this was no place for the Wicked Pickett. And this cornpone-voiced ofay, Rick Hall, standing there looking all nervous next to his beat-up old Chrysler— this is the man who's going to produce soul records on *Wicked Wilson Pickett?* When Atlantic Records' Jerry Wexler had taken Pickett to Memphis to record, that had worked out just fine: "In the Midnight Hour," "Don't

Fight It," "634-5789." But this Muscle Shoals, Alabama, this is peckerwood country for sure. Wilson Pickett, long a New Yorker by choice but originally a native of Prattville, Alabama, should know.

"Pickett was a very handsome man, but he looked like a tiger, a black panther or something," says producer Rick Hall today. "He was very intimidating. And I guess I was intimidating. Here I got my wing-tip shoes on; clodhoppers, he called them. And all the way from the airport, I'd see him looking at me out of the corner of his eye, and of course I'd look at him out of the corner of my eye. But I grew up tough too, on the street, you know, and we both had a little bit of wildness in us. Pickett was a very intense individual, as a singer and a human being, but with a real sense of loyalty to people he liked. As things turned out, we really liked each other, spent a lot of time together. But when we first got to the studio, back then we didn't have a paved road in front, and the carpet had been packed down by musicians going and coming until it was full of dust. Now when Pickett would sing, his whole body was like in knots, he's pounding and beating his foot, you know, and he's dancing. And when we got through with the first session, his face was all white; it looked like he had talcum powder on. I said, 'What . . . what . . . what's that on your face?' It was dust from the carpet."

The record that resulted? Pickett's memorable steamroller revision of "Land of 1,000 Dances," a major hit. "The energy and the sonority of that record to me is wonderful," says Jerry Wexler. "To this day, the projection is something that just leaps out of the record. And here's the anomaly: These players in Muscle Shoals were all Caucasians. How could authentic soul music and blues come out of a situation like this? I don't know how it did. But it did."

The "blackest" of singers—with a whiteface mask of Alabama dust.

1957

Sam Cooke becomes first major gospel star to cross over to secular music, performs his first hit "You Send Me" on *The Ed Sullivan Show*.

The funkiest kind of down-home dance record—with a backing band of white southern crackers. These are the sort of ironies that virtually *defined* the soul-music era—and, arguably, the entire history of rock and roll. The issue of race seems so evident and straightforward, so close to the surface in rock and roll, and particularly in soul music; but things are not always what they seem.

In a sense, the music community has long ignored what we might call the politics of race relations. White country yodeler Jimmie Rodgers recorded with black jazzmen Louis Armstrong and Earl Hines in 1930. Another white country singer, Jimmie Davis, a future Louisiana governor and composer of "You Are My Sunshine," recorded risqué, less-than-double-entendre blues with backing by black blues guitarists during the early and mid-thirties. Benny Goodman took the collaborations between black and white jazz musicians that were already common at after-hours jam sessions to the stage in 1935–36, when he hired black jazzmen Teddy Wilson and Lionel Hampton to play in his widely popular big band.

And yet . . . Goodman appropriated a black jazz style and captured the lion's share of both the money and the fame as the "King of Swing." Should he be considered a brave early exponent of equal-opportunity employment, a pioneer bringing black musicians into the pop-music mainstream? Or was he another white imitator and exploiter of black musical innovation? This is a political question, and as novelist William S. Burroughs reminds us, once a problem reaches the political stage, it is by definition insoluble; a politician who really solved problems would be solving himself right out of a job. Given what we know of jazz history, Benny Goodman seems an unlikely "King of Swing," but to see him as *either* a champion of civil rights *or* a white rip-off artist would be falling prey to a typically political myopia. Neither of these characterizations is entirely

1959

Isley Brothers' "Shout" and Ray Charles's "What'd I Say" bring the black church to the pop charts.

1959

Two black-owned record labels make their debut: Sam Cooke's Sar and Berry Gordy's Motown.

untrue; both are part of the bigger picture. The same could be said of Elvis Presley, or even Alan Freed.

Freed's appropriation of the term "rock and roll," originally black slang for sexual congress, was both a political act and a marketing ploy. Freed was known and loved, or hated, for playing original black recordings rather than white "cover" versions of the same tunes. But he intended the term "rock and roll" to be *inclusive.* A rubric like "race music" or "rhythm and blues" referred less to a particular musical style or group of styles than to the racial identity of the performers; "rock and roll" was meant to describe a kind of music, not to characterize or segregate those who were playing it. This was an attempt, almost utopian in retrospect, to let the music speak for itself, with white and black contributors distinguished only by their talent—and with Alan Freed, already being billed as "the King of Rock and Roll," leading the parade.

After the mid-fifties breakthroughs of black artists such as Little Richard, Fats Domino, and Chuck Berry, and of the independent labels that recorded them, the old-school-tie elements in the music industry began to reassert their control. By the early sixties, black artists hoping to break out of the "chitlin circuit" and win a broader audience were fighting the same battles all over again. Only the names had changed. Rhythm and blues was now being called soul music, and there was never any doubt about the racial identity of the featured performers. White singers and bands working in a similar idiom were labeled blue-eyed soul in case anyone missed the point. (Jerry Wexler, who originally coined the term "rhythm and blues," proposes a somewhat different, less politicized approach to the problem of race and categorization. "What determines a particular demographic or a particular market is not who plays the music or who sells the music, it's *who buys the music,*" he argues. "So-called rhythm and blues was

1961
Smokey Robinson and the Miracles' "Shop Around" is Motown's first million-seller.

bought by black people. It's an unfortunate truth of merchandising in a free-enterprise society that you need to target your audiences. So the categories were necessary then, and I believe they're necessary today. They're subject to accusations of political incorrectness, but I'd like to see how the gurus who would prescribe these things would go about merchandising a musically diverse catalog of recordings without these categories.")

In any case, the artists who were being labeled managed to invest even the terms that circumscribed their economic opportunities with meaning and dignity. Rock and roll had become, *in practice,* a somewhat different musical proposition from rhythm and blues. The beat tended to become heavier and more emphatic; blues- and gospel-derived melodic usages expanded to embrace more elements of pop songcraft; jazz content was minimized; lyrics began to address themselves to more specifically teenage concerns. Similarly, "soul," as defined by the music of the artists so labeled, came to represent a self-consciously "black" idiom, proudly displaying its roots in gospel singing and in the rhythm and dynamics of the holy dance or shout. But while the music, and to some extent the rhetoric, of soul spoke the language of black pride, the message specifically reached out to embrace all people of good faith. The early and mid-sixties were a crucial period for the civil rights movement, which seemed to be picking up steam as it successfully challenged segregationist attitudes and discriminatory laws that had been in place for almost a century. The soul era in music corresponds to the era of the racially mixed "freedom riders" who took the fight to the cities and towns of the Deep South, the era of the crusade for integration and equal opportunity exemplified by Martin Luther King.

But the soul-music story properly begins in the fifties, when a few key artists spearheaded the penetration of gospel's characteristic song forms and freedom of emotional expression into the pop marketplace. Ray

1961

Stax introduces Memphis soul music to the pop charts with the Mar-Key's "Last Night" and Carla Thomas's "Gee Whiz."

Sam Cooke, projecting relaxation and cool, making the pop-gospel crossover a two-way street.

Charles, who began his career crooning in the after-hours club-blues style of Nat "King" Cole and Charles Brown, began borrowing more overtly from his church background in the mid-fifties. His hits of this period, beginning with "I Got a Woman" (1955) and including "This Little Girl of Mine," "Drown in My Own Tears," and "Hallelujah, I Love Her So," were not simply gospel *influenced;* they were virtual rewrites of well-known gospel songs, with "my baby" serving as stand-in for "my Lord."

In 1959, the Isley Brothers' "Shout" and Ray Charles's "What'd I Say" scaled the pop charts, re-creating the give-and-take between preacher and congregation and condensing the gospel service's rising and falling levels of interaction and intensity into a pop single format. Sam Cooke, a born matinee idol who had female fans in ecstasies when he was still singing gospel with the Soul Stirrers, launched his own master plan to "cross over" gospel and pop with the founding of his Sar record label, also in 1959. Asserting that "real gospel music has *got* to make a comeback," Cooke saw the gospel-pop crossover as a two-way street. His own meteoric rise had already shown how a gospel-trained voice and gospel-inspired songs could be alchemized into pop gold. But Cooke also felt that gospel music could benefit from pop's production standards and arranging savvy. He wrote "Soothe Me," for example, for Sar artists the Simms Twins, stylistic models for future Stax soul stars Sam and Dave. At the same time, he crafted a gospel version of the song, retitled "Lead Me Jesus," for the Soul Stirrers. He recorded the Womack Brothers, featuring a teenage Bobby Womack, singing gospel and, in an identical style, rock and roll ravers like "Lookin' for a Love" and "It's All Over Now." The latter song became an early hit for the Rolling Stones, and Cooke's "Soothe Me" became something of a soul anthem when covered by Sam and Dave in 1966. Cooke was one of the first black artists to begin producing his own sessions, and one of the first to start his own pub-

1962

Southern soul music's definitive rhythm section, Booker T. and the MGs, scores the best-selling pop instrumental of 1962 with debut "Green Onions."

1962

Stax releases "These Arms of Mine," the label's first single by future soul star Otis Redding.

lishing company and record label. His Sar releases never matched the popularity of his own records, which were distributed by RCA, but long after his death in a questionable motel shooting in 1964, his example served as an inspiration for fellow soul artists.

Several other black artists founded their own publishing companies and produced records by themselves and others, notably the Impressions' Curtis Mayfield, whose Curtom publishing was founded the same year as Sar. But the most notable new black-owned label of 1959 would prove to be Motown. Founder Berry Gordy was an unabashed black capitalist who announced his intentions with the first big hit on his Tamla label, in 1959: "Money," sang Barrett Strong, "that's what I want." The lyric was by Gordy, whose first successes in the music business had been as a hit songwriter for Jackie Wilson ("Reet Petite," "Lonely Teardrops"). But the most crucial of Gordy's early alliances was his friendship with William "Smokey" Robinson.

Gordy happened to be around when Robinson and his vocal group, the Matadors, auditioned unsuccessfully for Jackie Wilson's manager in the summer of 1957. As the dejected group was leaving, Gordy stopped them and struck up a conversation. "Berry Gordy was street," Robinson has recalled, "but he was no jitterbug; he wasn't fly, wasn't the kind of cat who strolled with the limp walk. He'd come out of the same era as Jackie Wilson. He'd done his share of fighting, some of it in a ring. He'd opened a jazz record store that flopped, been married, had three kids, got divorced, but somehow, even though he was broke, the man had direction. He also had brilliance. I showed him a hundred songs I had written in my Big Ten notebook and he showed me that, for all my slick rhymes, I had no form. He explained that a song should tell a story with a beginning, middle, and end. He rejected almost everything I had—Berry will criticize you to death—

Berry Gordy, empire builder, outside the original Motown headquarters, Hitsville, U.S.A.

After helping aspiring producer Rick Hall convert an
old tobacco barn into
Muscle Shoals, Alabama's
first recording studio, soul
singer–songwriter Arthur

Alexander initiates his
string of hits, many of
which the Beatles and the
Rolling Stones would soon
cover, e.g., "Anna," "You
Better Move On."

**William "Smokey" Robinson,
a key player in the early
success of Motown as songwriter, producer, and artist,
preaching to the faithful
while his group the Miracles
do "Mickey's Monkey."**

but he set me straight. He became my teacher." Gordy also began managing and producing Smokey's group. When Robinson's bride-to-be, Claudette Rogers, joined the group, they changed their name from the Matadors to the Miracles.

After producing several records on the Miracles, leasing them to existing labels, and failing to see much of a cash return, Gordy started his own label. In 1961, the Miracles' "Shop Around," with Gordy himself on piano, gave Motown its first million-seller. Mary Wells's "My Guy," which became Motown's first number one pop hit in the UK in 1964, was written and produced by Robinson, who also wrote early hits for the Marvelettes, the Temptations, and Marvin Gaye and worked as producer on a variety of early Motown discs. Robinson was eventually rewarded for his role in building Motown with a company vice presidency.

Gordy's methods were innovative in a number of ways. Although most of his vocalists were quite young, raised in Detroit's inner-city neigh-borhoods and housing projects and lacking both social and professional polish, Gordy was determined to scale not only the record charts but the heights of traditional show business—supper clubs like New York's Copacabana; Las Vegas; and eventually Hollywood. Toward this end, he turned Motown into a virtual finishing school, hiring experienced teachers to drill his inexperienced young performers in music theory, choreography, and charm-school poise. "I worked on the Ford assembly line," Gordy explained to *Rolling Stone* magazine, "and I thought, 'Why can't we do that with the creative process?' You know, the writing, the producing, the artist development. . . . And when you got through and you came out the door, you were like a star, a potential star." Gordy also ensured productivity among his ever-growing staff of songwriters, arrangers, and producers by fostering an atmosphere of intense competition. Writer-producers like

1962

Detroit vocal group the
Contours top the r&b
charts with one of the
grittiest soul records ever
released on Motown,
"Do You Love Me?"

Smokey Robinson, Mickey Stevenson, and the extraordinary "H-D-H"
team of brothers Brian and Eddie Holland and Lamont Dozier were only as
secure as their most recent hit; if one of them took on a vocal group or solo
singer and failed to provide a hit, Gordy would give another production
team a shot. And there were always younger writer-producers, such as the
aggressive and multitalented Norman Whitfield, waiting in the wings.

Nevertheless, the backbone of Motown's unprecedented success as a
black-owned company making records for the broadest possible audience
was its incomparable group of session musicians, who dubbed themselves
the Funk Brothers. Whether the Miracles, the Marvelettes, Mary Wells,
Martha and the Vandellas, the Supremes, the Temptations, Marvin Gaye, or
the Four Tops were featured vocalists, the band was the same—and what a
band. The nucleus of key players came to Motown as members of pianist
Joe Hunter's combo, including the accomplished rhythm section of bassist
James Jamerson and drummer Benny Benjamin. The guitarists included
Robert White (prominent on the Temptations' "My Girl" among many
others), Eddie Willis (responsible for the guitar intro on the Temptations'
"The Way You Do the Things You Do"), and rhythm guitarist Joe Messina.
Miracles guitarist Marv Tarplin was another powerful contributor;
Smokey's "You've Really Got a Hold on Me" is built around interlocking
guitars, with Eddie Willis chording on the backbeat against Tarplin's simple-
but-eloquent melodic figures.

Drummer Benny Benjamin, whose recording career dated back to the
1940s, was familiarly known as Papa Zita. He was a musician of phenome-
nal technique, energy, and drive who could swing lightly, using brushes
rather than sticks, but was best known for his thunderous tom-tom fills and
the robust slap of his snare drum.

Everyone at Motown, however, seemed to agree that James Jamerson,

Motown's backbone, the
nonpareil Funk Brothers,
L to R, Benny Benjamin,
drums; James Jamerson,
bass; Joe Hunter, key-
boards; Larry Veeder, guitar; saxophonists Hank
Cosby (top) and Mike Terry.

87

1963

*The James Brown Show
Live at the Apollo,* a classic live soul album and
barn burner, released by
King Records.

1963

Motown lives up to its slo-
gan "Hitsville USA," with
chart successes by Martha
and the Vandellas, Mary
Wells, "Little" Stevie
Wonder, and the Supremes.

a jazz-trained bassist equally adept on the acoustic stand-up bass and the Fender bass guitar, was the band's real linchpin, its most consistently creative player. The other musicians might be given specific figures to play; Jamerson, given a chord sheet for the song and perhaps a run-through with voice and piano, created his own parts, and in the process became the most influential bassist of the sixties. Since Motown had a policy of giving its records a simple, heavily accented backbeat, often reinforced by tambourines, hand-clap patterns, and percussive rhythm-guitar strokes, even Benny Benjamin's drums occasionally receded into the background, especially on the churning, thickly orchestrated productions of Holland-Dozier-Holland. Jamerson, though, was always audible; as often as not, his lines were so incisively melodic that they were more memorable than the vocal melody, effectively becoming the record's "hook." Some of Jamerson's most distinctive work was on Four Tops records such as "I Can't Help Myself," "Bernadette," and "Standing in the Shadows of Love."

"My feel was always an Eastern feel, a spiritual thing," Jamerson once told an interviewer. "Take 'Standing in the Shadows of Love.' The bass line has an Arabic feel. . . . I studied the African, Cuban, and Indian scales. I brought all that with me to Motown." Jamerson's creativity could apparently be sparked by almost anything. "I picked up things from listening to people speak," he noted, "the intonation of their voices; I could capture a line. I look at people walking and get a beat from their movements." With a whole stable of arrangers at hand, Motown records were frequently elaborate, with strings and horns and backing voices, multiple guitars and keyboards, vibraphone and percussion all swirling over the basic pulse. Jamerson's bass parts were often the fulcrum on which the other parts seemed to hinge; no matter how complex the orchestrations, Jamerson always made the records swing—or rock. Although he was apparently well

1963

Smokey Robinson, inspired by Sam Cooke's classic "Bring It on Home to Me," writes one of his own with the Miracles, "You've Really Got a Hold On Me."

1963–66

Holland-Dozier-Holland, Motown's ace writer-producer team, score twelve #1 hits, placing twenty-eight records in the pop top 20.

paid for his session work, he was never given a songwriting or arranging credit—or royalty.

Jerry Wexler calls Jamerson "the greatest bass player in all popular music, from whom every other bass player took note, lessons, and licks. Berry Gordy and Motown," he adds, "found something that we [at Atlantic Records] didn't or couldn't do. . . . He went with his version of black music directly to the white teenage buyer. Motown has left its impact on people in a way that no other music has done. Gordy did make his records by a method that bore some relationship to the Stax and Muscle Shoals records, which was having a house rhythm section to build these records from scratch."

The "house band" concept was at the heart of sixties soul recording. Although the singers received star billing, and took the music to the stage backed by their own touring bands, the record-making process was fundamentally collaborative, dependent on the creative interaction of writers, producers, and small, handpicked crews of session musicians. At Motown, as in New Orleans in the earliest days of rock and roll, jazz-schooled musicians learned to adapt their chops to the more emphatic gospel rhythms and the classically and pop-influenced song structures of the Motown writers and producers, creating in the process a fresh rhythmic idiom that influenced generations of musicians around the world.

In Chicago, Chess Records developed a soul-era session band that purveyed jazzy, rhythmically supple grooves on records by Billy Stewart, Etta James, and Fontella Bass. The players included Memphis-bred drummer Maurice White, later the founder of the influential funk band Earth, Wind and Fire; guitarist Pete Cosey, later the dashiki-clad "special effects" guitarist in Miles Davis's mid-seventies electric band; and a superbly slippery bassist, Phil Upchurch, who scored a dance hit of his own with the

1964

Sam Cooke shot and killed in fishy-looking motel incident, apparently robbed of cash and other valuables, a never fully explained ending for the King of Soul.

1964

Curtis Mayfield writes and records with the Impressions the first of his exhortations to the civil rights movement,

"Keep on Pushing," to be followed by "People Get Ready" among others.

If Motown was Hitsville, then Stax records, located in a Memphis inner-city neighborhood, was Soulsville, U.S.A.

anthemic "You Can't Sit Down." Some of these players also appeared on Curtis Mayfield productions, such as Major Lance's "The Monkey Time" and the string of hits by Mayfield's own Impressions. Across town, the musicians at One-Der-Ful Records, a black-owned company with a more down-home ambience, worked up a harder, grittier groove behind incendiary soul singers like Otis Clay and Harold Burrage and get-down groups such as the Five Du-Tones and Alvin Cash and the Crawlers.

But Motown's only serious rivals, both in terms of creating a distinctive, influential sound and in crossing potential soul hits over to the pop charts, were in the Deep South: Stax/Volt, in Memphis, and a succession of studios and associated bands in the vicinity of Muscle Shoals, Alabama. Many of the Memphis and Muscle Shoals musicians, and most of the label owners and producers, were rebellious white southerners who had turned their backs on country and rockabilly and wholeheartedly embraced rhythm and blues. It's another irony of the soul era that Motown—owned, operated, and staffed by black writers, producers, and musicians—aimed at an audience of white teenagers and, a bit later, well-to-do adults who could afford an evening at the Copa, while southern soul, in which white musicians, writers, and producers played a crucial role, aimed to appeal primarily to blacks. "To me, Motown was white music," says Stax guitarist, writer, and producer Steve Cropper, who is white. "[Ours] was a form of community music that spoke for the black person. And it was a step above what people call the blues. It was slicker, but it wasn't too slick."

If Motown's Jamerson/Benjamin powerhouse was one of the music's premier rhythm sections, Stax's Booker T. and the MGs (for Memphis Group) was the other. Two of the musicians, guitarist Cropper and bassist Duck Dunn, had come out of the Mar-Keys, probably the first all-white band to tour the "chitlin circuit" promoting their own original r&b hit.

1965

Atlantic Records's Jerry Wexler brings soul man Wilson Pickett to Memphis to record at Stax, shows house band Booker T. and the MGs how kids in

New York dance the jerk; the result is "In the Midnight Hour," perhaps *the* Memphis soul classic.

That hit was "Last Night," a skeletal, unadorned, but rhythmically right-in-the-pocket instrumental that helped put the fledgling Stax label on its feet, along with the first hit by Rufus Thomas's daughter Carla, the uncharacteristically lush (for Memphis) "Gee Whiz." Both records made it into the pop top ten in 1961.

Sparks really began to fly the following year, when Cropper and Dunn were paired with two black musicians, organist/pianist Booker T. Jones and drummer extraordinaire Al Jackson Jr., whose father led a well-respected Memphis jazz and dance band. The foursome (but with Louis Steinberg on bass instead of Dunn) transformed an after-hours blues jam into "Green Onions," a seminal soul single that became the best-selling pop instrumental of 1962.

Atlantic's Jerry Wexler negotiated a distribution agreement for Stax/Volt, and the label was off and running. Wexler brought in Sam and Dave, who scored throughout the mid-sixties with soul classics like "Hold on, I'm Comin'" and "Soul Man," and, briefly, Wilson Pickett, who cowrote what many consider *the* Stax soul record, "In the Midnight Hour," with Steve Cropper. The MGs' guitarist collaborated with Eddie Floyd (like Wilson Pickett a former member of the Falcons) on a record that rivals "Midnight Hour" as definitive soul expression, "Knock on Wood." Both records featured a fractionally delayed backbeat in the drums that pushed and pulled against the percussive horn section and Cropper's surgically exact rhythm guitar, creating a sublimely understated rhythmic tension that periodically tightened and relaxed, tightened and relaxed. Drummer Jackson had experimented with a number of rhythms for "Midnight Hour," some quite abstract, others perhaps related to his abiding fondness for Jamaican rock steady. Wexler helped him decide, and made a permanent contribution to the MGs rhythmic idiom, when he demonstrated the way

Motown had its Funk Brothers; Stax had Booker T. and the MGs, with organist Booker T. Jones (seated) and, L to R, bassist Donald "Duck" Dunn, drummer Al Jackson Jr., and guitarist Steve Cropper.

1966

Otis Redding shows that "cover versions" can work both sides of the racial barrier with his top 40 version of the Rolling Stones' "Satisfaction."

1966

Percy Sledge's "When a Man Loves a Woman," a #1 pop hit, establishes Muscle Shoals, Alabama, as world headquarters for deep soul music.

northern kids were dancing the Jerk: with a heavy but slightly retarded accent on the second beat of each measure but not, as in conventional back-beat playing, on the fourth beat, which went largely unaccented, like the so-called weak beats, one and three. This was perhaps the most sophisticated development of the accented-backbeat style that had dominated both r&b and rock and roll from the first. In retrospect, it seems to lead inexorably to funk, which shifted the strong or accented beats from the backbeat, two and four, to former weak beats one and three.

In October 1962, Stax released its first single by Otis Redding, who'd come from Macon, Georgia, and sang very much in the tradition of fellow Maconites Little Richard and James Brown. "These Arms of Mine," an almost funereally slow soul ballad with a vocal that sounded torn from the heart, took awhile to win over disc jockeys, and it was almost a year before Redding successfully followed it up with another original ballad, "Pain in My Heart." But once he took off, Redding rapidly became Stax's front-running artist, and the clear favorite among the Stax musicians. He combined a pleading vulnerability (mostly on ballads) with an aggressively rhythmic, highly improvisational up-tempo style, interpolating "gotta-gotta-gottas" and "nah-nah-nahs" so freely that his creations frequently eclipsed the song's original melody and lyrics.

But Redding was more than a one-of-a-kind vocal stylist. He seemed to hear finished records in his head, not just songs; as often as not, the indelible horn lines that grace his performances were his own creations, and the arrangements as a whole took their cues from Otis's personal approach to the material. And he was consistently capable of inspiring musicians to stretch beyond what they thought they were capable of. His most perfect album, *The Otis Redding Dictionary of Soul,* includes an astonishing arrangement of the Tin Pan Alley standard "Try a Little Tenderness,"

Otis Redding's brass-driven shout and interpolations of "gotta-gotta-gotta" and "my-my-my" wrote a new "Dictionary of Soul."

1966

Stax songwriter David Porter makes a memorable trip to the studio bathroom; when partner Isaac Hayes yells for him to hurry up, Porter says

"Hold On I'm Comin'," a catchphrase the team proceeds to turn into a major hit for soul men Sam and Dave.

in which Al Jackson's metronomic tick-tock beat seems to operate on an entirely different rhythmic plane from the rest of the musicians and the vocal—at first. Gradually, the tempo begins to expand and contract, until suddenly the listener realizes that the band's rhythm and the drummer's have somehow meshed into a single, unstoppable groove. Far from calling attention to itself, this polyrhythmic legerdemain is employed entirely in the service of the song. When Creedence Clearwater Revival auteur John Fogerty gives Booker T. and the MGs his vote as the world's greatest rock and roll band, it's with performances like this one in mind.

Late in 1961, aspiring producer Rick Hall, an Alabama native who'd worked variously as a professional songwriter and a bootlegger, set up a makeshift studio in an empty Muscle Shoals tobacco warehouse. His first success was with Arthur Alexander, a former hotel bellhop who'd written a song called "You Better Move On." The gentle-sounding record, precursor of the country-soul style, became an international hit, and Alexander followed it in short order with performances like "Anna" and "A Shot of Rhythm and Blues." These had a tremendous impact in England; the Rolling Stones scored a hit of their own with a cover of "You Better Move On" and the Beatles recorded three of Alexander's tunes. As late as the last year of his life, John Lennon kept the personal jukebox in his Manhattan apartment well stocked with Arthur Alexander 45's.

Hall had recruited his studio band from among the white musicians who played r&b covers on the southern frat-party circuit. The original group left for Nashville, where they became some of the period's leading "Nashville Cats"; several turned up on Bob Dylan's *Blonde on Blonde.* By late 1962, Hall had a new band, and a new studio, Fame. The first song put on tape in the new studio became a widely influential soul hit, Jimmy Hughes's thrilling, heavily gospelish "Steal Away," which started a new vogue in

1967
Jerry Wexler signs Aretha
Franklin, takes her to
Muscle Shoals, and brings
the Muscle Shoals rhythm
section to New York to
record with her.

1967
Soul singer supreme Otis
Redding makes his break-
through with what he calls
"the love crowd" at the
Monterey pop festival; dies
in plane crash on Dec. 10.

"cheating songs" among both soul and country artists. But the record that decisively put Muscle Shoals on the map was Percy Sledge's "When a Man Loves a Woman," which featured key Fame musicians such as organist Spooner Oldham, bassist Junior Lowe, and drummer Roger Hawkins, although it was actually cut at a nearby demo studio. With this remarkable (and all-white) band in place, Hall was ready for all comers, and soon after Percy Sledge's archetypal soul ballad went to number one on the pop charts in 1966, Jerry Wexler sent Wilson Pickett to Hall. A string of smoldering soul hits resulted from the alliance—not just "Land of 1,000 Dances," but "Funky Broadway" and "Mustang Sally" and eventually "Hey Jude," which Pickett recorded at the suggestion of a session guitarist destined to make waves of his own, Duane Allman.

The core Muscle Shoals band by then included Oldham, Hawkins, bassist Tommy Cogbill (Duck Dunn's only peer in the mercurial, loping, only apparently laid-back Memphis style of soul bass), and ace rhythm guitarist Jimmy Johnson. When lead guitar was called for, Hall and Wexler would import Chips Moman, who had produced and engineered many of the early Stax hits and was about to make his mark as proprietor of Memphis's American Studio, or Bobby Womack, of Sar Records/ Valentinos/"It's All Over Now" renown. When Atlantic signed Aretha Franklin at the beginning of 1967, Wexler first recorded her with this band at Fame. Franklin and her then-husband, Ted White, didn't take to the red-neck ambience, so Wexler began flying Oldham, Johnson, Cogbill, and Hawkins up to New York for further sessions. These "Alabama pecker-woods" played on every one of the records that established Aretha as the Queen of Soul, from "I Never Loved a Man (The Way That I Love You)" to "Respect," "(You Make Me Feel Like) a Natural Woman," "Chain of Fools," and the soaring, inspirational "Ain't No Way."

Time out at a Wilson Pickett recording session in Muscle Shoals, Alabama, L to R, front row: unknown; bassist Tommy Cogbill; guitarist Jimmy Johnson. Middle row: guitarist Chips Moman; sax-ophonist Charles Chalmers; organist Spooner Oldham; producer Jerry Wexler; Pickett. Standing in back: producer-engineer Rick Hall, drummer Roger Hawkins.

1968

The assassination of Martin Luther King marks the beginning of the end of the cooperative effort between blacks and whites that was Southern soul.

Hits seemed to come pouring out of Memphis throughout the sixties. Chips Moman recorded O. V. Wright, James Carr, and Sam Cooke soundalikes the Ovations for Memphis's Goldwax label, and worked with artists as diverse as Bobby Womack, King Curtis, Dusty Springfield, and Elvis Presley at American. The combination of black, church-nurtured voices and white session players was a concrete embodiment of the rising aspirations and integrationist fervor of the times, and it was dealt a fatal blow by the 1968 assassination, in Memphis, of Martin Luther King.

The impact of this tragedy on the course of soul music as a whole has often been overstated. Certainly James Brown was already beginning the innovative streak that would redefine the modern rhythm section and usher in the funk era, and similar rhythmic crosscurrents had been simmering in New Orleans for some time. Motown producer Norman Whitfield had begun overhauling the Detroit sound through his work with the Temptations on records like "Beauty Is Only Skin Deep" and "I Know I'm Losing You." Sly and the Family Stone were already making records that combined rock and psychedelic elements with complex, angular funk rhythms, in a style that would soon inspire Whitfield to radically "psychedelicize" and funk up his Temptations productions, beginning with 1968's "Cloud Nine." And, lest we forget, the civil rights movement had already started to splinter. New leaders such as Stokely Carmichael and H. Rap Brown were emphasizing black pride and self-reliance; King's integrationist dream was beginning to seem to many in the movement like an outmoded and potentially self-defeating strategy of accommodation with the powers that be.

Nevertheless, the entire soul music enterprise in Memphis and Muscle Shoals was dependent on the goodwill engendered by Dr. King's fragile dream, and in the days, weeks, and months after the assassination,

A pensive Lady Soul, Aretha Franklin, whose trip to Muscle Shoals yielded the genre-defining soul hit "I Never Loved a Man (The Way That I Love You)."

95

1968
Otis Redding's posthumous "Dock of the Bay" is his first (and only) #1 pop hit.

1970
Just when Southern soul seems all but defunct, Al Green releases his first albums on Memphis's Hi label, *Green Is Blues* and *Gets Next to You.*

such goodwill was hard to come by. "Pickett was here in Muscle Shoals when Dr. King was shot in Memphis," Rick Hall remembers. "The whole mood and atmosphere in the studio suddenly changed, and in fact we called off the session, out of respect to Dr. King and everything. But there was a change from that night on. The rhythm and blues acts slowly stopped coming to work with us, and within a period of a year or so after that, we were cutting almost all pop acts: Paul Simon, Cat Stevens, Rod Stewart. I know that happened quite a bit at a lot of other studios in the South. For the black acts, it was, like, no longer cool to work with you anymore; they just quit coming. Prior to that time, we had worked with black acts almost one hundred percent." During 1968–69, says Jerry Wexler, "the rising aspirations of the inner city were looking toward other things than this kind of church-based music. There was a new spirit, it was more secular." And more overtly, rigorously black in both sound and message.

Soul music boasted not one but two poet laureates. One, Smokey Robinson, had been called America's greatest poet by no less an authority than Bob Dylan. Robinson's command of the language was incomparable, and his songs did not lack a social dimension, but his great subject was romance. Curtis Mayfield wrote plenty of love songs and clever dance numbers, but he also chronicled the civil rights struggle in language as powerful and heartfelt as that of the period's greatest self-determinist orators, celebrating the movement's gains while exhorting the faithful to "Keep on pushing/We can't stop now." Mayfield's "Keep on Pushing" was a hit in 1964 for his group the Impressions, who harmonized so richly and traded leads so smoothly that they sounded like a group considerably larger than a trio. Mayfield's subsequent Impressions hits, all stitched together by his understated, impeccable guitar figures, included "Amen" (the only one Curtis himself didn't write), "People Get Ready" (covered passionately by Bob

1970

Motown (finally) addresses the war in Vietnam and the psychedelic movement with Edwin Starr's "War" and "Stop the War Now" and the Temptations'

"Psychedelic Shack," all recorded by the company's most topical songwriter/producer, Norman Whitfield.

Marley, among many others), "Woman's Got Soul," the celebratory, decidedly funky "We're a Winner," and "We're Rolling On." The final title, recorded early in 1968, solidified the bass-heavy "rumbling funk" sound Mayfield would carry into the seventies. It was his last "message" song before the King assassination, and the last to celebrate the struggle with such open-hearted buoyancy and hope. In the early seventies Mayfield would find another subject worthy of his talents in the celluloid adventures of "Superfly," an inner-city dope dealer who was caught in the middle of a pitiless power struggle and "just trying to get over"—a far cry from the sweetness and optimism of "Keep on Pushing," but equally relevant to its time and milieu.

By the mid-seventies, Stax was bankrupt, its equipment sold at public auction. Booker T. and the MGs split up, with Cropper, Dunn, and Jones taking on session work in Los Angeles. Soul's master drummer, Al Jackson Jr., stayed in Memphis to work with producer Willie Mitchell on the city's last great string of soul hits, by the charismatic, prodigiously gifted vocalist Al Green. When Jackson died of gunshot wounds in 1975, apparently after surprising a burglar in his own home, and Al Green abandoned secular music to preach the gospel, in 1979, there could be no doubt that the soul era was over.

A Rolling

Rehearsing for the Newport Folk Festival appearance that prompted folk purists' cries of "traitor" and "Judas," all because of a little electricity. L to R: unknown; guitarist Mike Bloomfield; drummer Sam Lay (hidden); bassist Jerome Arnold; Bob Dylan; Al Kooper.

David Gahr

Stone

"Folk rock? I've never even said that word. . . . The word 'message' strikes me as having a hernialike sound."
Bob Dylan

"I remember playing Bob this song 'I've Been Trying' by Curtis Mayfield and the Impressions, and the look on his face when he was listening to this. I told him, 'They're not saying anything much and this is killing me, whereas you're rambling on for an hour and you're losing me.'"
Robbie Robertson, the Band

"The Beatles were a strong influence. They kept us moving, they kept giving us something to strive toward. They were going from one direction to another, not wanting to be locked into a box, and we didn't either. So we changed musical styles quite frequently. I think changing musical styles was part of the adventure of the sixties; things changed all the time."
Roger McGuinn, the Byrds

In August 1964, journalist Al Aronowitz and his pal Bob Dylan called on the Beatles at their New York hotel, leaving them several hours later in a haze of marijuana and tobacco smoke. "When I first met Dylan, in 1963, he just scorned the Beatles, thought they were bubblegum," says Aronowitz, one of the first journalists to specialize in writing intelligently about popular music,

1961

Hibbing, Minnesota's
Robert Zimmerman rein-
vents himself as Bob
Dylan, arrives in Greenwich
Village, and is soon per-
forming in coffeehouses.

1962

Bob Dylan, the folksinger's
debut album, is released
by Columbia Records to
general indifference, but
attracts considerable attention in folk-music circles.

and an important behind-the-scenes figure throughout the sixties. "I would argue with Bob, I would tell him that today's hits are tomorrow's folk-music classics. Then when I met the Beatles, I kept talking to Lennon about Bob Dylan; I thought they should meet. When the Beatles came back to the U.S., they were staying at the Delmonico Hotel on Park Avenue, and John called me. He said, 'Well, where's Dylan? Bring him around.' I called Bob in Woodstock, and it was like Dylan was doing *me* a favor, you know. Of course, as long as I've known Bob, I don't think I've ever heard him give me or anybody else a straight answer about anything." (Indeed. In a later inter-view, Dylan was quoted as saying of the Beatles, "They were doing things nobody else was doing. Everybody else thought they were for the teenagers, that they were gonna pass right away, but it was obvious to me that they had staying power.")

"Bob and his road manager, Victor, drove down from Woodstock," Aronowitz continues, "and we drove over to the Delmonico in Bob's blue station wagon. Allen Ginsberg later asked me if the meeting was 'demure,' and that's exactly the word for it. They didn't want to step on one another's egos. Well, pretty soon the conversation turned to drink; Bob always liked cheap wine, so he said, 'You got any cheap wine?' Of course they only had champagne and expensive liquors, so Bob had to settle for something expensive to get drunk on, which he immediately did. Then somehow the conversation got around to, ah, drugs. They offered us some pills, and I was against pills; I followed the hippie line that pills were man-made, whereas marijuana grew naturally from the ground. I couldn't imagine that any-body making such hip music could not be a pot smoker; in 'I Want to Hold Your Hand,' I thought John was singing 'I get *high*.' He explained that he was singing 'I can't hide.' Finally, we did talk him into trying a joint of mar-ijuana. We handed the joint to John, and he handed it to Ringo and made

1963

Peter, Paul and Mary, a folk/cabaret act put together by Albert Grossman, begin the popularization of Dylan with their hit version of "Blowin' in the Wind."

1964

Bob Dylan, folk music's rising star and outstanding topical/protest songwriter, puts his "finger-pointing" songs on the back burner, announcing, "From now on, I want to write from the inside of me."

a remark about Ringo being his royal taste tester. That shows you the Beatles' pecking order. Then Ringo started smoking. After awhile he started giggling, and pretty soon we started laughing at the way Ringo was laughing, and that's all it was, one big laugh. Paul got high and he seemed to think it was the first time he had ever done some real thinking, so he had Mal Evans follow him around with a pad and pencil and write down everything he said.

"But that meeting between Bob and the Beatles influenced each of them. Bob went electric, and the Beatles started writing much grittier lyrics. And of course they became total potheads; their subsequent albums started reeking from the aroma. When Bob and I heard they had smoked a joint at Buckingham Palace, he gave me a verbal wink, saying, you know, maybe we never should have turned them on. But the Beatles more or less effected a de facto decriminalization of marijuana, because whatever the Beatles did was acceptable, especially for young people. Pretty soon everybody was smoking it, and it seemed to be all right." But wait a minute: What was actually *said* when Dylan and Aronowitz turned on the Beatles? Did they talk music? Did they discuss each other's work? "Yeah, they talked about records and music, but I don't remember exactly what was said," Aronowitz admits somewhat sheepishly. "I was a total pothead myself."

In mid-1964, the Beatles were still very much a teen-oriented pop group, uniformed and carefully coiffed, the four lovable mop-tops. Bob Dylan was still the folk poet and champion of acoustic music, celebrated as the spokesman for a generation because of what Dylan himself called his "finger-pointing songs"—"Masters of War," "A Hard Rain's A-Gonna Fall," "Blowin' in the Wind," "The Lonesome Death of Hattie Carroll," "Talkin' John Birch Society Blues." Invited to appear on television's top-rated variety show, hosted by granite-faced Ed Sullivan, Dylan angrily withdrew

1964

Capitol releases debut album *Meet the Beatles* in the U.S.

1964

February 7: Beatles arrive in the U.S. and are greeted by carefully orchestrated teen "hysteria" at New York's JFK airport.

12-string guitarist Roger McGuinn, whose fusion of Bach, Beatles, Beach Boys, and Dylan made the Byrds' "Mr. Tambourine Man" a pop hit, and the definitive folk-rock record.

when the producers refused to let him sing his ditty about the ultra-right-wing John Birchers, which gave him even more cachet among the left-leaning, work-shirt-wearing, social-activist folk-music crowd. But all was not as it seemed, and, in any event, the times were a-changing.

Apparently, folk music's great white hope had always loved rock and roll. Growing up in Hibbing, Minnesota, Dylan (née Robert Zimmerman) faithfully attended rock and roll shows, including one of Buddy Holly's last performances, and wrote in his high school yearbook that his principal ambition was "to join the band of Little Richard." He seems to have played the occasional rock and roll gig during this period, including a stint as the Jerry Lee Lewis–inspired pianist in a group with future teen idol Bobby Vee. But by the time he had dropped out of the University of Minnesota and headed for New York's Greenwich Village at the beginning of 1961, young Robert Zimmerman had reinvented himself (not for the last time) as Bob Dylan, folksinger. White rock and roll was temporarily dominated by clean teen idols, and subsequent developments such as the girl-group phenomenon, Motown, and southern soul were just beginning to emerge. "Folk music was very hip at that point," the Byrds' Roger McGuinn recalls. "It was part of the beat movement, wearing goatees and black turtlenecks and sunglasses at night."

Inspired equally by the on-the-road populism of Okie troubador Woody Guthrie and the existential dread of primal Delta blues, Dylan found a ready audience for his early topical songs in New York. He was soon swept up in the civil rights movement, but the more he became a media icon, the more restless he became. In the wake of the Kennedy assassination, his writing took a more personal turn. "I don't want to . . . be a spokesman," he said at the time. "From now on, I want to write from the inside of me."

1964

April 4: *All* of America's top 5 records are Beatles' discs, a feat never repeated by anyone.

1964

Rolling Stones arrive in New York City to begin their first American tour, with a bevy of British "beat groups" following in their wake.

"It wasn't a rejection of protest music," argues poet Allen Ginsberg, "because he continued writing music that was relevant in that way. But he didn't want to be limited, he didn't want to be stereotyped as the protest boy. Because he could expand much beyond that as a poet, and as a singer. In songs like 'Tambourine Man,' 'Gates of Eden,' Dylan immediately took lyrics from moon/croon/spoon/June/I love you high-school-romance stereotypes, to psychological investigations into the nature of consciousness itself. Into the nature of identity, which is his specialty. Into making many masks of identity, even referring ultimately to the tambourine man himself, who is, what? Historical poetry, the tradition of minstrelsy, the trickster hero who appears and disappears . . . 'through the smoke rings of my mind, down the foggy ruins of time. . . .' The tradition back to Mercury, Hermes, the trickster, the bearer of messages, the one who played jokes on the gods, which has been a persona of Dylan all the way through, as with many great poets, like Gregory Corso."

When Dylan "went electric" in 1965, beginning with the release of his *Bringing It All Back Home* album and its influential opening track, the Chuck-Berry-on-amphetamine surrealist protest song "Subterranean Homesick Blues," the Beatles' burgeoning sense of independence and risk-taking may have provided some encouragement. But as it took shape, Dylan's new electric music had little to do with the Beatles' *musical* style. The Byrds, who took the lead in adapting Dylan's songs for pop radio beginning with their hit single version of "Mr. Tambourine Man" in early 1965, were influenced by the Beatles' use of folk-music-style passing chords; "Mr. Tambourine Man" combined these with enriched mop-top harmonizing, a Beach Boys beat, and a *soupçon* of Bach. Dylan himself had little interest in such niceties. His electric music was not guitar-band pop rock; it was a wildly original, high-energy brand of electric blues, as gritty

1964

Bob Dylan and the Beatles (especially John Lennon) form a mutual admiration society after being introduced by journalist Al Aronowitz.

1964

The Animals' "House of the Rising Sun" tops the chart, an early indication for Dylan that folk and rock & roll can success-fully mix.

and unpolished as the rural folk music that had inspired his earlier acoustic work.

Al Kooper switched from guitar to organ for Bob Dylan's "Like a Rolling Stone" and created from his relative unfamiliarity with the instrument one of the most influential keyboard styles of the sixties.

For accompanists, Dylan chose open-throttle electric blues players such as guitarist Michael Bloomfield and the rhythm section of the Paul Butterfield Band, r&b journeymen like organist Al Kooper and bassist Harvey Brooks, and those supremely soulful purveyors of hard r&b and transcendental bar-band Americana, the Hawks, subsequently the Band. These bristling, aggressive players helped Dylan find the confidence to explode previous rock and roll song forms. He was writing lyrics of unprecedented complexity and scope that seemed to come rushing out as intensely as the crackling, driven music that supported them, accommo-dating poetic influences as diverse as Hank Williams and Arthur Rimbaud, Jack Kerouac and Robert Johnson. When it came to recording, a raw infor-mality reigned, as in the music itself. Or was it chaos?

"The Dylan sessions were very disorganized, to say the least," according to participant Al Kooper. "I was invited to the 'Like a Rolling Stone' session by the producer, but only to watch. Only through sheer ambition did I end up playing on it; the fact that I could do that is a testa-ment to how disorganized it really was. I had planned to play guitar on that session until Mike Bloomfield sat down and started playing. I went 'whoah,' because I had never heard any white person play like that before. That finished off my guitar career just like that, in one afternoon. So still being ambitious and wanting to play on the record, I seized the opportunity to play the organ. I was a mediocre keyboard player, but musically Bob is a primitive. He's not a Gershwin, somebody that uses eloquent musical terms, he's more blues-derived and primitive. So my primitive organ play-ing fit in with that very well. During the playback of that keeper take of 'Like a Rolling Stone,' Dylan said to the producer, Tom Wilson, 'Turn up the

1965

Byrd David Crosby introduces Beatle George Harrison to Indian music and the work of Ravi Shankar at a Los Angeles LSD party.

1965

Columbia producer Tom Wilson replaces the folk-style accompaniment on Simon and Garfunkel's "The Sounds of Silence" with electric guitars,

bass, and drums while the singers are away; the new version is a #1 hit and a major success for "folk rock."

organ.' Tom said, 'Oh man, that guy's not an organ player.' And Dylan said, 'I don't care, turn the organ up.' And that's how I became an organ player. Maybe a year later, Bob and I were in Los Angeles, playing at the Hollywood Bowl, and we sat in this hotel room listening to all these records that imitated the sound we'd got. And I was laughing, 'cause they were imitating me not knowing what I was doing."

Kooper was also on hand for the celebrated Dylan performances at the 1965 Newport Folk Festival, his first with full-band backing. The folkies were at war; distinguished folklorist Alan Lomax and Dylan's manager, Albert Grossman, actually came to blows over Lomax's less-than-welcoming stage introduction for another Grossman act, the Butterfield Blues Band. This was the beginning of the "let's boo Bob Dylan" craze that persisted through much of 1966, but Kooper insists the booing from the *audience* (as opposed to the booing from folk purists backstage) had little or nothing to do with Dylan "going electric."

"The Butterfield Band and the Chambers Brothers had already played electric sets at the festival," Kooper recalls, "and the crowd hadn't booed them. The board of directors didn't like it, they were going berserk, but this was really not known to the crowd that was there. Most of these people had come to see Bob Dylan. He was the star of the show, and he played on the last night. The folk acts that preceded him that night were pretty much something these kids endured, as opposed to appreciated. They came on a sort of spring-break mentality to see their hero. And after the Georgia Sea Island Singers, Son House, and Robert Pete Williams had all played for forty-five minutes to an hour, Dylan comes out with this electric band and plays *three songs*—that was all we had rehearsed. And we didn't especially play that good; the beat got turned around on 'Maggie's Farm,' for example. We played for fifteen minutes and left the stage, and

1965

The Byrds record "Mr.
Tambourine Man" with
Beatles harmonies, a
Beach Boys' beat, and
a bit of Bach in the guitar
intro, resulting in a #1 hit.

1965

Dylan headlines the
summer's Newport Folk
Festival backed by an
electric band, explicitly
embracing rough-edged
r&r and splitting the folk

music community into
supporters and scoffers;
the latter boo him.

people went nuts. I didn't hear any boos, but they certainly were unhappy, and they were yelling, 'More, more, more.' Peter Yarrow from Peter, Paul and Mary, who was the MC, came over to Dylan and said, 'You gotta do another one.' So Bob went out with an acoustic guitar and played 'It's All Over Now, Baby Blue,' which was great drama. Because it was; it was all over now, baby blue."

After playing a few more shows with a band that included Kooper, Brooks, and two of the Hawks, guitarist Robbie Robertson and drummer Levon Helm, Dylan decided to dispense with his New York session men and go with the Hawks as his backing group. Although they were only in their mid-twenties, the Hawks were road warriors, having joined Arkansas rockabilly Ronnie Hawkins in their mid-teens and played with him in dives across America and their native Canada. The group boasted two riveting soloists, Robertson and the brilliant organist Garth Hudson, as well as a funky, flexible, but eminently solid rhythm section consisting of Helm; the slippery, highly intuitive bassist Rick Danko; and rhythm pianist Richard Manuel, who was also the group's most soulful singer.

"We were from a different side of the tracks," says Robertson. "It hadn't meant anything to us when the Beatles came along, just more of the same with longer hair. Folk music was happening in the coffeehouses, and we were in the bars, on a more dangerous side of town. We weren't really aware of just what Bob Dylan *did*. I know I'd never heard anybody with such long songs and so much to say before. I remember playing Bob this song 'I've Been Trying' by Curtis Mayfield and the Impressions, and the look on his face when he was listening to this. I told him, 'They're not *saying* anything much and this is killing me, whereas you're rambling on for an hour and you're losing me.' But I liked it that when I talked to him about having some violence and dynamics in the music, about getting

Three-fifths of the Band as young Hawks, L to R: Levon Helm, Rick Danko, Robbie Robertson.

1965

Folk rock reaches a commercial peak and arguably an artistic nadir with Sonny and Cher's "I Got You Babe" and Barry McGuire's "Eve of Destruction."

1965

Bob Dylan's classic rock and roll single "Like a Rolling Stone" is the first hit song more than five minutes in length—twice as long as the average single.

really quiet and then exploding, it pushed a button in him. Because just making electric folk music wasn't enough; it needed to be much more violent than that."

Violent it was. Through the latter part of 1965 and the first half of 1966, Dylan and the Hawks toured the world, playing music with overwhelming power and colossal nerve. They found immediate acceptance in the southern U.S. and on the West Coast. Elsewhere, the crowds were divided between those who came to listen and those who came to boo: "Traitor!" "Judas!" The routine took its toll on the musicians; Levon Helm left before the European leg of the tour and was reunited with the other Hawks only after they'd settled in Woodstock, once Dylan was off the road. But as he reeled from plane to stage to hotel in a pot-and-speed-driven rush of antic partying and sleepless nights, growing visibly thinner by the week, Dylan took a certain perverse pleasure in fanning the flames.

At London's Royal Albert Hall, with the Beatles looking on admiringly, Dylan told the audience, "Folk music was just an interruption and was very useful. This is not English music you're listening to; you haven't actually heard American music before." When the French showed signs of lionizing him for what they perceived as his "vietnik" stance against the war, he appalled them by draping the stage for his Paris concert with an immense American flag. "I think he always has gotten his greatest kicks out of confounding his audience," says Al Aronowitz. In its confrontational dynamics and speed-frazzled edginess, the music made by Dylan and the Hawks was punk before its time. Rock and roll would never be quite the same again.

In August 1966, Dylan had an accident on his motorcycle and took advantage of the interruption to retreat from public performance. In a whirlwind eighteen months, he had toured the world and recorded the

1965
Beatles play to an audi-
ence of almost 60,000
fans at New York's Shea
Stadium

1965
Beatles' classic *Rubber
Soul* released.

three albums on which his reputation largely rests: *Bringing It All Back Home;* the luminous, from-the-hip *Highway 61 Revisited* (with Kooper and Bloomfield); and the epic *Blonde on Blonde,* cut with Kooper, Robbie Robertson, and a crew of ace Nashville session men and described by Dylan himself as "that wild mercury sound." After the accident, and the wired whirlwind that had preceded it, both Dylan and the Hawks were ready to relax. Hanging out at the Hawks' "Big Pink" house, near Saugerties in upstate New York, Dylan and the others reinvestigated their roots, making home recordings of folk, blues, country, and soul evergreens and their own compositions, frequently writing together in varying combinations. The results of this period were certainly more low-keyed than the music that preceded it, but Dylan's *John Wesley Harding,* the collaborative *Basement Tapes,* and the Band's *Music from Big Pink* and *The Band* (the "brown album") were perhaps, in their quieter way, even more inspired and impressive.

John Lennon plays on as American police lead an enthusiastic fan offstage, nearing the end of the Beatles' final concert tour in 1966.

The Beatles, too, had abandoned touring following a last U.S. swing that ended in August 1966 in San Francisco. Nobody was booing them, except for a few Christian fundamentalists outraged by Lennon's "Beatles bigger than Jesus" tempest in a teapot. But in growing musically, they had failed to connect with a more "adult" concert audience; why play live when you couldn't hear your own music over the screaming of pubescent girls? In the studio, having won decisive control of their own musical destiny, they were able to create sounds to satisfy their own sense of adventure.

The transition from what Dylan scathingly referred to as "I'm hot for you and you're hot for me ooka dooka dicka dee" music had been gradual. John Lennon, who seems to have most readily taken Dylan's

1965–66
Dylan tours the world
backed by a rough-and-
tumble band of ex-
rockabillies, the Hawks,
soon better known as
the Band.

example to heart and was always, in any case, the most literate and abrasive Beatle, weighed in with a series of more or less unflinching self-portraits — "I'm a Loser," "Help," "In My Life," "Nowhere Man" — and at least one thinly disguised account of his own extramarital exploits, "Norwegian Wood," the first Beatles tune to feature George Harrison's Indian sitar.

The Beatles had first encountered Indian music when visiting Los Angeles in 1965. "We were all doing LSD and sitting in a big shower in this house in Bel Air, playing guitars," Roger McGuinn remembers. "David Crosby started playing this Indian sort of music and George said, 'What's that?' And Crosby told him about Ravi Shankar. Peter Fonda was up there, and in the middle of this LSD trip he decided to show John the scar from when he'd apparently shot himself in the stomach, and John flipped out, he didn't like it at all. He kicked Fonda out of the house. But it seems Peter had said something like, 'I know what it's like to be dead,' and John used that in 'She Said She Said,' which he wrote when he went back to England."

"She Said She Said" was among the many highlights of *Revolver,* the first fruits of the Beatles' decision to stop touring and concentrate on studio recording, and arguably the artistic high point of their career as a group. The Indian influence was in full flower on Harrison's "Love You Too," while his "Taxman" was one of the Beatles' most impressive hard-edged rockers, distinguished by the composer's sizzling electric guitar leads. McCartney's interest in the electronic tape collages of composer Karlheinz Stockhausen and Lennon's restless imagination and experimental flair were evident in touches like the backward guitar solo on "I'm Only Sleeping" and the use of "found sounds" and overlapping tape loops on John's *Tibetan Book of the Dead*–inspired bardo travelogue "Tomorrow Never Knows."

Beatle George Harrison and Indian friend examine a tamboura, the drone instrument that makes the oscillating buzz tone behind the sitar and other lead instruments in Indian music.

1966
Dylan, after being injured
in a motorcycle accident,
takes a long vacation from
touring.

1966
Bob Dylan and the Band,
off the road and kicking
back in Woodstock,
jam almost daily in the
basement of the Band's

"Big Pink" house, making
the recordings eventually
released as *The Basement
Tapes*.

McCartney may have already made his "Decision for Pop," in Greil
Marcus's phrase, but if his crooning to a string quartet on the sentimental
"Eleanor Rigby" was little more than stylish MOR, he still had it in him to
rave Little Richard–style on his brass-driven "Got to Get You into My Life."
The British music-hall influence, as much a part of the Beatles' brew as
skiffle-style folk music and basic fifties rock and roll, distinguished "Yellow
Submarine," a song for children of all ages, while Lennon's "Dr. Robert"
continued in his tell-it-like-it-is vein with its decidedly adult tale of a
swinging New York doctor who was a dab hand at writing amphetamine
prescriptions.

With the recording studio as their stage, the mid-sixties Beatles and
Bob Dylan created a kind of rock and roll art music, explicitly designed for
listening and thinking rather than dancing and romancing. Almost immediately, this Dylan/Beatles "axis" sparked a brief but memorable flowering
of folk-rock. The Byrds, the idiom's musical trailblazers and most accomplished exponents, took their lyric cues from Dylan, expanded the range
and richness of Beatlesque harmonizing, and soon moved on to their
epochal fusion of Indian shimmer and Coltrane-style modal improvising
with a single inspired by their first tour of England, "Eight Miles High."
Other groups, such as the Lovin' Spoonful, accomplished their best work in
the mid-sixties folk-rock idiom they helped define. But the example of
Dylan and the Beatles also played a wider role, inspiring rock musicians to
experiment with new ideas, and to seize control of their own artistic direction by writing their own songs and, whenever possible, arranging and producing their own recordings.

"The mid-sixties was a very fortunate period to be a part of," says
Robbie Robertson. "The Beatles were making very interesting records, there
was a whole wave of amazing music coming from Motown and Stax, and

1966

The Beatles play their last
concert in San Francisco
and sequester themselves
in the studio, producing
their masterpiece *Revolver*.

Dylan was writing songs with much more depth than what had come along before. Everything was changing, all these doors were being opened, and it made you think, 'I could try *anything, right now.*' Revolutionary times are very healthy for experimenting and trying stuff—and for being fearless in what you try."

Delta bluesman Willie "Sonny Boy Williamson" Miller, who put the Yardbirds and the Animals through "some bloody hard paces" when they backed him on English dates, relaxes after one such show with an unidentified lady friend, dressed in a tailored suit and bowler hat he picked up on London's Savile Row.

Cross roads

5

"'Feel' is the word. One of the things the Yardbirds learned from playing with Sonny Boy Williamson was what feel was all about. And tempos. Sonny Boy told them that his idea for tempo was looking at how animals or people walk, relating the physical movement to the feel of the tempo in the music. That's something the English bands didn't know about. So from then on, everything the Yardbirds did had that kind of feel. You went for the groove."

 Giorgio Gomelsky, Yardbirds manager

"I always liked the wilder blues guitarists. I liked Buddy Guy and I liked Freddie King, and Otis Rush, 'cause they sounded like they were really on the edge, not really in control, and at any time they could hit a really bad note. I liked that a lot more than I did B. B. King; I got into B. B. later, when I realized that polish was something too."

 Eric Clapton

"Those English boys want to play the blues so bad. And they play it so bad."

 Sonny Boy Williamson, on his return from England,
 as recounted by Robbie Robertson

"I hope they don't think we're a rock and roll outfit."

 Mick Jagger, 1962

Rolling Stones Mick Jagger and Brian Jones, in matching stripes for an early television appearance.

1938

Legendary Mississippi Delta bluesman Robert Johnson dies, reputedly from poisoned whiskey, after recording a series of singles destined to inspire generations of rockers— "Me and the Devil Blues," "Cross Road Blues," "Hell Hound on My Trail," "Come on in My Kitchen," "Sweet Home Chicago."

New movements in rock and roll have traditionally defined themselves in two ways: by choosing sources of inspiration distinctly different from whatever is current or "hip," and by forging a personal style from these sources that runs counter to prevailing musical orthodoxy. The international success of the Beatles and the "invasion" of British pop-rock bands that came riding in on their coattails represented such an orthodoxy to the generation of British musicians coming up immediately behind the Merseybeat tide. Though most of these musicians were from middle-class suburban backgrounds and had attended art school—then roughly the British equivalent of an American liberal arts education—they found a new set of heroes and musical values in the black American subculture of the blues.

Several generations of American bluesmen had undertaken the challenging task of adapting the expressive subtleties found in blues singing to the single-string style of electric lead guitar. The style began, for all intents and purposes, with Texas guitarist T-Bone Walker; it continued to diversify with the recording debuts of players such as B. B. King, Matt "Guitar" Murphy, Freddie King, Otis Rush, Buddy Guy, and Albert King in the 1950s. Having discovered the work of these and similar players on hard-to-find American imports, British guitarists bitten by the blues bug went on to discover the work of an earlier, "deeper" generation of electric blues performers, men like Muddy Waters and Howling Wolf, and from a still earlier time, the recordings, legends, and lore of country blues guitarists such as Charley Patton, Son House, and Robert Johnson. Beginning as off-night entertainment in clubs devoted to folk music or traditional jazz, British blues musicians went on to form bands such as the Rolling Stones, the Animals, and the Yardbirds. A few gifted and highly motivated guitarists—Eric Clapton, Jeff Beck, Jimmy Page—made it their business to learn everything they could about blues music and blues culture, and in the process they devel-

1958

Muddy Waters and his electric guitar leave British folk fans shaken on the seminal bluesman's first visit to England.

1961–64

Journeyman guitarist Jimi Hendrix hones his chops on the American r&b circuit, backing Little Richard, the Isley Brothers, Jackie Wilson, and Sam Cooke.

oped into something of a breed apart. They were among the first exponents of rock and roll to define themselves primarily as instrumental virtuosos and then refuse to settle for the subservient sideman's role that had traditionally been the rock and pop guitarist's lot. Enter the guitar hero.

The folk-music revival of the fifties, and its subsequent commercialization into a kind of alternative pop, had provided a crucial impetus to the development of blues-based rock and roll on both sides of the Atlantic. The same folk clubs and festivals that had nurtured Bob Dylan, the future members of the Byrds, and other folk-rooted rockers also took the lead in presenting traditional American bluesmen to their first white audiences. One result was that Big Bill Broonzy and Muddy Waters both made early visits to England, but there was some confusion about the culture they represented. Broonzy had been leading a jazz-oriented small band on records for some twenty years and was a dapper, urbane Chicagoan, though with Mississippi Delta roots. For "folk" performances he reverted to a much earlier style and traded his sharp suits for a field hand's overalls and hat, which duly impressed his new audience as marks of "authenticity." Muddy Waters, on his first tour of England in 1958, appalled traditional jazz and folk music buffs by playing the same style of screaming electric guitar familiar to his fans on the South Side of Chicago. "His rocking blues and electric guitar was meat that proved too strong for many stomachs," British blues authority Paul Oliver noted wryly. When Waters returned to Chicago, he relearned some of the traditional blues he had grown up playing, and when he next appeared in England, in 1962, he brought his old acoustic guitar. "The first thing they wanted to know," he later recalled, "was why I didn't bring the amplifier. Those boys were playing louder than we ever played."

The mixed signals were soon sorted out, more or less, and by the time bluesmen like John Lee Hooker and Sonny Boy Williamson crossed the

Big Bill Broonzy, sporting the urbane threads he favored when performing in Chicago.

1962
The Rolling Stones make their debut at London's Marquee Club on July 12, with "sixth Stone" pianist Ian Stewart.

1963
The Rolling Stones enjoy their first British hit with a winter single written by Lennon and McCartney, "I Wanna Be Your Man."

Atlantic, there were British blues bands to back them up, most notably the Animals, who were from Newcastle, and London's Yardbirds, with Eric Clapton on lead guitar. The experience of backing the often irascible Williamson (who made some scornful comments regarding Britain's blues hopefuls to the Hawks' Robbie Robertson after he returned home) precipitated a crisis of conscience for Clapton, then at the beginning of his career.

"It was a frightening experience, because this man was real and we weren't," Clapton said some years later. "We didn't know how to back him up, and he put us through some bloody hard paces. I was very young, and it was a real shock. I realized we weren't being true to the music; I had to almost relearn how to play. But it taught me a lot. It taught me the value of that music, which I still feel."

Nevertheless, being British, and once-removed from the day-to-day realities of the blues, probably helped the best of the British blues guitarists achieve a certain level of originality, not just in their own playing but in how they arranged and presented the music in a group context. The Rolling Stones, who quickly moved to the head of the British r&b pack after their formation in 1962, lacked a really fluent lead guitarist, but boasted two of the most idiomatic and versatile rhythm guitarists ever to come out of England in Keith Richards and Brian Jones. With their superbly seasoned rhythm section of bassist Bill Wyman and jazz-loving drummer Charlie Watts, they turned their potential weaknesses into strengths, with the band becoming an elemental but subtly modulated rhythm machine behind Mick Jagger's harmonica and vocals. The Animals and Belfast's Them featured outstanding, gritty lead vocalists in Eric Burdon and Van Morrison, respectively, and each band developed a tightly integrated, highly distinctive ensemble style as well.

The Yardbirds were more of an improvising unit, and thus more

1964

The Animals' "The House of the Rising Sun," the first American hit by a British r&b group, attracts the admiration of Bob Dylan, among others.

1964

The Rolling Stones fulfill a burning ambition to record at Chess Studios, and can hardly believe it when Muddy Waters, Buddy Guy, and Chuck Berry drop by.

dependent on the sustained invention of their stellar lead guitarists—first Clapton, then Jeff Beck, then Jimmy Page. But not entirely dependent; early on, the group perfected the "rave-up," an improvisational strategy that found the whole band accelerating tempos in tandem, building up to a dynamic peak, then bringing the music down to a hypnotic, slowly simmering riff that would sooner or later begin building toward an explosion again. The key player in the rave-up style was not the lead guitarist but the group's virtuosic bassist and musical director, Paul Samwell-Smith.

"If the Yardbirds played blues material faster than the originals, or slower, it was to convey some kind of an emotion," says manager Giorgio Gomelsky, who also ran several early r&b clubs and was one of the scene's genuine creative spark plugs. "The Yardbirds were breaking up the old format, extending it. I thought that was very important because it allowed us to develop from the blues in more experimental directions, taking risks. I had a background in jazz and avant-garde music, so I very much wanted to see that happen. As long as the music had the right feel, there was a certain authenticity about it."

All of these musicians were coming of age at a time when British pop music was enjoying an unprecedented international popularity and influence. In defining their own ambiguous relationship to the machinery of the pop-music business, they also defined what became innovative approaches to rock and roll.

"Lulu, Herman's Hermits, all that crap, they were just a bloody nuisance," says an unrepentant Jeff Beck. "I couldn't stand those records, they were like an audio nightmare. I don't consider that the British ever played rock and roll, really. At least their interpretation of rock and roll didn't fit my interpretation. My own favorites were about ninety percent black." The Rolling Stones had started with similar purist intentions. "I hope they don't

The Yardbirds, early on, picking and singing around the old swimming hole, or its suburban equivalent; that's Eric Clapton in the crewcut, far left.

1964

Belfast soul man Van
Morrison arrives in London
and begins recording as
the vocalist for one of the
British r&b boom's most
convincing bands, Them.

1965

Keith Richards comes up
with the basic guitar part
for "Satisfaction" during
the Rolling Stones' third
American tour.

think we're a rock and roll outfit," Mick Jagger worried in 1962, when the
Stones were still sitting on stools while performing.

Purists or not, these bands were absorbed willy-nilly into the British
"beat boom." The Animals were the first of the British r&b groups to score
a major international hit, with their moody, dramatic reworking of a folk-
blues tune about a New Orleans whorehouse, the "House of the Rising
Sun." The Animals weren't cute, and didn't try to be. They disdained the
Beatles' squeaky-clean image and teen-idol grooming. Seizing on just this
sort of distinction, the Rolling Stones and their ambitious young manager,
Andrew Loog Oldham, presented the group as a kind of anti-Beatles. It was
Oldham who coined the phrase, "Would you want your daughter to go out
with a Rolling Stone," which the tabloid press was only too happy to exploit.
But when it came to breaking onto the singles charts, still the name of the
pop game in the mid-sixties, Oldham and his band were not so picky. They
were delighted when the Beatles gave them a Lennon-McCartney reject, "I
Wanna Be Your Man," which became their breakthrough British hit in the
winter of 1963. They packed their early albums with covers of American
hits, but were less than convincing at straight blues (except perhaps for
their pungent take on Howling Wolf's "Little Red Rooster") and soul music
(Mick's "Cry to Me" sounds forced and anemic alongside Solomon
Burke's). Black rock and roll, as exemplified by Chuck Berry, Bo Diddley,
and the Valentinos' "It's All Over Now," proved more amenable to the
Stones' revisionism. This winning combination of blues colorations and
country twang was especially well suited to Keith Richards, who demonstrated an exceptional aptitude for riffcraft. Once Jagger and Richards
became the Stones' in-house songwriting team, Keith's lean-and-nasty riffing emerged more clearly as the band's musical foundation.

When the Stones left their residency at the suburban Crawdaddy

The Animals, with gritty lead
vocalist Eric Burdon, scored
hit singles with material as
disparate as the folk ballad
"House of the Rising Sun"
and the Brill Building pop-
protest of "We Gotta Get
out of This Place."

1965

Them releases one of British r&b's most enduring singles, pairing the Chicago blues standard "Baby Please Don't Go" with Morrison's "Gloria."

1966

With *Aftermath,* their first complete album of original songs, the Rolling Stones leave blues and r&b covers behind while retaining an r&b-based *feel.*

Club for the national touring circuit, booker Giorgio Gomelsky replaced them with the Yardbirds. Once again, a group that was interested in playing blues (and in experimenting with it) was faced with the choice of staying on the relatively low-paying club circuit or coming up with a hit single as an entrée to better gigs.

"The kids were buying two-and-a-half-minute songs, so we had to do this," says Gomelsky. "And we didn't know how; none of the blues bands knew how to do it because that was not their desire." After several blues covers failed to take off, Gomelsky talked the group into recording a commercial tune, "For Your Love," written by a young, pre-10 C.C. Graham Gouldman. It was a ballad with harpsichord accompaniment! Upon its release, Clapton left the Yardbirds to pursue his blues muse. "Some of the band began to see a future in being internationally famous," he later said, "and I couldn't see what the rush was all about, what was so wonderful about competing with the Liverpool sound."

Clapton's replacement, Jeff Beck, was not the same sort of purist. He had been refining what he calls "this sort of, like, Martian guitar style" while indulging in twenty-minute Bo Diddley–based jams with his previous group, the Tridents. "I had fallen in love with blues," says Beck, "but I had also listened to a lot of Les Paul and was quite a fan of Cliff Gallup, the guy who played guitar with Gene Vincent. I didn't really want to just play pure blues. It was too much like tunnel vision." Indeed, once Beck clicked with the Yardbirds, he seemed to radically redefine the parameters of rock and roll guitar playing with every single, from "The Train Kept A-Rollin'," a metallic rave-up version of a rockabilly/r&b original, cut at Memphis's Sun studio during an early American tour, to the still-bracing "Shapes of Things," a blast of antiwar apocalypse the Yardbirds recorded at the Chess studio in Chicago. Fuzztone and feedback, dive-bomber runs and harmonic sustain,

The Yardbirds' short-lived "dream lineup," ca. 1956. Standing left to right are rhythm guitarist/bassist Chris Dreja and drummer Jim McCarty; seated are guitarists Jimmy Page and Jeff Beck and vocalist Keith Relf.

1966

The Yardbirds, briefly featuring the unexcelled twin-guitar lineup of Jeff Beck and Jimmy Page, do their own sullen version of the Who's guitar-destruction routine for director M. Antonioni's "Swinging London" film *Blow Up.*

1966

The Yardbirds' classic LP is released in Britain as *Roger the Engineer,* and in the U.S., with several songs missing, as *Over Under Sideways Down.*

sounds like explosions and buildings collapsing, all were part of Beck's expressive arsenal. At the time, the guitarist could not read music, a factor that may have helped him imagine extravagant sonic effects not reproducible in musical notation.

"Our biggest problem recording in England was getting a really good drum sound," Gomelsky remembers. "And the engineers would want you to turn the guitars down, so when we toured America, we decided to go into an American studio every time we had the opportunity, to see how they were doing it." The Stones had paved the way for the Yardbirds and other British bands by recording at Chess in Chicago with engineer Ron Malo, and at RCA in Hollywood, with Dave Hassinger. This combination of British blues revisionism and American sonic expertise resulted in some of the most innovative and enduring records of the mid-sixties, culminating in 1966 in two outstanding albums, the Stones' *Aftermath* and the Yardbirds' *Roger the Engineer.* Unfortunately, both albums were severely truncated for their initial American release by corporate record labels hoping to squeeze a bit more product out of their licensed English money-makers. Not even the Beatles escaped this fate; the British *Revolver* and various British EP's were scrambled together to make two American albums, *Revolver* and *Yesterday and Today.* Consumer advisory: *Seek out imports or reissues of albums with the original British track configurations.*

The year 1966 brought change and upheaval to the British r&b scene. The Rolling Stones' *Aftermath,* their first album made up entirely of original songs, made them rock stars second only to the Beatles, and it was the Beatles, rather than other blues-based bands, who now represented their only serious competition. In June, the Yardbirds lost their inventive bassist, Paul Samwell-Smith, and replaced Jeff Beck with session man Jimmy Page, who had recorded with everyone from Donovan to Lulu and was some-

1966

Clapton records the *Bluesbreakers* album during his brief stay with John Mayall, his last all-blues disc until the 1994 bestseller *From the Cradle*.

1966

Eric Clapton, Jack Bruce, and Ginger Baker form "super group" Cream, rock's definitive "power trio."

thing of a virtuoso at the studio console as well as on the guitar. The band also sacked their manager, Giorgio Gomelsky, and fell under the baleful sway of pop producer Mickie Most, who saddled them with banal bubblegum ditties in the studio and effectively prevented them from building on the astonishing innovations that had made them such trailblazers in 1965 and early '66.

Meanwhile, Eric Clapton stayed with blues purist John Mayall just long enough to record the 1966 *Bluesbreakers* album before leaving to start his own "blues trio." But the jazz chops and assertively exploratory bent of the group's bassist and drummer, Jack Bruce and Ginger Baker, soon transformed Cream into something far removed from the blues band Clapton had originally envisioned. "We were just three musicians who got together and had to come up with a repertoire," Clapton recalled some twenty years later. "I was throwing in Skip James and Robert Johnson [blues] songs, Jack was composing and Ginger was composing, and so this melting pot came together which was completely hybrid. When we played in front of an audience, we began to realize that they actually wanted to go off somewhere, and that we had the power to take them there."

Appropriately, Cream became known as the archetypal "power trio." Playing through stacks of Marshall amps at staggering volume levels, Clapton was soon stretching his improvisational abilities to the limit. Often, the guitarist's grounding in blues and his internalized sense of structure provided the glue that held the music together while Bruce and Baker spun elastic variations in meter and tempo. In the studio, the band ranged widely, exploring polytonality, a sophisticated concept even in the jazz world, on "I Feel Free"; crafting superior pop-rock on the single "Badge"; pioneering "heavy blues," a prototype for heavy metal, in the blues-based sludge-riffs that anchored "Sunshine of Your Love" and "White Room."

Eric Clapton described Cream's music as a "melting pot . . . completely hybrid"; the guitarist is on the left, with bassist Jack Bruce in the middle and drummer Ginger Baker on the right.

1966
Jimi Hendrix makes his
London debut, presenting
Britain's finest blues-based
guitarists with a new standard of excellence and
innovation.

Live, almost anything could happen, from inspirational epiphanies to shambling chaos. Clapton has expressed considerable reservations about Cream's legacy, but the band did such innovative work in so many musical areas, taking so many chances along the way, that the adulation of its many die-hard fans does not seem entirely misplaced.

Clapton, who was being touted as God himself in an epidemic of London graffiti, met his match in the fall of 1966, when Jimi Hendrix made his London debut. "Cream was playing at London Polytechnic, and Chas Chandler from the Animals brought this guy around," says Clapton. "He was dressed really freaky, and he spent a lot of time arranging his hair in the mirror, but at the same time he was very genuine, and very shy. I took to him straightaway, but then he came up and asked if he could jam and just blew me away. Ginger and Jack didn't take to it kindly, they thought he was trying to upstage me, but I was so floored by his technique and his choice of things to play that I fell in love straightaway."

Jeff Beck, perhaps the most advanced and inventive of the British blues-based guitarists, compares hearing Hendrix for the first time to "a bomb blowing up in the right place. He just blew the place wide open, and I went away from there thinking I ought to find something else to do, go back to panel beating or something. Then I got to know him and found out that he wasn't this immovable force, that we could talk music, and he became a great source of inspiration. He was doing things so up front, so wild and unchained, and that's sort of what I wanted to do, but being British, and the product of these poxy little schools I used to go to, I couldn't do what he did."

Hendrix, an African American guitarist from Seattle, had acquired his blues roots not from listening to records (though he did plenty of that), but from touring and recording as a sideman with Little Richard and the

1968

The Yardbirds dissolve; guitarist Jimmy Page recruits John Paul Jones, Robert Plant, and John Bonham to become the

New Yardbirds . . . who soon change their name to Led Zeppelin.

1968

Cream disbands in a haze of egos and chemicals.

Isley Brothers, among others. He was playing clubs in Greenwich Village in 1966 when Animals bassist Chas Chandler heard him, signed on as his manager, and took him to England, where the leading guitarists of the day followed him from gig to gig, hanging on every note. Even Clapton was still borrowing phrases wholesale from his American blues heroes. Cream's *Disraeli Gears* album is known among blues aficionados as "the Albert King tribute" because Clapton's playing on it was so evidently affected by "Born Under a Bad Sign" and King's other Stax recordings; his work on *Bluesbreakers* had been similarly indebted to Freddie King. But Hendrix had already alchemized his many blues influences into an approach that was unmistakably his own, a point not lost on the British guitarists who admired him.

Jimi Hendrix, with his guitar and his favorite amplifier setup, the Marshall stack.

Nevertheless, it was a British group concept, the power trio, that determined the shape Hendrix's own band would assume. Like Cream, the Jimi Hendrix Experience featured a drummer with strong jazz leanings— Mitch Mitchell, who, like many sixties drummers, was profoundly affected by Elvin Jones's thrashing, polyrhythmic workouts behind John Coltrane. And like Cream bassist Jack Bruce, the Experience's Noel Redding was a forceful but melodic player who got around the frets as fluently as a lead guitarist. (In fact, Redding had played lead guitar in his previous band.) The Experience took blues-based, improvisational rock to perhaps its ultimate level of development. Hendrix himself expanded the tonal and sonic resources of the electric guitar so spectacularly that his work remains definitive a quarter-century after his death. Subsequent rock guitarists have taken the instrument in different directions and redefined its role in the band, but nobody has come close to equaling Hendrix at his own game, let alone surpassed him.

Perhaps the most lasting legacy of mid-sixties British r&b has been

1968

Led Zeppelin begins to forge a new "heavy" blues on their first album, recorded in October in some thirty hours.

1969

Robert Plant borrows a phrase from Blind Lemon Jefferson and Robert Johnson for the Led Zeppelin opus "Whole

Lotta Love," asking to have his lemon squeezed "till the juice runs down my leg."

heavy metal, a stepchild no one seems eager to claim. The "heavy" approach to blues, which involved slower, more ominous tempos and the reduction of elemental blues phrases to thick guitar and bass unison riffs, was initially one of those sixties side trips that musicians explored for a short time before moving on to something else. It was one of the many facets of the power-trio style epitomized by Cream and the Jimi Hendrix Experience. The Jeff Beck group, with young Rod Stewart on vocals, further refined the approach, which Beck prefers to call "supercharged rhythm and blues."

Led Zeppelin, formed by Jimmy Page and originally billed as the New Yardbirds, made the "heaviest" blues-rock yet. But as a graduate of the mid-sixties school of innovation, Page was determined to avoid being pigeon-holed. A devoted student of the blues, he was also fond of Celtic folk music, and intrigued by Indian and Arab music: "I saw a parallel between the bending of guitar strings in blues music, and the emotional quality of that, with what was being done in Indian music. Once I started to kind of digest the whole system of Indian music and learned what was involved, I realized it was far too complicated for someone who was really a rock and roll guitarist. But *ideas* from Indian music were well worth incorporating, tunings and such. I always thought our mixing of the electric with acoustic music was [another] thing that really made us stand out as a band. Musically, we weren't afraid to go in any direction whatsoever. I guess that was the way we kept ourselves really alive as musicians." In the studio, Page adds, "I was extremely conscious of building and maintaining the atmospheric quality of the song from square one. No matter how many guitar parts I might layer on in the studio, I followed the tune's overall theme and ambience in my mind. Sometimes I did get carried away a bit, but fortunately I always managed to catch myself. That's what it's all about, catching yourself."

Page, and Zeppelin bassist John Paul Jones, another former session

An early Led Zeppelin gig, with singer Robert Plant, bassist John Paul Jones, and guitarist Jimmy Page; drummer John Bonham is unseen but was rarely unheard.

1970

Black Sabbath, borrowing their name from a lurid mid-60s horror film, link the hoodoo traditions of the blues to a B-movie version of European occultism and take blues-based rock one step beyond — into heavy metal.

pro, brought enormous versatility and solid musicianship to Led Zeppelin. Vocalist Robert Plant's all-out intensity and unselfconscious rock-god preening and the thunder of John Bonham's atavistic drumming proved the perfect foils for Page and Jones's more calculated expertise. Zeppelin not only became enormously popular and influential, especially in America; their music has retained its popularity over the years since Bonham's death and the band's official breakup in 1979. In 1995, Page and Plant were at it again, delving ever deeper into Arabic intonation and North Mississippi trance-blues with a vitality few musicians of their generation have been able to sustain.

White blues will always be a problematic notion. Certainly the best blues-based guitarists to come out of the sixties — and Americans such as Duane Allman, Michael Bloomfield, and Robbie Robertson must rank near the top of any such list — learned to play with a genuine feel for the idiom. Pure blues guitarists as exalted as B. B. King, Robert Jr. Lockwood, and Ike Turner have praised Clapton's feel. "You know it's the blues when he plays it," B. B. has said. But the most effective blues-based rockers are often those who, like Keith Richards, make up for a lack of flashy chops with a deeply felt, highly personal sound and conception. Richards can pick up any guitar, play a single chord or run, and sound exactly like himself and nobody else.

But as Muddy Waters once said, "They got all these white kids now. Some of them can play *good* blues. They play so much, run a ring around you playin' guitar, but they cannot vocal like the black man." Clapton's *playing* suggests that he hears more of the music's recondite intricacies than most white blues musicians, who often sound like they think blues is a diatonic, equal-tempered idiom instead of a modal, microtonal one. But good blues *singing* involves subtleties that are deeply imbedded in the blues cul-

1970

Jimi Hendrix, 27, dies in London, at the same age as star-crossed bluesman Robert Johnson.

1971

Duane Allman soars into the improvisational strato- sphere with his double- guitars/double-drums unit on the Allman Brothers Band's *At Fillmore East.*

ture's spoken idiom. Suffering for your art has nothing to do with it; if you didn't grow up in that culture, your singing is going to sound like what it is: an imitation.

Few things are certain in rock and roll; one certainty is that as soon as somebody comes up with a good idea, somebody else will simplify it. In this sense, limitations can help breed originality. Case in point: Black Sabbath, who came roaring out of Birmingham, England, in 1969–70 with a debut album (*Black Sabbath*) and a single ("Paranoid") that virtually define heavy metal to this day. Like the original *Black Sabbath*, a 1964 hor- ror film directed by Italian goremeister Mario Bava, the band celebrated a sort of cheesy, comic-book demonology, conflated with a superficial under- standing of some of the occult elements in blues lore. Sabbath's detractors would undoubtedly argue that the group's understanding of blues *as music* was equally superficial; they reduced its call-and-response format and riff- based structures to a dark, churning, supremely heavy sound that was prac- tically *all riff,* topped by Ozzy Osbourne's inimitable demonspew. But the music's simplicity made it just that much more effective. It was an approach almost anybody could emulate, and in fact, Sabbath's riffmaster, Tony Iommi, became one of rock's most widely imitated guitar stylists, though he was rarely acknowledged as such.

In Bava's *Black Sabbath,* Balkan hunter Gorca (Boris Karloff) gets bit- ten by a vampire and eventually initiates his entire family into the ranks of the undead—beginning with his little grandson, whose piteous cries lure other family members to their doom. Likewise, the heavy metal infection spread wherever Black Sabbath and similar bands appeared. Young white males seemed especially susceptible to Sabbath's lurid sagas of sorcery and satanism, sex and drugs, death and destruction; many of them returned home from Sabbath shows thinking, "*I could do that.*" Sooner or later, rock

Black Sabbath's original riffmaster and reigning heavy metal guitar god Tony Iommi, wielding his ax like an ax.

126

1971
In October, a motorcycle accident claims the life of Duane Allman.

1979
Led Zeppelin disbands following the death of drummer John Bonham.

fans who had confined themselves to more rarefied pleasures awoke with a shock to find themselves surrounded by thrash-maddened rivetheads, some of them barely recognizable as someone's little brother, somebody's son, the kid down the street. There can be no escape; the undead are everywhere. Just keep telling yourself: It's only a movie, only a . . .

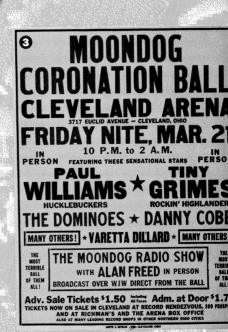

③ **MOONDOG CORONATION BALL**
CLEVELAND ARENA
3717 EUCLID AVENUE — CLEVELAND, OHIO
FRIDAY NITE, MAR. 2?
10 P.M. to 2 A.M.
IN PERSON FEATURING THESE SENSATIONAL STARS IN PERSON
PAUL WILLIAMS ★ **TINY GRIMES**
HUCKLEBUCKERS ROCKIN' HIGHLANDER
THE DOMINOES ★ **DANNY COBB**
MANY OTHERS! ★ VARETTA DILLARD ★ MANY OTHERS

THE MOST TERRIBLE BALL OF THEM ALL!
THE MOONDOG RADIO SHOW
WITH **ALAN FREED** IN PERSON
BROADCAST OVER WJW DIRECT FROM THE BALL
THE MOST TERRIBLE BALL OF THE ALL!

Adv. Sale Tickets $1.50 Including All Taxes Adm. at Door $1.7?
TICKETS NOW ON SALE IN CLEVELAND AT RECORD RENDEZVOUS, 300 PROSP
AND AT RICHMAN'S AND THE ARENA BOX OFFICE
ALSO AT MANY LEADING RECORD SHOPS IN OTHER NORTHERN OHIO CITIES
SMITH & DETROIT — CLEVELAND, OHIO

② IN PERSON ALAN FREED AND ROCK AND ROLL STARS
THE PLATTERS·FRANKIE LYMON AND TEENAGERS·RUTH BROWN
BUDDY KNOX · JIMMY BOWEN·CLEFTONES·NAPPY BROWN·CADILLACS
BOBBY CHARLES·MAUREEN CANNON·DUPONTS·ROBIN ROBINSON
"DON'T KNOCK THE ROCK" "BILL HALEY AND COMETS
ALAN DALE·ALAN FREED·TREMERS·LITTLE RICHARD·DAVE APPELL

IN PERSON ALAN FREED
AND **GREAT STAGE SHOW** OF
ROCK "N" ROLL STARS
ON THE SCREEN "DON'T KNOCK THE ROCK"
PARAMOUNT

Delinquents of Heaven
Hoodlums from Hell

Delinquents of Heaven, Hoodlums from Hell

"*The god's companions are described as a troupe of freakish, adventurous, delinquent and wild young people, who prowl in the night, shouting in the storm, singing, dancing, and playing outrageous tricks on sages and gods. They . . . mock the rules of ethics and social order. They personify the joy of living, courage, and imagination, which are all youthful values. They live in harmony with nature and oppose the destructive ambition of the city and the deceitful moralism which both hides and expresses it. These delinquents of heaven are always there to restore true values and to assist the "god-mad" who are persecuted and mocked by the powerful. They personify everything which is feared by and displeases bourgeois society, and which is contrary to the good morale of a well-policed city and its palliative concepts.*"

Alain Danielou, *Shiva and Dionysus*

"*They had a riot. They tore the hall up like you never seen a hall torn up before in your life. They broke about twelve store windows, stole the suits. They caught kids taking the beautiful chromium water fountains home. We had police. Didn't mean nothing. I had to go and get Italian hoodlums to break jaws.*"

Teddy Reig, tour manager for Alan Freed

"*Rock 'n' roll smells phony and false. It is sung, played, and written for the most part by cretinous goons and by means of its almost imbecilic reiteration . . . it manages to be the martial music of every sideburned delinquent on the face of the earth.*"

Frank Sinatra, 1957

"*Tutti frutti, good booty*
If it don't fit, don't force it
You can grease it, make it easy"

Little Richard, 1955, original lyric for "Tutti Frutti"

That Midget Could Dance

Two longtime partners, one black, one white, are sitting in an otherwise empty Chinese restaurant. Outside it's raining, one of those gray weekday afternoons that reduces everything colorful to monochrome, even the brightly painted signs and ideograms that line the streets of New York's Chinatown. Inside, two nondescript trench coats are stretched on chairs, drying, as the two men drink their warm sake and regale a visitor with tales from "back in the day." Paul Williams, the saxophonist, had a 1948–49 rhythm and blues hit with "The Hucklebuck," and later led touring bands for some of the biggest stars in fifties r&b/rock and roll. That's Williams's band rocking behind the likes of Big Joe Turner, Amos Milburn, Ruth Brown, and other r&b front-runners on early-fifties videos from Harlem's Apollo Theater. And the other gentleman, Mr. Williams's friend:

"You should tell him," growls the graying but still impressively bear-like Teddy Reig, "that I'm not a gentleman. See," he says, turning to face the visitor squarely, "the only thing I know is show business. I ran away from home when I was fifteen, and I've been learning it all my life. And I'm sorry to say. . . . See, Paul was a musician. And I made a honker out of him. A lot of those other sax players, they couldn't read a note if it was as big as a bomb. They just honked and they got lucky. But Paul was a musician. This I swear."

According to some people, turning Paul Williams into a honker was only one of Teddy Reig's *minor* transgressions. In Chuck Berry's autobiography, Reig shows up unbidden at the beginning of Berry's recording career and appoints himself the young rocker's manager, a job that, according to Chuck, consisted largely of pocketing stacks of bills off the top of each night's concert receipts. Later, Reig was tour manager for some of the earliest and wildest rock and roll package shows, including those booked by Alan Freed. He produced records for a variety of companies, some of which had more than a casual connection to organized crime. Reig has been there, that's for sure; he knows where the bodies are buried.

"Detroit, 1948," says Reig, sounding like a "Dragnet" voice-over, "I'm producing for Savoy, for old man [Herman] Lubinsky (owner of Savoy Records). I should have owned the joint; I didn't, that's all. After I'd produced Stan Getz and Charlie Parker for him, Lubinsky sent me out to

Detroit to check on this band. Paul was the saxophonist. I took him down the street to a coffee shop and said, 'Fella, I don't want that band but I want you. Let's get a good understanding. You don't know me and I don't know you, but I'm crazy. But if you listen to me, I'll make you a lot of money. *But,*' I said, 'the days of playing horns are over. Now you got to entertain and bullshit.'"

WILLIAMS: "He wanted one note. Bam. Bam. Bam. Maaan . . ."

REIG: "It was honking and screaming, that's what it was. Anyway, we had a buddy who had a record shop on Hastings Street; that was a major black strip in Detroit. We would sit in the back, buy a bottle, drink it up, and play records. Then we'd take the records we wanted back to the rooming house, and to be very honest, we took patterns, changed the notes. We stole. And we cut the first records on Paul in the living room of a two-family house, where a guy had his studio. Lionel Hampton was an inspiration; he was sort of the big-band version of honking and screaming. Hamp was the first guy to turn his drumsticks around, play with the thick end of the sticks. He'd play theaters and give everybody a fit, 'cause they couldn't get him off the stage. He'd get into a groove and wouldn't want to come out of it. If they closed the curtains, Hamp would take the band out in the audience and keep playing. Saxophone players would be flying through the air, jumping off the stage. He had to work with his musicians, tell them what he wanted, in order to get them to play like that, because everybody was still trying to play 'good swing music' in those days. . . . But he got something going, and the people *loved* it."

Reborn as a screamer and a honker, Paul Williams made several singles for Savoy under Reig's direction. The big one was "The Hucklebuck," which borrowed, none too subtly, a phrase from Charlie Parker's bebop composition "Now's the Time" as its key riff. Reig produced both records. "The one was jazz, the other was rock and roll, and we were hungry," he says. "And Lubinsky owned everything anyway." Williams says the title "The Hucklebuck" came from one of his musicians, "that crazy little drummer" Benny Benjamin, who would later be the spark plug in Motown Records' rhythm section, the Funk Brothers.

"Paul got his own band together, and we had a little rehearsal," Reig continued. "Hey, I had all the games down. I taught him some choreography—kicking with the feet, hitting a note and bending with it. Bought six uniforms for fifty dollars and we're off on the road, to Baltimore. Paul has a record out, he's the hottest thing in town; he gets the last part of the show. So he's playing the baritone, trying to remember all the little things about bending and dipping. The theater had a microphone that retracted into the floor, and the lower he'd blow, this guy Charlie would be under the stage at the pully, pulling the mike down lower and lower. Paul built to a crescendo, the house was in an uproar, till finally he's blowing right down to the floor, and the microphone disappears under the flap. And people were screaming, running up onstage. I'm closing the curtains, and I grabbed Paul's arm and got him out of there. After that we were so hot, I made the theater owner my partner, and we booked dances. The first dance, we had around five thousand people there, and every five minutes the fire department would come in. I'd give them a bunch of tickets to count. But in my pockets I had thousands of tickets they didn't know about. Then there was a shooting or something. Man, before it was over, Paul Williams had closed up every dance hall in Baltimore; there wasn't one left he didn't close with a riot."

WILLIAMS: "The word got out. 'Man, that saxophone player down there blowed the microphone into the floor! Blowed it away!' And that was it—lines three or four blocks long, firemen, policemen, people running up onstage, stone crazy. I'd play three tunes and never get to finish the third one."

"Yeah, when they'd run up onstage, I'd have to close in on 'em to keep my man alive," Reig adds cryptically. "Now, eventually, we played more clubs, and we had a broad singing 'I know how to hucklebuck,' and a midget dancing the hucklebuck on top of the bar. That midget could dance, but he was the biggest pain in the ass for his size you ever seen."

Reig's experiences on the wilder edge of rhythm and blues served him well when rock and roll broke loose. Alan Freed, an early acquaintance of Reig's, was only one of a number of white disc jockeys playing black records for a largely teenage audience in the early fifties. His impact was minor compared to that of jocks like Gene Nobles and Hoss Allen of Nashville's WLAC. Then, on March 21, 1952, Freed produced the first concert of the rock and roll era, "Moondog's Rock and Roll Party and Coronation Ball." Thirty thousand Cleveland teenagers, eighteen thousand holding tickets, showed up at the designated arena, which seated only ten thousand. The musicians were all black, as many as half the teenagers were white, but race was not the issue. The kids outside just wanted to get inside; fearful police pulled the plug on the show. The result: The first rock and roll concert was also the occasion of the first rock and roll riot.

Freed arrived at New York City's radio station WINS in 1954, already a star, but in New York he would only burn brighter. "He'd go to all these record companies and get their acts to play his concerts for free," Reig reports. "They couldn't do enough for him. He used to drink, and on his way home one night he hit a tree. It was like all the record companies had a convention, who's gonna pay for what. He buys this house, this *estate*, something like thirty rooms, beautiful oceanfront property. And he decides he needs a swimming pool. Some distributor pays for that. He stubs his toe on a case of whiskey, says, take it home, it ain't my brand. Insane. But he was the godfather.

"St. Nicholas Arena in New York, that was nuts. The Brooklyn Paramount . . . but the pièce de résistance was Orange, New Jersey. Freed's show was in an armory. Paul, I was holding shopping bags full of money, standing next to these other bags and pushing money down with my feet. There were so many people outside, and inside a guy at a little table, selling tickets. Ha! The door flew open, and they just knocked him over, the tickets, the money, everything. Teddy Powell, who was helping us, made a run for it with the money box and almost didn't get out of there alive. At the Brooklyn Paramount, the kids came in, and they tore the hall up like you never seen a hall torn up before in your life. They broke about twelve store windows, stole the suits. And all the fancy furniture out in the lobby . . . Paul, they caught kids taking the beautiful chromium water fountains home. We had police. Didn't mean nothing. I had to go and get Italian hoodlums to break jaws. At one point, I'm sitting there minding my own business, and somebody yells, 'Fight! Fight, Teddy, hurry!' I fly through there and I see a kid and a man, and I tried to break 'em up. The man started swinging at me, I threw three punches and broke his nose, closed his eye, he was bleeding like a pig. You know who it was? The treasurer for the Paramount theater chain. The kid had called him a motherfucker, and he was going to beat the kid up. I went and beat him up. Well, maybe it's

Alan Freed at one of his innumerable in-person record hops, spinning platters for "the kids."

good he didn't get a look at what was going on up in the box seats. Everybody was doing *everything* up there: fucking, sucking, smoking, drinking. A lot of those theaters, they had to nail up the boxes. When we played the Paramount, I told the manager, 'I don't want no money, all I want is the concession to fix the seats.'"

According to Teddy Reig, "Freed had these little gimmicks he used on the radio. He would push a button, bang and scream and holler, push the button again and the record would come back on. Then some guy would buy the record, bring it back to the store and say, 'Hey, this ain't the record. I want the one with the guy screaming.' And there'd be arguments in the record shops, fights, every damn thing. It was so ridiculous; I've never seen anybody have the impact Alan Freed had. And the guy was just *drunk* with power. That's what killed him."

In the days B.C.—Before the Cleanup that followed the congressional "payola" hearings of 1959–60—streetwise hustlers like Teddy Reig, disc jockeys who profited from the sales of records they played, and record company owners who kept most of their artists' performing and songwriting royalties for themselves represented business as usual. Publishers' representatives had been slipping money or favors (including spurious "composer" credits on likely hit songs) to bandleaders and popular vocalists for decades in order to get their songs preferential treatment—a "push." When the cult of the personality disc jockey began to bloom in the early 1940s, due to groundbreaking radio shows like Al Jarvis's "Make Believe Ballroom" and the "Lucky Strike Hit Parade" (later "Your Hit Parade"), the song pluggers were waiting. But during the late forties and early fifties the music game was suddenly overrun by newcomers—independent record companies springing up far from the traditional music-business power centers, upstart performers who seemed to come pouring out of the backwoods and the back of town across America, upstart disc jockeys with power to burn, broadcasting this new music far and wide. Older Tin Pan Alley types saw their long-standing stranglehold on "the business" being broken, their profit margins eroding. And rock and roll, despised by "good music" types and authority figures, provided a conveniently broad target for their wrath.

"Rock and roll smells phony and false," griped Frank Sinatra in 1957.

"It is sung, played, and written for the most part by cretinous goons and by means of its almost imbecilic reiteration, and sly, lewd, in plain fact, dirty lyrics . . . it manages to be the martial music of every sideburned delinquent on the face of the earth." Rock and roll had supplanted Sinatra's crooning in the hearts of the young, as his sagging record sales during the first half of the fifties confirm.

Behind the scenes, powerful forces were in conflict. Virtually all the old-line, prerock songwriters belonged to the American Society of Composers Authors and Publishers (ASCAP), which kept track of and collected members' royalties. The proliferation of independent, street-level record companies after World War II brought a new crop of songwriters to the fore, most of them country or r&b oriented, few of them considered worthy ASCAP material by that organization's old guard. The rejected tunesmiths flocked to ASCAP's rival organization, Broadcast Music Inc. (BMI), originally founded by a coalition of radio broadcasters to counter a 1941 ASCAP strike. ASCAP ignored BMI for more than a decade, but by the mid-fifties the burgeoning popularity of rock and roll had made BMI, for the first time, a serious rival. The late-fifties' congressional hearings into payola, or pay for play, were undertaken at the urging of ASCAP-affiliated lobbyists, who sent stars like Sinatra in to dazzle the lawmakers and testify against the demon Rock.

Contrary to popular legend, the payola hearings did not bring ruin to Alan Freed; they were more like the final nail in the coffin. Freed's real troubles began on May 3, 1958, when his traveling package show, headlined by Jerry Lee Lewis, played the Boston Arena. The twenty-odd policemen on duty, faced with an unruly crowd of about five thousand teenagers, warned the kids about dancing in the aisles and standing on their seats—behavior that had erupted into violence at previous concerts when police overreacted. The Boston police turned up the houselights in the middle of the show, and for a moment everything stopped. Freed, acting as MC, came out to take charge of the situation. According to several witnesses, he also commented, from the stage, "I guess the police here in Boston don't want you kids to have a good time." Apparently the comment didn't stir up any action in the hall. But outside, after the show, some fifteen people were reported stabbed, beaten, or robbed by roving gangs. The arena was in a rough part of town where muggings were frequent, and there was no evidence that any of the marauders had attended or wanted to attend the concert. Nevertheless, Freed was served with two indictments for inciting a riot.

One charge was based on an antique anti-anarchy statute and was subsequently dropped by the commonwealth. The other hung over Freed's head for more than a year. On November 12, 1959, that case too was dropped. But in the meantime, Freed had been forced out of the concert business, and the congressional payola hearings were at hand. Feeling the heat, Freed's employer, radio station WABC, demanded that all its disc jockeys sign pledges stating they had never accepted money or valuables in exchange for airplay. Freed, claiming the pledge was an insult to his integrity, refused to sign. On November 21, he was fired. Finally, in May 1960, Freed was arrested and charged by New York State under a commercial bribery statute. This was one of the few courses open to Freed's enemies; there would be no federal regulations making payola illegal until later in the year. When he pleaded guilty to some of the charges, he was fined three hundred dollars and given a six-month suspended sentence. A slap on the wrist, perhaps, but by this time Freed was washed up as a power in the music industry, and suffering with a bad case of (possibly alcohol-related) uremia. He continued to work in radio, but in relative obscurity. The IRS was after him, hoping to collect taxes on undeclared payola from 1957–59, when he succumbed to the uremia on January 20, 1965. Freed was forty-three.

Drunk with power though he may have been, Alan Freed was undoubtedly made the scapegoat for rock and roll's sins, real and imagined. Of course he had accepted record company payments in exchange for playing records; was there a major-league disc jockey who hadn't? Arrangements of this sort were so commonplace, in fact, that according to WLAC's powerful r&b disc jockey Hoss Allen, the more popular DJ's were openly carried on record company books as "consultants." They received regular payroll checks for their services, with federal withholding taken out and everything entirely aboveboard.

Not so aboveboard, perhaps, was the practice of record companies assigning co-composer credit, with all the attendant royalties, to disc jockeys and others who might help "break" a record. Freed, for example, was credited by Chess Records as a co-composer of Chuck Berry's breakthrough hit "Maybelline," along with Berry himself and one Russ Fratto. According to Teddy Reig, "Next door to Leonard Chess and Chess Records was a guy who had a stationery store, and although Leonard didn't realize it at the time, this guy was doing all the printing for the Chicago numbers racket. He was lending Leonard money, which led to the syndicate having a beef with Leonard. So Leonard gave this guy Russ Whatever a third of the writing credit on 'Maybelline,' Freed pushed the hell out of it, and the syndicate took a walk."

Unfortunately, it was a short walk. Recording engineer Malcolm Chisholm, who began working at Chess in the mid-fifties, has recalled repeated attempts by a Chicago gangland faction to "muscle in" on the Chess brothers' operation. But the tough, scrappy Leonard Chess, raised in a *shtetl*, or Jewish ghetto, in Poland, stood his ground. According to Chisholm, the hoods subjected Leonard Chess to several systematic beatings. Each time, he reminded them that all they could do was kill him, and that Chess Records would die with him. He was stubborn; so were the hoodlums. Finally, a Chess representative made a special trip to New York City in order to meet with a certain record mogul, a "Mr. Big" whose ties to organized crime were well known within the industry. Mr. Big (who frequently employed Teddy Reig as a producer) made a few phone calls and determined that the Chicago mobsters preying on Chess were "wildcatting"—acting for their own personal gain without the knowledge or approval of their higher-ups. He had them called off. During the next few years, the radio stations owned by the Chess brothers devoted substantial airtime to records from Mr. Big's family of labels. Naturally, this was purely coincidental.

By the late fifties, the independent labels that had nurtured rock and roll from birth were under attack from all sides. The mob wanted a piece of the action; the major record labels and music publishers were determined to regain their dominance of the hit parade; clergymen and local politicos were out for blood; and congressmen were probing rock's Achilles heel, the payola issue. Privately, many indie-record men argued that payola was their only means of competing with the major, corporate labels on something approaching an equal footing. The indies couldn't afford to hire an army of

Alan Freed gets behind the drums to give Chuck Berry a lift; after Leonard Chess gave Freed co-composer credit on Berry's first single, "Maybelline," the influential disc jockey helped "break" the record.

promotion men, or buy their own distributorships, as many of the majors were doing. They *could* afford to slip a disc jockey a few greenbacks, or a regular, nominal consultant's fee. Pay-for-play rates were hardly exorbitant; often a bottle of good liquor would be enough to get a record an airing. And as long as Chess and Sun releases shared airtime with products from the likes of Columbia and RCA Victor, the fans could vote with their pocketbooks. The trouble with this arrangement, from the point of view of what we might call the pop-music establishment, was that the teenagers seemed to prefer indie-label originals by Little Richard or Fats Domino to the sort of white-bread cover versions churned out by the likes of squeaky-clean Pat Boone. This teen preference was shared by Alan Freed.

One Hundred Percent Men

All the payola in the world couldn't seem to persuade Alan Freed to play a record he didn't like. And the records he liked were usually by black artists. Even during the early fifties, when it seemed every r&b smash inspired a sanitized white-pop remake, Freed played only the black originals. When white rockers with something of their own to say came riding in on Elvis Presley's blue suede coattails, Freed's package shows continued to feature overwhelmingly black lineups. At Freed's concerts, black and white teenagers mixed and mingled as freely as the authorities would allow. The girls greeted favorite performers with screams and squeals; often the girls were white, and the performers were black mojo men, strutting their stuff. Early rock and roll shows and tours like Freed's brought instant integration and raised the specter of "the white man's worst nightmare"—miscegenation.

Basically, that was the real fear: a black man fondling Daddy's little white girl. And like most deep, dark fears, this one had some basis in fact. "I'd made love to nearly a thousand women over the past few years, women of every color, religion, and nationality," writes Charles Connor, the drummer with the Upsetters, of his days on the road with Little Richard. "We'd partied more than any band in history." They could afford it; Richard kept the party going by dipping into the bags of cash with which most groups were paid in those days. Bobby Byrd, one of James Brown's Famous Flames, recalls approaching Richard for a loan when Brown opened for him in New Jersey; Brown and his men hadn't made enough money from the show to get back home to Macon, Georgia. "He [Richard] opened the trunk of his car," says Byrd, "reached in, and scooped out a handful of dollars without even looking. The trunk of the car was *full* of loose notes of all denominations!"

Among their fellow performers, Richard and his Upsetters were as notorious for their after-show bacchanals as for incendiary musical performances. Etta James, still a teenager when her "Roll with Me Henry" hit the r&b charts, had heard the stories. When she was booked on a tour headlined by Richard, she was determined to see for herself. She heard loud voices and much merriment from behind the locked door of Richard's dressing room, but several older performers took it upon themselves to "protect" her. This only piqued James's curiosity, and one night she hauled a chair out into a theater hallway, braced it against Richard's dressing-room door, stood on tiptoe, and peered in through the transom. "And honey," she says, her eyes widening as the memory hits her, "the things I saaaaw . . ."

What did Etta see? Charles Connor describes a typical scene: "The kitchen was closed on concert nights, and when women poured in the back after the shows, we had our pick. We'd make love to chicks all over that kitchen. They'd be sitting around on barstools waiting for us, some of them almost naked. A hundred more would be screaming outside the door, wanting to get in. Sometimes Little Richard would have his boyfriends with him, or he'd sit on a table and watch us. . . . It had been part of our success and a way of letting off steam after we brought down the house all over America and in Japan, the Philippines, and Australia. People just seemed to lose all control when Richard performed. They got a natural high from seeing sweat flying off him and his long hair flying over his face. Thousands of women took off their panties and threw them at us. We'd be playing and dodging panties. Sometimes they'd land on one of my cymbals. I'd pick them up with a drumstick and wave 'em in the air, and that would just make the women crazier—a dozen more panties would come flying at us."

Richard, of course, was an outsider's outsider—black and bisexual and proud of it, the self-designated King *and* Queen of Rock and Roll. Had he belonged to an earlier generation of performers, he would have had to keep his sexual predilections well hidden under a veneer of highly stylized masculinity, and doubtless subordinate his natural exuberance to a smoother crooning style. But Little Richard was a rocker, and this is one

Members of the Upsetters, Little Richard's hard-rocking road band; "we'd partied more than any band in history," drummer Charles Connor recalls.

way you can tell: Rockers don't sublimate their idiosyncracies, they exaggerate them, revel in them. "We decided that my image should be crazy and way-out," he writes in his sizzling autobiography, "so that the adults would think I was harmless." Whether this was closer to image making or typecasting is debatable. In any event, Richard and his musicians decided that what was good for the goose would be good for the ganders.

"Richard wanted us to look like no other band we'd seen before," says Connor. "So we started dressing in bright red or yellow shirts, and white or navy blue trousers, and we got our hair 'gassed' and curled like Richard's. At shows we'd wear pancake makeup and earrings. He intended his band to look gay and act like sissies. First of all, it set us apart from other bands. But it also had practical benefits. If one of us saw a beautiful lady in the audience, he'd say in a little friendly voice, 'I wanna see you backstage at intermission.' If she had any boyfriends around, they'd figure, 'He's a sissie, I don't have to worry about him.' Then once we'd get these girls alone, we'd be one hundred percent men."

The Upsetters may have been the first rock and roll musicians to discover that *girls actually liked* performers who dressed in gender-bending frills and finery but were "one hundred percent men" underneath. Rockers as musically disparate as the Rolling Stones, Alice Cooper, David Bowie, Prince, Boy George, and cross-dressing "alternative" icons such as Nirvana's Kurt Cobain and the Leaving Trains' Falling James Moreland would keep "glam" current from the sixties to the nineties. Looking back, it seems that Little Richard and his cohorts—including rough-and-ready tour manager Teddy Reig and the supreme rabble-rouser, Alan Freed—did more than invent and popularize a new music. They were pioneers of what we might call the rock and roll lifestyle.

Musically, rock and roll was not so much a departure from tradition as an evolutionary synthesis. For a hypothetical (and highly unlikely) listener well versed in the history of jazz, gospel, hillbilly, western swing, Latin music, blues, and r&b, fifties rock would have held few surprises. And this wasn't the first time social problems such as juvenile delinquency had been linked to popular music. In the 1920s, jazz was blamed for the drinking and promiscuity of the flappers. The association of leather jackets, sideburns, motorcycles, and delinquency with bop and r&b was in the grand tradition

1 Etta James, a.k.a. Peaches, was a teenager when her first rock and roll hits won her a place on package tours headlined by Little Richard: "Honey, the things I saaaaw . . ."

2 Sam Cooke was drop-dead, supperclub cool at watering holes like the Copa; for r&r/r&b gigs, like this 1964 show at Comiskey Park, the jacket, tie, and cuff links came off and the sexy soul man took charge.

3 Richard at the piano, flashing his megawatt smile, eyes aglitter with visions of the backstage bacchanal to come.

4 Prince, whose calculated androgyny and gospel-inspired showmanship owe much to Little Richard's example, once asked a concert audience, "Don't you wish your boyfriend had an ass like mine?"

4

of Hollywood myth making. Leather-clad Marlon Brando and his pack of cyclists in *The Wild One* (1950) provided nascent rockers with a look and an attitude; in 1955, James Dean embodied the *Rebel Without a Cause;* and teen hoodlum Vic Morrow terrorized a teacher to a Bill Haley soundtrack in *The Blackboard Jungle.* Nor was there anything new in the spectacle of teenage concertgoers screaming, swooning, and jitterbugging in the aisles to music with a heavy, emphatic beat. Charismatic bandleaders such as Benny Goodman and Gene Krupa, and their standup vocalists, including young Frank Sinatra, were the pop stars ("matinee idols") of the late thirties and early forties, and their teenage fans ("bobby-soxers") were an energetic and sometimes volatile bunch. All this was business as usual.

It was *not* business as usual when Little Richard hit town, trailing a young retinue of varying races and varying sexual persuasions. It wasn't business as usual when Alan Freed presided, with a kind of avuncular glee, over a theater full of white girls who were investigating the mysteries of the orgasm, encouraged by black men given to advertising their lovemaking prowess in songs. This was what rock's powerful opponents would not tolerate, and as the fifties became the sixties, it seemed that what America's rich popular culture had given us, America's moral watchdogs were taking away. Freed was out of the picture by 1960; Little Richard, perhaps sensing that the shit was about to hit the fan, was back in Bible school. The Elvis Presley who returned from his U.S. Army tour of duty was no longer the sneering, ducktailed "hillbilly cat," decked out in Beale Street's gaudiest pimpwear. The new Elvis celebrated his return to civilian life by donning a tux and singing a television duet with . . . Frank Sinatra? Apparently, Elvis (or his management) was out to prove that he could be as malleable as any of the impeccably coiffed and manicured "teen idols" being manufactured to order by the corporate music business. Even Buddy Holly seemed ready to follow Elvis into the pop-music mainstream, if his sessions with strings and the last demo recordings he made before his fatal plane crash are accurate barometers of his intentions.

But not even the icy demise of two exceptionally talented singer-writer-guitarist-performers (Holly and Ritchie Valens) and a clever disk-jockey-turned-songwriter (the Big Bopper) in a single 1959 plane crash added up to a rock and roll apocalypse, "the day the music died." The years between that crash and the arrival of the Beatles as spearheads of a "British Invasion" were fallow years for rock and roll only if you confined your listening to top-forty radio. Rock and roll—the hard stuff, the genuine article—has often ruled the best-seller lists, but just as often it has been "bubbling under," as *Billboard* magazine would say. It's easy to forget that even during the giddy years of the original rock and roll explosion, the best-selling pop records were often easy-listening fodder like "Volare" and "Cherry Pink and Apple Blossom White." During the post-Freed, pre-Beatles years, rock and roll, especially black rock and roll, was "bubbling under" with a vengeance. For those who followed the music faithfully, even when it drew them away from their transistor radios and out into the night, the years around the turn of the decade were as full of fresh and wondrous sounds as any comparable time period in the music's history.

In 1960, when I was fifteen, I attended a show whose talent roster now reads like some arcadian dream. Sam Cooke and Jackie Wilson were the headliners, preceded by two less celebrated but equally distinctive voices from an era blessed with an unequaled abundance of great singers—Jesse Belvin, who was a prime influence on the young Stevie Wonder, and Marv Johnson, who was one of writer-producer Berry Gordy's pre-Motown protégés. The competition was fierce, with no quarter asked or given.

Marv Johnson was smooth, understated, almost self-effacing, but he sang and moved with a sensuous elegance. Jesse Belvin quieted the exuberant audience with an impossibly soulful "Funny (How Time Slips Away)." It was his last performance. Later that night, he died in a flaming collision on a dark Arkansas highway, and some of us missed him as much as we missed Holly and Valens. Jackie Wilson squeezed every drop of emotion out of his ballads and punctuated his up-tempo vocal gymnastics with faultless splits, spins, and knee-drops. The crowd had been shaken and stirred again and again by the time Sam Cooke made his appearance, dressed in tie and tails, as if for an evening at the Copa, and radiating a supremely confident cool.

This was no supper club—it was a dingy auditorium basement set up with flimsy restaurant tables and folding chairs—but Sam Cooke knew exactly where he was. The Tin Pan Alley show tunes that knocked 'em dead at the Copa were passed over and Sam Cooke the Soul Man took charge.

Halfway through the opening number he shed his tuxedo jacket. Next came the tie. Loosening his collar, singing like God's favorite angel, Cooke slowly, teasingly peeled off his formal white gloves. Around me, women were tensing, some rising halfway out of their chairs. Cooke pretended to hesitate, then nonchalantly tossed the gloves into the audience. One landed on my table, and half a dozen women, each the size of a football linebacker, landed on top of me. Down I went, followed by the table, the chairs, and the women, who fought for the glove tooth and nail while I squirmed on the bottom of the pileup. The eventual victor went running through the crowd, hooting, crowing, waving the glove high above her head like the battle trophy it was. Cooke, who had somehow remained dapper through it all, made a graceful exit, leaving the hall in pandemonium.

A few years earlier, the same show would most likely have been billed as a rock and roll event. Alan Freed had sent out package tours with comparable talent rosters, playing to teenage audiences that often were overwhelmingly white. But by 1960, black and white pop music seemed almost as segregated, and as mutually exclusive, as they had been before the anomalous events of the mid-fifties. When my white friends in Little Rock went out to a rock and roll show, they would catch a package tour like Dick Clark's Caravan of Stars, which generally featured a talent lineup as white as the audience it attracted. Cooke and Wilson were playing the "chitlin circuit," which meant playing for black audiences in segregated, second-class venues. In Little Rock, for example, Cooke and company were denied use of the municipal auditorium and had to settle for the facility's unprepossessing basement. The only white face in the audience was mine.

I had no way of knowing, but across America, up in Canada, and over in the U.K., in every town and every city, there were kids like me. We were loners, outsiders in our communities, strangers in our own homes, and we lived for rock and roll.

As the sixties unwound, America's corporate music business took steps to ensure that rude upstarts like Alan Freed and Sam Phillips and Leonard Chess would not catch them napping again. Disc jockeys would no longer play whatever they liked; now there were program directors and playlists to tell them what they could and couldn't air. By the end of the sixties, the major labels would control an enormous chunk of America's record-distribution network, and most of the hit-making fifties indies, including Sun and Chess, would be history.

"And that's just what it is: history," says Sam Phillips. "We were all beginners, just beginners, and we were *making history.* Oh, there was all sorts of resentment. First it was 'sinful,' and second it was affecting our children. *Yes, it was.* But it was giving them some individuality, giving them some say-so about their emotions and not having them just be a product of their parents right up until they were twenty-five years old. All this had an awful lot to do with the total psychological change that took place in this country because of rock and roll and r&b—which was for the better, I don't give a damn what anybody says."

For kids like me, it wasn't a question of better or worse. We were rockers, and that was that. To outsiders, we seemed to have been infected by some viral mania, a point of view deftly satirized in tunes like Huey "Piano" Smith's "Rocking Pneumonia and the Boogie Woogie Flu" and in the warnings of Dr. Ross, an early Sam Phillips discovery, concerning the "boogie disease": "The doctor says I may get better, but I'll never get well." But for us, for all the outsiders who had been touched and transformed by this music, it was more consuming than any mere infection. Rock and roll was our community and our calling, our inspiration and our mode of expression. Rock and roll was our very lives, our reason for being.

Rock was our religion. But what kind of religion was it?

Safety Zone

The ancient Greeks enshrined philosophical dualism in their hierarchy of gods and myths, identifying spiritual forces or powers that embodied two basic tendencies in society and culture: the "balanced, rational" Apollo and the "intoxicated, irrational" Dionysus. The cult of Dionysus is among the oldest of the world's religions, with roots in the even more ancient pre-Aryan cult of Shiva. Both Shiva and Dionysus were given appropriate nicknames. Shiva was the Howler, the Noisy One, the "Ithyphallic" (god with a hard-on), or Skanda, literally "the jet of sperm." In an archaic Indian text, the *Shiva Purana,* the god is described as "magnificent, completely naked, his only ornament the ash with which his whole body is smeared. Walking about, holding his penis in his hand, he showed off with the most depraved tricks." When Shiva encountered the most revered wise men of his time, "they were shocked to see the god abandon himself in obscene acts. . . . The priests and sages used indignant language, but the power of their virtue could not prevail against Rudra (Shiva), just as the brightness of the stars cannot prevail against the light of the sun."

Like Shiva, like Pan, the Greek Dionysus is often represented as a horned god. These are gods of ecstasy and rampant sexuality; their methods include "music, dance, and prophecy," which "emerge like blessed miracles from Dionysiac madness," according to Walter F. Otto's *Dionysus: Myth and Cult.* "Madness is a cult form which belongs to the religion of Dionysus. The god who sends the mind reeling, the god who appears to mankind in the most urgent immediacy is welcomed and feted by the women in an absolute ecstasy and excess of rapture. They respond to his coming with the behavior of the insane. . . . Dionysus was the god of the most blessed ecstasy and the most enraptured love. But he was also the persecuted god, the suffering and dying god, and all whom he loved, all who attended him, had to share his tragic fate."

The prospect of coming to a bad end did not deter Dionysus's attendants and camp followers, any more than a similar prognosis will dissuade a true rocker from pursuing a chosen course. According to E. R. Dodds's *The Greeks and the Irrational,* "the use of wine and the use of the religious dance" were "the two great Dionysiac techniques," and the god's followers indulged in plenty of both. "The aim," says Dodds, was "to satisfy and relieve the impulse to reject responsibility, an impulse which exists in all of us and can become under certain social conditions an irresistible craving." Dionysus was sometimes referred to as Lusios, "the Liberator" — "the god who by very simple means, or by other means not so simple, enables you for a short time to *stop being yourself,* and thereby sets you free. . . . And his joys were accessible to all, including even slaves." Dodds notes that Apollo "moved only in the best society . . . but Dionysus was at all periods a god of the people." Another Dionysian epithet was Master of Illusions; as such, "Dionysus came to be the patron of a new art, the art of the theater. To put on a mask is the easiest way of ceasing to be one's self." (In the Lemonheads' song "My Drug Buddy," Evan Dando and temporary Lemonhead Juliana Hatfield propose a similar rationale for ingesting mind-altering chemicals:

"I'm too much with myself/I wanna be someone else.")

The horned god, whether manifesting as Shiva, as Dionysus, or as Pan, was frequently accompanied by a wild and crazy crew of ravers, "freakish, adventurous, delinquent and wild young people, who prowl in the night, shouting in the storm, singing, dancing, and playing outrageous tricks on sages and gods." One can imagine them raising their fists in unison, each with two fingers protruding as "horns," like enraptured fans at a heavy metal concert.

In *Shiva and Dionysus,* Alain Danielou paints a vivid picture of these "delinquents of heaven"; they are "dancers, musicians, acrobats, practical jokers and lazy. They press the grape and get drunk. They are perpetually overexcited . . . ecstatic demons for whom eroticism is a form of expression." Their coming is heralded by the music of pipes, flutes, cymbals, and especially drums, the more thunderous the better. "Certain rhythms and their gradual acceleration play an important role, as well as the sudden changes in rhythmic formula causing a psychological shock to the dancers," writes Danielou. "A very high level of sound is useful in inducing states of trance. . . . The dance and noise of the drums have the effect of creating a safety zone and of driving away ill-omened influences." Accounts of the dancing make it sound like a wilder, more frenzied version of the Lambada, hyped as "the forbidden dance" and best described as having sex with one's clothes on. "The rhythm of the sexual act is included among those of the dance," Danielou notes. "The procreative act, the act of life, is thus opposed to the powers of destruction and death."

Among the Greeks, the god Apollo was everything Dionysus was not—balanced, rational, responsible, and, according to some classicists, "hostile to anything in the nature of ecstasy." The god Apollo spoke to humans in measured tones through his chosen oracles or mediums. Dionysus might speak to anyone, inciting them to ecstatic behavior that was liable to spread like wildfire. But even among the Greek rationalists, according to Otto's *Dionysus: Myth and Cult,* it was "a commonplace to say that no one ever creates anything great without a dash of madness." The patriarchal white-bread America of the 1950s was faux-Apollonian to a fault. "Father Knows Best" was the watchword; even when Father was hunting Communists and atheists under the living room sofa, or watching the skies for flying hubcaps manned by little green un-American aliens, he proceeded *calmly* and *rationally*. If "Don't worry, be happy" was a familiar bromide of the eighties, its fifties counterpart was "Don't worry, *everything's under control.*"

Rock and roll challenged the dominant norms and values with a *genuinely* Dionysian fervor. Compared to an ancient Dionysian revel—trances, seizures, devotees tearing sacrificial animals to pieces with their bare hands and eating the meat raw—a rock and roll performance is almost tame. But in a culture whose idea of musical entertainment was Perry Como, Doris Day, and "Your Hit Parade," the appearance of an Elvis Presley, let alone a Little Richard, was radical, unprecedented. In time, rock and roll concerts would become what Hakim Bey, a self-described "poetic terrorist," calls "temporary autonomous zones." A TAZ is a zone of freedom, a kind of functional anarchy that manages to exist within a more or less repressive mainstream culture precisely because it is of limited duration and scope. A rock and roll tour is a *portable* TAZ, creating a temporary Dionysiac community in a different location night after night.

Memphis, 1975, early in the morning on the Fourth of July: Dad and Mom are in bed asleep; the tykes are dreaming of parades and fireworks displays. But in a luxury hotel out near the airport, there's electricity in the air. It's one of those hotels that resemble a huge, multistoried shell, with cantilevered balconies on each floor jutting out over a huge central atrium that's carpeted in Astroturf. When you walk out the door of your room, you're standing on a balcony, looking out over a railing at all the rooms above and below. And despite the early hour, doors keep opening and shutting on one floor or another. Fans, members of the press, the curious, the insomniacs, all can feel the electricity. They're awaiting the arrival of the Rolling Stones.

The band, flying in aboard their own passenger jet, are hours late, as usual. By the time they do begin trickling into the lobby, there's only one young, inexperienced desk clerk on duty. Up to the desk, which is fully visible from every floor, marches Stones tour manager Peter Rudge—wired, frazzled, constitutionally impatient. The desk clerk mutters something; Rudge's response is clearly audible from ten floors up: "What do you bloody *mean* you can't find our reservations?" The desk clerk is mumbling, turning red with embarrassment. Rudge is already red, and not embarrassed in the least. "You want to see our reservations?" he barks, hefting a bulging attaché case onto the desk. "*Here's* our bloody reservations!" The case is full of greenbacks, some banded neatly, many loose. For a brief, frozen moment, it's raining dollars; they heap up on the desk, tumble off onto the Astroturf, flutter in the breeze as Mick Jagger and others crowd up behind Rudge. "*There's* your reservations," snaps the tour manager. The clerk gives up and summons a couple of bellboys, who scurry across the Astroturf, scooping up stray bills and stacking them neatly next to the pile on the desk.

The Stones disappear into various rooms, but just as I'm about to shut my door I hear an unmistakable clang of guitar chords. From my balcony I can see Keith Richards, who's several floors (and untold chemicals) higher. He's leaning over the edge of his balcony with a guitar in one hand and a bottle of Jack Daniels in the other; his amp is in his room, turned up loud enough for everyone in the hotel to hear it. Soon Ronnie Wood shows up, and after playing and swaying dramatically on the edge of the abyss, Keith joins him in the room. You can still hear them playing after they've shut their door.

The next day, the Stones take over the coliseum for a show that includes strutting New Orleans funk from the Meters, Boston white-boy r&b from the J. Geils Band, a set from octogenarian Memphis bluesman Furry Lewis (added to the bill at the Stones' demand), some fireworks, and a couple of elephants. The Stones, as is their wont, wait until after sunset to start their set. By the second or third tune, the crowd on the floor of the stadium has been transformed from a reasonably orderly rock and roll audience into a turbulent, undifferentiated ocean of humanity. You can wade into that crowd and feel your individual identity slipping away as you merge with a huge, protoplasmic organism; the music's pumping rhythms seem to make actual physical waves ripple across the sea of flesh.

Later that night I'm sitting in the hotel bar talking jazz with Charlie Watts, who always says he doesn't do interviews but will jaw for hours about Count Basie's rhythm section or the alto saxophone since Charlie Parker. Suddenly Keith Richards is standing over us, swaying unsteadily, decked out in velvet and scarves and grimy jeans, the ever-present whiskey bottle in

2

1. Keith Richards in mufti, displaying some of the scarves he often draped over hotel lamps and furniture to "personalize" his temporary quarters.

2. "We all need someone we can lean on," sings Mick Jagger, as guitarist Keith Richards, glimmer in his eyes, hits a power chord and lets it ring; Mick 'n' Keef were "the Glimmer Twins," and Richards reckoned that "a touch of glimmer can be more addicting than smack."

3. Sam Cooke, Jackie Wilson, Jesse Belvin, and Marv Johnson, four of r&r's great voices, share a package with two of the most soulful vocal groups (Midnighters, Falcons) and a single white face, Jerry Lee Lewis.

4

4. Fans at a heavy metal concert, displaying the clenched fist and the two-fingered sign of the horned god Dionysus, or Pan.

3 Cherrington and Allen Promotions Presents
CHARLOTTE'S GREATEST!

Rock n' Roll
★ SHOW ★

WED., JUNE 3 | 19 GREAT ACTS | 8:30 P.M.

INTERNATIONAL FAMOUS
Jerry Lee Lewis
"GREAT BALLS OF FIRE"
"WHOLE LOT OF SHAKING GOING ON"
And MANY OTHERS!

Sam COOK
"YOU SEND ME"
"EVERYBODY LOVES TO CHA CHA"

Jackie WILSON
"THAT'S WHY"
"LONELY TEARDROPS"

HANK BALLARD And
The MIDNIGHTERS
THE HANK MOORE ORCHESTRA
"KANSAS CITY"

The FALCONS
"YOU'RE SO FINE"

Jesse BELVIN
"GUESS WHO"

Marv JOHNSON
"COME TO ME"

Baby WASHINGTON "THE TIME"
With CLIFF DRIVER and His BAND

hand. "Hey, Charlie, c'mon with us," he says to the drummer. "Ronnie and me, we're gonna get off that plane, *drive* to the next gig, go through Arkansas, see a bit of the country." Watts gives him one of those steely, impenetrable looks that pass between Rolling Stones and, speaking very deliberately, says, "You must be mad." End of conversation. Keith grins, takes a slug of Jack, and exits.

The following afternoon, with the Stones' Dallas show hours away, Keith and Woody find themselves in the Fordyce, Arkansas, jail, along with two traveling companions, one a bodyguard, the other, possibly, a bagman. Frantic phone calls crisscross the country. Lawyers commandeer private planes and fly in from both coasts. Stones troubleshooter Bill Carter, an Arkansan and ex-Secret Service man, huddles with the local judge and police behind closed doors. When it's over, everyone is all smiles. Would anybody mind if Keith and Ronnie pose, gaunt and unshaven, behind the judge's desk, with Keith wielding his honor's gavel? Nobody minds at all. In a matter of minutes, Keith and Ronnie are on their way to the airstrip. The Dallas show goes on, later than scheduled but no later than many another Rolling Stones show.

The last time I caught part of a Rolling Stones tour, I found Carter, a new tour manager, and a clutch of longtime Stones roadies sitting around the backstage buffet table, looking noticeably grayer and unexpectedly glum. These were the guys who sweated and wheedled and connived and generally did what had to be done to see that the Rolling Stones got where they were supposed to go, more or less when they were supposed to get there. More than fifteen years had elapsed since that July 4 in Memphis. The new tour, a multizillion-dollar extravaganza, was running like clockwork. Nobody was about to take any unscheduled side trip; even big bad Keith had been behaving himself. Surely, I thought, my friends around the table were finding their jobs a lot easier. "Oh, it's a *lot* easier," said one of the long-time roadies. "*Too* goddamn easy. It's boring, is what it is. It's still hard work, mind you, but now it's *predictable* work. I might as well be punching a time clock in a fooking *bank*."

As I looked at the familiar faces around the table, noticing this one's new wrinkles, that one's receding hairline, the spreading midriffs under their regulation rock-crew T-shirts, the scene reminded me of something.

After a minute or so, I had it: These guys reminded me of Paul Williams and Teddy Reig, brothers of the road, getting together on a rainy afternoon to talk about how crazy, how nerve-racking, how much *fun* their lives had been, "back in the day." Williams and Reig are no longer with us; as I write this, the Rolling Stones are touring America again. This time, instead of sampling an Arkansas jail, they're *playing* in Arkansas, in the same over-grown cattle barn in Little Rock where I saw so many shows as a teenager. Like many of the earlier rock rebels who struck a chord, copped an attitude, and ignited Dionysian frenzies wherever they went, the Rolling Stones have become mere musicians—*professionals.*

And that's the beauty of rock and roll. The lifestyle can be perilous, the rate of attrition remains high, but the survivors can go on practicing and perfecting their craft while the younger generation's best and brightest assume the Dionysian mantle and get on with the main program, which is liberation through ecstasy. Somewhere, in some sleazy bar or grimy practice room or suburban garage, young musicians wielding guitars or turntables, drum kits or beat boxes, sequencers or samplers, are creating the music for tomorrow's rock and roll revelry. Now that women have belatedly been accepted as guitarists, bassists, drummers, songwriter-auteurs, and "not just another pretty face," we're witnessing the birth of a whole new style of rock and roll frenzy and transcendence. Even the media overkill surrounding the much-hyped "riot grrrls" can't rob the term of its Dionysiac import. Don't let the faux-Apollonians fool you. As rockers, we are heirs to one of our civilization's richest, most time-honored spiritual traditions.

We must never forget our glorious Dionysian heritage.

The Grateful Dead's Jerry Garcia, Phil Lesh, and Bob Weir (from left), playing "r&b with a large amount of weirdness inserted into it" for "people who were taking LSD and dancing their hearts out."

Eight Miles High

6

"It was incredible because of the formlessness, because of the thing of people wandering around wondering what was going on . . . and stuff happening spontaneously and people being prepared to accept any kind of thing that was happening and add to it. Everybody was creating."

> Jerry Garcia, the Grateful Dead, on the first Acid Test, 1965

"Recently, it has become possible for man to chemically alter his mental state and thus alter his point of view. . . . He then can restructure his thinking and change his language so that his thoughts bear more relation to his life and his problems, therefore approaching them more sanely. It is this quest for pure sanity that forms the basis of the songs on this album."

> 13th Floor Elevators, from the liner notes for their first album,
> *The Psychedelic Sounds of the 13th Floor Elevators*, 1966

"Psychedelic music is music that expands your awareness, your consciousness. It's that simple."

> Phil Lesh, the Grateful Dead

"Nobody can define psychedelic music. Psychedelic is when the person that is listening to it is on acid."

> Paul Kantner, the Jefferson Airplane

"Americans invented the blues: This is what we have got to be proud of. It ain't the nuclear stuff, it's not putting the man on the moon, it's the blues. And when the blues ran up against psychedelics, rock and roll really took off."

> Ken Kesey, author and Merry Prankster

The All-Seeing Eye on the cover of the debut album that launched the 13th Floor Elevators.

1938
Dr. Albert Hoffman invents
LSD in a Swiss lab.

1965
Bastion of the Beats,
North Beach, California,
proliferates with new
music clubs like the
Peppermint Tree and

Mothers, which feature
topless dancers and show-
case up-and-coming bands
such as the Byrds.

LSD-25 was a gift to the burgeoning youth culture of the sixties from a most unlikely Santa, the CIA. Originally synthesized in 1938, lysergic acid diethylamide, "acid" for short, was classified as a "psychedelic" or "mind-manifesting" substance after clinical tests discredited an earlier theory that it mimicked so-called psychotic states. Caught up in these clinical tests were several bright young men who later became "counterculture gurus," among them poet Allen Ginsberg and novelist Ken Kesey. If the CIA was disappointed that LSD proved ineffective as an agent of covert or psychological warfare—the effects were simply too unpredictable—the "guinea pigs" recruited for testing found other uses for it.

Novelist, beat-scene maker, and psychedelic booster Ken Kesey, riding the magic bus: "The sixties just won't be over until the fat lady gets high."

"I went to the Stanford Research Institute every Tuesday for many weeks," says Kesey. "They would give me one thing or another, which could be LSD-25, or LSD-6 or mescaline, or it might be a placebo; and they would pay me twenty bucks. There were about a hundred of us that went through the program. Not long after that, Ginsberg said this was all coming from the CIA, but nobody believed that, like nobody believed a lot of other conspiracy stuff."

When the experiments were called off, the guinea pigs revolted. "There is something very American about this," argues Kesey, who was a college athlete and wrestler. "When they said, 'Hey, we've got a new territory over there, and we'd like to have some explorers to go over and check it out,' it seemed like the most American thing to do—like crossing the continent in covered wagons, or going to the moon. Then after we'd come back and given our report to King George, the king said, 'Don't let anybody else go up there; I don't like the way these people look.' But the experiment was already in progress, and us guinea pigs decided, 'Well, if you guys don't have the balls to carry on with this, we'll do it on our own.' And it's still going on."

1965

The North Beach club Mothers, which features a Hieronymus Bosch decor, debuts the first light show seen in a West Coast club.

1965

The first of the "Acid Test" events — $1.00 cover gets you in, the LSD is free — is presented by Ken Kesey and friends at a house in San Jose, California.

Kesey and various friends began throwing LSD "parties" in San Francisco's bohemian North Beach. Before long, the parties had become "happenings," the Kesey crew (which included fifties beat-movement avatar Neal Cassady, immortalized as Dean Moriarty in Jack Kerouac's *On the Road*) had dubbed themselves the Merry Pranksters, and a scruffy electric band had become an integral part of the proceedings. This was the Grateful Dead, one of those mixtures of schooled and self-taught musicians that often seems to make for a favorable group chemistry (no pun intended) in rock and roll. Like many of San Francisco's sixties rockers, Dead guitarists Jerry Garcia and Bob Weir had played folk music and bluegrass. (Their earliest musical involvement had been with fifties rock and roll.) Organist Ron "Pigpen" McKernan and drummer Bill Kreutzmann preferred hard-edged r&b. When Phil Lesh was drafted by Garcia to replace an earlier bassist, he had never played the instrument before; *his* background was largely in classical and electronic music — and, according to Garcia, in big-band jazz.

Rock and roll has always thrived on a certain amount of musical diversity, most notably in the interaction of self-taught blues or country musicians with jazz-trained session players so characteristic of the fifties. But rarely had a rock or r&b band included musicians from so many different backgrounds, with such heterogeneous areas of expertise. In the sixties, such bands became the rule rather than the exception. In the case of the Dead, the diversity helped prepare them for a different kind of playing and a different kind of audience, beginning with the first of the "Trips Festivals" presented by Kesey and friends, which took place December 4, 1965, at a private house in San Jose. The LSD came free with the one-dollar admission; at the time, the substance was not illegal.

"Before, when we were playing the bars, what we did was basically r&b with a large amount of weirdness inserted into it," says Garcia. "We

Beat legend Neal Cassady, the inspiration for the Dean Moriarty character in Jack Kerouac's *On the Road,* partied with Kesey, the Merry Pranksters, and the Grateful Dead during the Acid Test days.

1966

The 13th Floor Elevators
undertake the "quest
for pure sanity" with their
first album.

1966

George Harrison of the
Beatles takes up the
sitar under the tutelage
of Indian musician Ravi
Shankar.

started as a dance band; when we took off from an r&b song on a twenty-minute improvisation, the bartenders loved us because the audiences would dance themselves silly and afterward they would be dying for a drink. But then we burnt out on the club scene and got involved in the Acid Tests. Since everybody paid their dollar to get in, including the performers, and nobody was coming to see *us,* we had maximum freedom; we could play absolutely anything, or nothing at all. Of course, we were experimenting with LSD ourselves. I don't think playing high ever yielded much of musical value, but it did instill in us a love for the completely unexpected. So right around then, the idea of having a set list, even having fixed arrangements, went completely out the window. We were playing to people who were taking LSD and dancing their hearts out, and it was easy, because we were playing from that flow."

Drugs and music making have interacted in a variety of ways throughout human history, but specific musical developments have rarely been attributed to the effects of drugs. Louis Armstrong's lifelong fondness for marijuana may have had something to do with his extraordinary sensitivity to tonal richness and detail, but nobody characterizes Armstrong's brilliant improvisations as "psychedelic" or "pothead" music. Heroin may have had something to do with the ability of modern jazzmen like Charlie Parker to reel off the most complex and rococo flurries of notes while maintaining an air of slightly bemused or disengaged "cool," but we don't call bebop "junkie jazz." Nevertheless, LSD is a special case, and not just because it is so much "stronger" in its effects than, say, THC, the psychoactive component in marijuana. From a pharmacological or medical point of view, the difference between the effects of smoking marijuana and taking a hit of LSD may be one of degree rather than kind. But an LSD trip, given a sufficient dosage and a lack of inhibiting factors (such as a chemical antag-

1966

The Beatles' final American concert is held August 29 at San Francisco's Candlestick Park.

1966

John Lennon of the Beatles meets his future wife/collaborator Yoko Ono at a London gallery, exhibiting her work.

onist), is quite capable of "shaking" an individual to the core of his or her being. It can be a life-changing experience, revealing (not merely "suggesting") that environmental and psychological (external and internal) realities are not at all as they had seemed. The results can be personally empowering, or highly destabilizing, depending at least in part on the degree of understanding and preparedness one brings to the experience.

"For some people, taking LSD and going to a Dead show functions like a rite of passage," says Jerry Garcia. "Each person deals with the experience individually; it's an adventure that you can have that is personalized. But when people come together, this singular experience is ritualized. I think the Grateful Dead serves a desire for meaningful ritual, but it's *ritual without dogma.* You know, we don't have a product to sell; but we do have a mechanism that works." Beginning around 1965, rock musicians made use of this working mechanism to explore their own relationship to music making, and the relationship of music to pure sound. LSD can provide alternative modes of processing sensory input; "Feel purple! Taste green!" blared ads for *The Trip,* one of the first acid-exploitation B movies, written by a young Jack Nicholson. More to the point, one could "explore" apparently simple sounds, "get inside" them. "When you're high, you like to blow flutes and knock rocks together," says Kesey. "You like to listen to the purity of a sound."

LSD also seems to slow down the passage of time, or render it plastic. There is a tendency to perceive music more as a flow than as a linear succession of discrete events or moments. The tripster/listener now "has the time" to appreciate sonic detail, the specific, sensuous texture of each sound. A sound that is particularly rich in harmonic overtones, such as the buzz and shimmer of drone strings on an Indian sitar or tamboura, may be especially appealing. But almost any sound can be interesting once one

161

1966

The first "psychedelic" rock hit, the Byrds' "Eight Miles High," is released in April; the same month, the Beatles record their first overtly psychedelic track, John Lennon's "Tomorrow Never Knows."

1966

Brian Wilson of the Beach Boys responds to the Beatles' challenge with the acid-drenched *Pet Sounds* album.

Composer Karlheinz Stockhausen, whose tape collages and electronically generated sounds inspired *Sgt. Pepper* and other landmarks of studio experimentation in sixties rock.

"takes the time" to examine it carefully. There is a sense of playfulness about all this; the musician and listener cooperate in the creation of a kind of virtual reality, a sonic playpen in which sounds can be investigated and toyed with in a spirit of childlike delight and wonder.

This playful, plastic, participatory immersion in what we might call the sonic bath strongly suggests that a redefinition of music is in order: Music is simply organized sound, or more specifically, *sound organized by consciousness.* It follows that any sound can be musical as long as it is contextualized as such. This definition may seem radical from a pop-music point of view, but it has been accepted in modern classical and avant-garde circles for years. "Noise music" was part of the anti-art program of Dada and the Futurists during the first two decades of the twentieth century. In the thirties and forties, Edgard Varèse, John Cage, and Harry Partch were composing with "noises" derived from specially constructed instruments or sound machines; "found" and electronically generated sounds on tape; and, in Cage's "Imaginary Landscapes," from radios tuned to different stations. In the late fifties and early sixties, composers such as Karlheinz Stockhausen refined the art of tape-collage while John Coltrane and La Monte Young, each in his own way, adapted the sonic drone and repeating melodic cycles of Indian and Arab music as a fresh format for improvisation.

The spread of LSD from the CIA's "controlled experiments" into the culture at large undoubtedly accelerated the penetration of these and other rarefied influences in rock and roll. Bob Dylan led the way on the lyric-writing front, transforming what had largely been teen-oriented dance music with social and psychological resonances into a forum for "investigations into the nature of consciousness." But Dylan showed little interest in effecting a similarly radical transformation of the music itself, once his exploded song-forms gave him sufficient room in which to work. That task

1966
London's "hippie underground rock club" UFO opens December 23.

1966
Revolver displays the Beatles' experimental studio techniques: artificial double tracking, tape loops, tape saturation, and guitar turning into a seagull.

1967
"Underground radio" begins in San Francisco as KMPX broadcasts progressive rock.

he left for others, and by 1965 there was no shortage of volunteers. Emboldened by the experience of LSD, encouraged by an audience that actually seemed to *crave* experimentation, a generation of rock and roll musicians embarked on a journey to the music's outer limits, and beyond.

From the very beginning, psychedelia was a cultural moment—in plain English, a fad—as well as a process of genuine musical innovation. The first rock and roll band to espouse the psychedelic cause openly was almost certainly Austin, Texas's 13th Floor Elevators, who were presenting their reverb-drenched r&b as a "quest for pure sanity" in 1965 and early 1966, before Kesey's Acid Tests, before "Eight Miles High" and *Revolver* and more than two years before the Grateful Dead's tentative first album. And already, in the band-written liner notes to *The Psychedelic Sounds of the 13th Floor Elevators,* their first album (released by International Artist [sic] of Houston in 1966), we find warnings about "those people who for the sake of appearances take on the superficial aspects of the quest." Various songs on the album are said to illustrate "the difference between persons using the old and the new reasoning. The old reasoning, which involves a preoccupation with objects, appears to someone using the new reasoning as childishly unsane. The old system keeps man blind to his animal-like emotional reactions. . . . The new system involves a major evolutionary step for man." This is Dylan's "Ballad of a Thin Man" ("Something is happening, and you don't know what it is/Do you, Mr. Jones?") writ large indeed, us versus them inflated into a gnostic cosmology in which the material world and its institutions incarnate darkness and death and only the Knowers are cognizant of the divine spark within.

This response to the psychedelic experience is interesting for several reasons. It is a direct response, as yet unmediated by the marketing efforts of Dr. Timothy Leary and other self-appointed tripster gurus. In contrast to

Bob Dylan at the piano, the instrument he used to bang out the tolling chords of his "Ballad of a Thin Man," the psychedelic era's us-versus-them anthem.

163

1967

The Gathering of the Tribes, or Human Be-In, held January 14 at San Francisco's Golden Gate Park, draws 20,000 plus and inaugurates a tradition

of the era: free music-in-the-parks. The peaceful fest is policed by the Hells Angels, unofficial enforcers of Haight-Ashbury.

1967

In June the Beatles' *Sgt. Pepper's Lonely Hearts Club Band* released to much highbrow acclaim.

Leary's adumbration of Eastern reality maps such as the *Tibetan Book of the Dead,* it is a *Western* response, representing an insurgent strain of do-it-yourself spirituality and individual contact with the ineffable at least as old as Christianity itself. Finally, it is a response that needs to be factored into any genuine understanding of what went on in the sixties. For behind the media-friendly facade of peace, love, and flowers, the sixties were a period of violence, conflict, and paranoia, with battle lines being drawn in the streets. For every Woodstock, there was an Altamont, for every "All You Need Is Love" and "Sunshine Superman" there was an "Ohio" (on the shooting of demonstrating Kent State students by the National Guard) and a "Born under a Bad Sign." Given a choice between meditative quietism and rocking the foundations of consensus reality, rock and roll would almost have to choose the latter in order to remain true to itself.

If any single artist epitomized both the spirituality and the insurgency of the times, that artist was saxophonist John Coltrane. Though he entered the decade with impeccable jazz credentials and the blessings of his former employers Miles Davis and Thelonious Monk, Coltrane had experienced a spiritual awakening and began to view his music more as a "quest for pure sanity," a development that alienated the jazz traditionalists. A composer of gorgeously lyrical melodies, Coltrane increasingly used his precomposed themes as launching pads for no-holds-barred group improvisations, headlong leaps into the sonic bath. His example encouraged rockers in "the quest," inspiring ferocious outpourings of freely improvised "energy music." (Coltrane had investigated LSD himself and was responsible for turning other jazzmen on, most notably Ornette Coleman, who says Coltrane gave him his first "hit.") But Coltrane's most important contribution to the new rock was on a how-to, nuts-and-bolts level: He showed musicians how to improvise practically endless melodic variations by

Saxophonist John Coltrane, whose restless, innovative career epitomized the sixties artist as spiritual seeker and inspired rock musicians such as Roger McGuinn, Eric Clapton, and Duane Allman.

1967

The Box Tops' big hit "The Letter" features a teenage Alex Chilton, of later Big Star renown, on lead vocals.

1967

Self-appointed tripster gurus such as Dr. Timothy Leary turn the counter-culture on to Eastern reality maps like the *Tibetan Book of the Dead.*

superimposing a variety of scales, modes, and textural variations onto a single root-chord or drone. This was an ingenious Western adaptation of the *principles,* as opposed to the merely exotic colorations, of Indian and Arabic music, which were the source for many of the scales or modes Coltrane employed. Rock musicians have rarely been comfortable with the complex, rapidly changing harmonies or chord sequences of conventional jazz and the Tin Pan Alley songwriting tradition; Coltrane opened up a world of possibilities beyond the major, minor, and blues scales that had long been the rockers' stock-in-trade, bringing extended improvisation within their grasp for the first time. Among the beneficiaries were guitarists such as Eric Clapton, Roger McGuinn, Jimi Hendrix, and Duane Allman—Coltrane freaks all.

The first "psychedelic" rock hit was the Byrds' "Eight Miles High," written in 1965 and released as a single in April 1966—the same month the Beatles recorded their first overtly psychedelic track, John Lennon's "Tomorrow Never Knows," later included on the *Revolver* album. At a press conference celebrating the release of "Eight Miles High," Byrds guitarist Roger McGuinn spoke at some length about the record's Coltrane influence. He was trying to emulate Coltrane's soprano saxophone style on his electric twelve-string guitar, he announced, right down to "the sound of valves [on the saxophone] opening and closing." What McGuinn apparently did not mention at the time was the source of the four-note melodic motif that leads from the opening vamp into the song proper and later recurs at appropriate intervals, lending this carefully thought-out composition an exceptional thematic coherence. The four-note figure was originally the opening phrase of Coltrane's composition "India."

Lyrically, "Eight Miles High" was a deliberately cryptic account of the Byrds' first visit to England. You had to be "in the know" to understand that,

The Byrds, whose "Eight Miles High" ran afoul of a censorship movement aimed at cleansing the airways of "drug songs."

165

1967

An estimated 100,000 people emigrate to San Francisco's Haight-Ashbury district in the first half of the year, preceding the Summer of Love.

1967

John Coltrane, 40, dies July 17 of liver ailment, having exerted a spellbinding influence on a generation of rock and jazz musicians and composers.

1967

The Beatles' manager, Brian Epstein, 32, dies August 27 from an overdose of sleeping pills.

for example, the "small faces" referred to were actually an up-and-coming British band, or that the title was a reference to the cruising altitude of transatlantic flights. (The actual figure would be closer to "Six Miles High," but the Beatles had recorded "Eight Days a Week" and somehow "Eight" sounded more poetic. . . .) Unfortunately for the Byrds, the record ran afoul of one of those tiresome, periodic efforts to "cleanse" the airwaves, the target this time being overt references to drugs. A leading record-industry tip sheet identified "Eight Miles High" as a drug song and recommended that it be dropped from playlists; radio stations were happy to comply, and the de facto censorship undoubtedly prevented the record from becoming the hit it should have been (though it did climb to number fourteen on the *Billboard* charts). "If we'd wanted to write a drug song, we'd have written a drug song," McGuinn protested. More recently, David Crosby, one of the architects of the Byrds' forays into Indian music and Coltrane, asked rhetorically, "Did I think 'Eight Miles High' was a drug song? No, I *knew* it was. We denied it, of course. But we had a strong feeling about drugs, or rather, psychedelics and marijuana. We thought they would help us blast our generation loose from the fifties. Personally, I don't regret my psychedelic experiences. I took psychedelics as a sort of sacrament."

The Beatles' "Tomorrow Never Knows" also treated the psychedelic experiment as a kind of sacrament. But rather than construct his own scaffolding of metaphor and explication, Lennon in effect gave his endorsement to Timothy Leary's manual for tripping, based on the *Tibetan Book of the Dead*. A Tibetan Buddhist conception of the afterlife may or may not be an appropriate metaphor for what Westerners could have expected to encounter on LSD if left to their own devices. But this much is clear: The dialogue on psychedelics was now a media dialogue, one in which rock music would play a central role.

Although the Grateful
Dead's eponymous debut
album is recorded in just
three days, the band
soon is booking extended
studio time to master
recording technology that
will change their sound.

Musically, "Tomorrow Never Knows" was a truly revolutionary piece of work, the result of unprecedented studio experimentation. Tape loops were overlaid, piled one upon the other until the master tape was almost saturated. Guitars were distorted, fed back, speeded up, mixed with sounds made by wineglasses and other everyday objects. There was more Stockhausen than Coltrane in this "quest for pure sanity," but in another, more fundamental sense, "Tomorrow Never Knows" and "Eight Miles High" are very much alike. They exemplify the musical impact of the psychedelic experience on rock and roll before media stereotypes began to dictate what the with-it acidhead should see, feel, listen to, and wear. And, like most of the enduring rock and roll to have emerged from this particular moment in time, both records are built on inspired songwriting and craftsmanship. Even when the songs diverged radically from traditional song forms, the very conciseness of the pop singles format kept the sonic experimentation from degenerating into mere self-indulgence.

Many bands soon abandoned the singles format in favor of more open-ended explorations, resulting in "profound" album-length noodling to no particular purpose. Today, these records are little more than quaint period pieces—a criticism that can arguably be leveled at that sacred cow of psychedelia, *Sgt. Pepper's Lonely Hearts Club Band*. Although the album remains a marvel of the record-making process, achieving unheard-of effects without recourse to today's computer-assisted multitracking technology, the effects are not always organic. One often has the impression that these effects are cosmeticizing or disguising the songs' superficiality, and that the music's sheer cleverness is too often an end in itself. "Tomorrow Never Knows" may have borrowed its central metaphysical conceit rather uncritically, but at least here the song and the sounds and effects are working toward the same end and are very much of a piece. On *Sgt. Pepper*, with

1967

The psychedelic rock poster, strobe lighting, and laser show are as prevalent as marijuana and acid.

1967

The Monterey Pop Festival in Monterey, California, presents Janis Joplin and Jimi Hendrix, Otis Redding and Ravi Shankar.

one or two exceptions, the extraordinarily creative songwriting that so distinguished *Revolver* and *Rubber Soul* is in critically short supply.

The Beatles created their psychedelic rock entirely in the studio, without having to worry about how and whether the new sounds might translate in concert. In San Francisco, the situation was very different. The Grateful Dead, the Jefferson Airplane, Big Brother and the Holding Company (with Janis Joplin), and most of the other San Francisco bands had developed along with an audience that largely shared their backgrounds, their values, and their choice of chemical stimulation. They played both for and with the dancers, and their song arrangements expanded (or exploded) according to the evolving dynamic of the city's unique dance-concerts, which took place weekly in old ballrooms like the Avalon and Fillmore, and frequent free concerts in the parks. Many of the musicians had been coffeehouse folkies and were not well prepared for the demands of extended improvisation. But the nurturing Bay Area ambience gave them room to grow and learn; the audiences neither expected nor valued flash and polish and were willing to forgive stumbling and wrong turns as long as they were *going somewhere.* The light shows, poster art, and underground comics that flourished along with the rock bands also relied on the local milieu for inspiration and support. This was a kind of rock and roll renaissance, remarkably free of commercial constraints and pressures. The corporate record labels ignored it for a while, but inevitably they descended on the scene like robber barons, signing up all the popular bands, beginning with the Jefferson Airplane.

Most of these bands were so thoroughly oriented toward live performance that they did not immediately feel at home in the recording studio. On tape, limitations that hadn't mattered in the dance halls—sloppy ensembles, directionless jamming, the difference between improvising off the energy of

The Jefferson Airplane, one of the more musicianly and spontaneous of the San Francisco bands, with one of the psychedelic sixties' ubiquitous light shows behind them.

1967

Rolling Stone magazine is founded in San Francisco during the heyday of the underground press. The first issue has John Lennon on the cover.

the dancers and the moment and improvising solos that would stand up musically to repeated listening—were glaringly evident. The Grateful Dead's first album was a stiff, ramshackle affair, but they had wisely negotiated a contract that allowed them practically unlimited studio time and soon got down to work learning to use the technology for their own ends. Jefferson Airplane, a band with perhaps too many ex-folkie troubadors for its own good, at least had recourse to a diverse songwriting output, plus an accomplished and inventive jazz-stoked rhythm section. Big Brother and the Holding Company were in many ways a punk band before their time—rough, ragged, loud, and snotty, specialists in garage-band mayhem. The media soon singled out their vocalist, Janis Joplin, for praise, with predictable results: band splits, chanteuse goes out on her own. As has often been the case throughout rock's history, several of the less-hyped "second tier" San Francisco bands have proved especially influential among subsequent generations of rockers: Santana, Quicksilver Messenger Service, Moby Grape.

In Los Angeles, Beach Boy Brian Wilson responded to the Beatles' challenge with his own acid-drenched studio creations: *Pet Sounds* and the sonically devastating "Good Vibrations." If the Byrds failed to follow up on the promise of mid-sixties masterworks like "Eight Miles High," "Why," and "5D (Fifth Dimension)," opting to return to their folk and country roots, L.A. bands such as Love, the Doors, Clear Light, and Kaleidoscope remained committed to their own versions of "the quest." In London, an underground flourished briefly around the UFO Club, where the reigning masters of psychedelic weirdness were unquestionably Pink Floyd. Like the San Francisco bands, the Floyd, Soft Machine, and their fellow travelers originally developed their music in conjunction with an audience of tripsters, as a kind of underground alternative to the pop-music bandwagon. But the honeymoon would be even briefer than in San Francisco.

Janis Joplin gets a hug from Fillmore impresario Bill Graham.

169

1967

The Jefferson Airplane's "Somebody to Love" leads an intimidated reviewer to label Grace Slick the only man-hating songwriter who is also a misogynist.

1968

West Coast concert promoter Bill Graham opens the Fillmore East in New York City after his San Francisco rock theater, the Fillmore, proves successful.

"The first night of UFO was December 23, 1966," recalls record producer Joe Boyd, an American who had arrived in Britain in 1965 to open a London office for Elektra records (U.S. home label for the Butterfield Blues Band, the Doors, and Love, among others). "And in three months the club went from being nonexistent to being the club that defined which groups were hot, which groups would go down well on the university concert circuit; by spring 1967, Pink Floyd was already on the record charts. For maybe eight to ten months in all there was a real underground scene, coming out of the art schools for the most part, with venues that weren't normal venues, an audience that wasn't a normal audience, and light shows, which were not a normal part of presenting groups. And it took less than a year for it to become part of the mainstream of the pop-music industry."

A number of bands that began in the heady period of 1968–1970 continued to make highly experimental music. In Britain, Hawkwind chased the psychedelic dragon's tail through years of personnel changes and individual and collective ups and downs. They even survived the defection of their personable, gruff-voiced singer-bassist Lemmy, who subsequently formed pioneering thrash-metal band Motorhead with the idea of creating a sound so brutal it would wither your lawn. In Germany, Can, Faust, and Neu grounded their sonic experimentation in the modular repetition-structures employed by La Monte Young, Terry Riley, and other avant-garde minimalists, taking their cues from the first rock band to incorporate these influences successfully, New York's Velvet Underground.

But in most art forms, periods of feverish experimentation inevitably give way to periods of reflection and retrenchment; what goes up must come down. The spate of drug-related deaths that decimated rock's ranks during the late sixties was bound to have a sobering effect. And in their search for musical values that would provide some solid grounding in the

The Rolling Stones ca. 1967, looking a bit befuddled by all the peace, love, and psychedelia seeping into their more hard-edged world.

1968

The Byrds' *Sweetheart of the Rodeo* and Bob Dylan's *John Wesley Harding* albums segue psychedelia into a more country-oriented roots mode. The

Band's *Music From Big Pink* (1968), The Dead's *Workingman's Dead* (1970), and Neil Young's *Harvest* (1972) also exemplify the shift.

1968

The Beatles found Apple Records.

trip's inevitable aftermath, many musicians turned to the sustaining verities of the tradition, to their folk and country roots. The Byrds' *Sweetheart of the Rodeo* (with the star-crossed country-rock innovator Gram Parsons) and Dylan's *John Wesley Harding* (both from 1968) set the tone for this back-to-the-roots movement. Equally crucial were the first two albums by Dylan's former backing group, the Band (née Hawks). *Music From Big Pink* (1968) and *The Band* (1969) were steeped in Americana, sounding superficially like the aural equivalent of a nineteenth-century tintype. A closer listen revealed a group that was experimental as well as firmly rooted; the "little black boxes" that guitarist Robbie Robertson and organist Garth Hudson fed their signals through were hardly traditional instrumentation, and what sounded like a rustic jew's harp turned out to be an electric keyboard instrument, a clavinet, played through a wah-wah pedal. Even the Grateful Dead returned to their roots in folk, country, bluegrass, and jug-band music in 1970 for two of their most consistently rewarding albums, *Workingman's Dead* and *American Beauty*. Once country rock reared its head, the neo-folkie harmonies of Crosby, Stills, and Nash and the early-seventies proliferation of introspective, folk-based singer-songwriters were sure to follow. The Eagles were just around the bend.

For all its brevity and evanescence, the "quest for pure sanity" in sound has left a surprisingly rich and lasting legacy. The recording-studio experimentation that flourished during this period, fueled by the healthy competition between bands and artists from Los Angeles and San Francisco to London and Berlin, is one aspect of this legacy. Another is the freedom that rock musicians won to explore these experiments without undue commercial and record-company pressures—freedom that was in many cases hard-won, and which, like most freedoms, has had to be fought for again and again.

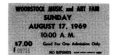

The *musical* impact of psychedelia has been pervasive, not just in progressive or album rock but in idioms as different as funk (Sly and the Family Stone, George Clinton and Parliament-Funkadelic) and contemporary electronic dance music of the trance, ambient, and acid house persuasions. It's true that the main lines of rock and roll's development have largely rejected psychedelia's more extended forays into formlessness. For the most part, the bands that applied their search for new sounds in the service of the song, rather than indulging in freak-outs for their own sake, have been the bands with the most lasting influence. But this is only part of the story.

"So many of the fundamental assumptions behind the way people approach making music today wouldn't be there if it hadn't been for the music of the psychedelic era," says Joe Boyd, who now runs his own highly eclectic label, Hannibal Records. "The foundation of rock and roll was always this standard guitar-bass-drums structure, which came out of rhythm and blues and jazz. What psychedelic music did was to open the music up to Indian and Arabic influences—guitar solos based on modal scales replacing chord-based improvisation, the introduction of the drone. With Pink Floyd you had a definite classical influence coming in. You had an opening up to avant-garde jazz, so you had dissonances coming in. The long-term effects have been so pervasive. I would compare it to reggae, which has been incredibly influential on pop music, so that today very few drummers or bass players are *not* influenced by the reggae way of hearing rhythms. It's become so much a part of the way everybody plays that people just don't notice it anymore, and I think the same is true of those influences from the psychedelic era. They've become so much a part of the musical landscape that they're just accepted as being part of the way music is played and recorded."

Altamont: The Rolling
Stones' free concert at a
deserted speedway east
of San Francisco on
December 6 ends in
tragedy when a member

of the Hells Angels, once
again providing "security,"
stabs a man to death.

Right now, in a town or city near you, the quest for pure sanity goes
on. Meanwhile, the original conspirators are still wondering whether they
understand *what really happened.* "Why we got away with it I don't know,"
admits the Airplane's Paul Kantner. "Maybe when you're dealing with
authority, you just have to go on and do what you want, and then see what
you get. Sometimes the laws fall before you like cards if you just go take
what you want. On the other hand, we once supposed that this was an *ongoing* CIA investigation, of introducing LSD into the culture to see how it
would affect people; that they would keep us from getting arrested, just so
we could continue with the experiment as they observed us from afar. And
we certainly got away with everything we wanted to get away with—everything and more."

Ken Kesey echoes and amplifies these sentiments: "I don't know; it's
been examined and reexamined over and over. What I do know is that this
revolution in consciousness changes you at the core of your soul. And I
know that we're not finished with it yet: The sixties just won't be over until
the fat lady gets high. This is hard for a lot of fat ladies to acknowledge, but
it's the truth."

Walk on the

Iggy Pop, who described his band the Stooges as "juvenile delinquent kids...running wild in America," taking the show to the audience and paving the way for punk rock to come.

Wild Side

7

"*Rock should rock in every conceivable way. It should have heart, it should have a beat and move you, and it should be done well enough so you can listen to it twenty years down the road and it will still have its force and power, like a good short story that you go back to. At the time, people thought the Velvet Underground was being very negative and bleak and dark and anti, whereas I thought we were an accurate reflection of things that were happening, and were going to happen on a larger scale. I thought I was being very realistic, and compassionate. I think one of the things people forget about the songs is how compassionate they are.*"

Lou Reed, the Velvet Underground

"*The sound of the Velvet Underground really comes from the work that was done with La Monte Young in the Theater of Eternal Music. . . . We found out what a great orchestral noise we could get out of bowing a guitar. We applied it to viola and the violin, and then I filed the bridge of the viola down and played on three strings . . . it made a great noise; it sounded pretty much like there was an aircraft in the room with you. . . . Lou and I had an almost religious fervor about what we were doing—like trying to figure ways to integrate some of La Monte Young's or Andy Warhol's concepts into rock and roll.*"

John Cale, the Velvet Underground

"What our band did was basically make a big noise and create some movement with that noise. Slowly I came up with a kind of concept. A lot of it was based on the attitude of juvenile delinquency and general mental grievance that I'd gotten from these dropouts I was hanging out with, mixed in with the sort of music that I like: hard r&b, hard rock and roll, and the exciting elements of jazz, 'cause I was starting to listen to John Coltrane, and the unpredictability of that. And then an added element was to find something simple, monolithic, metallic, like a big machine—like the drill presses at the Ford plant, stamping out fenders. I'd listen to that and think, 'God those are impressive sounds, big sounds.' And they're so regular and simple, I thought, 'Those are sounds that even we could master.'"

Iggy Pop, the Stooges

"In suburbia you're given the impression that nothing culturally belongs to you, that you are in this wasteland. I think most people who have an iota of curiosity about them develop a passion to escape, to get away from our desperation and exhaustion with the blandness of where we grew up and try and find who one is and find some kind of roots."

David Bowie

Far from his native suburbia, David Bowie spreads his arms like wings and is transformed into the Other, a possibly transsexual alien who knows how to rock and roll.

There are two kinds of "success," two ways of "making it" in rock and roll. One is pretty much your standard all-American success story: Seize the time, ride the zeitgeist, hit the nail on the head, take the money and run. This is the way of hit records and mass adulation, the way of Elvis and the Beatles—the way of "pop." The alternative doesn't sound like nearly as much fun: Be an innovator, march to the beat of your own drum, go against the grain of the times, make your statement, sit back and starve and hope you become a legend before you die of old age (or malnutrition). This is the way of "art."

1963
Welshman John Cale moves to NYC; joins La Monte Young's Theatre of Eternal Music, a.k.a. the Dream Syndicate.

1963
After graduating from Syracuse University as an English major, Lou Reed takes a job writing pop tunes for a budget album label, Pickwick Records.

1964
John Cale meets Lou Reed when Pickwick Records recruit a band to promote Reed's pseudonymous dance single "The Ostrich."

From a pop point of view, art means nothing. This is one of the ways we can tell the difference between pop music and rock and roll, for in rock, the way of art is very much a viable alternative, if not an invitingly lucrative one. It even has its rewards, provided you live long enough to enjoy them.

Before we finally take leave of the sixties, where we have perhaps been spending too much time for our own good, we need to roll up our sleeves and sift through some of that overhyped decade's rock and roll trash; it's time to have a look at the losers. Just as yesterday's sleazy sex-and-violence B movies have a way of becoming today's classic film noir, some of the rock that sixties listeners and critics ignored and/or reviled has proved at least as influential as the work of the period's commercial and critical icons, and arguably more so. Ever since the epochal arrival of punk in the mid-seventies, the music of sixties punk precursors—suburban garage bands like the Seeds, the Standells, Count Five, and ? and the Mysterians (who at least scored one or two hit singles each) and the more artistically ambitious Velvet Underground, Stooges, and MC5 (who never even made *Billboard*'s Hot Hundred)—has enjoyed an ever-increasing influence and esteem. But make no mistake: Back in the day, these groups were generally and heartily despised. The Velvets and Stooges were variously described as decadent, crude, dark, negative, abrasive, nihilistic, and incompetent; "the only thing this will replace," predicted Cher when the Velvets first visited Los Angeles, "is suicide." Still, this was recognition, of a sort. The garage bands weren't even taken seriously enough to dismiss.

Then there was the makeup-wearing, fishnet-hose-and-spandex-sporting "glam" movement, spearheaded by the likes of Pink Floyd founder/singer/guitarist Syd Barrett, in his frilly lace cuffs and eye shadow; T. Rex main man Marc Bolan, with his fey androgyny; and the early David Bowie, warbling "Space Oddity" and posing for the cover of his *The Man*

Syd Barrett, the acid mastermind behind Pink Floyd, shirtless in eyeliner, a harbinger of glam.

177

1965
The Velvet Underground makes its formal debut at a New Jersey high school (with Sterling Morrison on guitar and Maureen Tucker on drums).

1965
Artist Andy Warhol becomes VU patron and manager after hearing the band play Greenwich Village's Cafe Bizarre.

1966
VU is the centerpiece of Warhol's multimedia "happening," the Exploding Plastic Inevitable, which features light shows and bullwhip dancing.

Who Sold the World in a dress. It is no accident that these early glam rockers were British; in America, cross-dressing was considered as threatening and out-of-bounds as the Velvet Underground's songs about hard drugs, sadomasochism, and leather.

"Radio stations in mainstream America would not touch that kind of stuff," recalls Danny Fields, who signed the Stooges and the MC5 to their first recording contracts and later managed the Ramones. "It's a very conservative industry; the promoters were conservative, the radio stations were and are very conservative. Sexual ambiguity was more acceptable in England, where there's always been this camp tradition. In America it was all horrifying, deep-seated righteousness and biblical homophobia. It was an atrocious sensibility that's rampant in America to this day, and people rebelled against it. But there was no way to break through on musical merit once you put on lipstick."

The early glam exponents, the garage rockers, and the more "artistic" protopunks had at least this much in common: They were all outsiders, not just in society at large, but in the pecking order of rock and roll itself. If the mainstream of rock seemed rebellious to those on the outside looking in, the sixties "losers" were rebelling against the rebellion. In the long run, their stance made them heroes. In the short run, they were scum.

In many cases, they were *self-made scum:* Lou Reed with his B.A. in literature from Syracuse, fellow Velvet John Cale with his prestigious classical-music background, ex-suburbanite art student David Bowie, not to mention the musical progeny of America's suburban garages.

"These were middle-class, spoiled, creative young people, and they took the record companies by surprise," says Danny Fields. "Suddenly the record execs were dealing with people who were as spoiled, demanding, and obnoxious as their own children; these were not some people out of the

1966

Former UCLA film students Jim Morrison and Ray Manzarek, the latter a classically trained keyboard player, recognize each other on the beach and, with Morrison's recitation of a few lines of his poetry, the idea for the Doors is born.

projects that they could herd in and out of the studio and pay disgraceful royalties to; they were people who knew about art and who *knew about lawyers.* The record companies had to adjust very quickly."

In 1965, two of the Velvet Underground's founding members, Lou Reed and original percussionist Angus MacLise, described their band as "the Western equivalent to the cosmic dance of Shiva. Playing as Babylon goes up in flames." Reed had already written many of the songs the group would record for its first album, *The Velvet Underground and Nico,* which was finally released in March 1967, almost a year after it was completed. In fact, he had written "Heroin" while still in college, under the influence of cutting-edge literature such as Hubert Selby's *Last Exit to Brooklyn,* William Burroughs's *Naked Lunch,* and the work of his college mentor, the poet Delmore Schwartz, whose advice and example Reed took to heart. "In the unpredictable and fearful future that awaits civilization," Schwartz had written, "the poet must be prepared to be alienated and indestructible." Especially when the poet spins his tales of drugs, kinks, and hincty high jinks in the first person, backed by bracingly intense, in-your-face music that fairly snarls, as Johnny Rotten would snarl a decade hence, "We really *mean* it, man."

"I had no intention of letting the music be anything other than troublesome to people," says the Velvets' John Cale. "We really wanted to go out there and annoy people." Lou Reed recalls that pop artist Andy Warhol, the V.U.'s early sponsor and the nominal producer of their first album, "pulled me aside when we were going to record, and his only advice to me was, 'Everything's really great, just make sure you keep the dirty words in.' And I knew what he meant: Keep it rough. Don't let them tame it down so it doesn't disturb anyone. Andy wanted it to disturb people and shake 'em up; so did we."

Even denizens of the Exploding Plastic Inevitable have gotta eat; whip dancer Gerard Malanga, artist and patron Andy Warhol, and the Velvet Underground's John Cale (L to R) visit the local greasy spoon, somewhere in America.

179

1966

Called up before his local draft board, young James Osterberg, in his words, "queers out" by insisting he is gay; the U.S. military rejects the future Iggy Pop.

1967

After being delayed for nearly a year by record label executives, *The Velvet Underground and Nico,* the band's first LP, is released by Verve.

Before long, armed with a "punk" attitude that lavished "hatred and derision" (Cale's words) on the West Coast hippie bands and considered making audiences "uptight" a valid artistic goal, the Velvets were soon shaking *themselves* up. Nico, their ice blond German chanteuse, had been Warhol's addition to the Velvets' lineup and was never entirely accepted into the band. After album number one, her position was no longer ambiguous: She was out. She went on to record *Chelsea Girl* with Reed, Cale, and V.U. guitarist Sterling Morrison, and four subsequent albums arranged and partly composed by Cale, beginning with the hypnotic, autumnal *The Marble Index.* The somber lyricism of Nico's work with Cale and the others did not carry over to the second V.U. album, *White Light White Heat,* which had all the grinding, lurching momentum of the intravenous amphetamine rush hymned in Reed's title song. In the studio, minus Warhol, the Velvets turned their amps up to eleven and fought each other for sonic supremacy thoughout the seventeen minutes twenty-five seconds of "Sister Ray." Partway through, Cale's organ took off with a tremendous surge of power amid the guitarists' howling feedback. He was the clear winner of the volume battle, but lost the war a few months later when Reed, over the protests of Sterling Morrison and drummer Maureen Tucker, asked him to leave the band. Two subsequent Velvet Underground albums, with the mercurial, multitalented Cale replaced by bassist Doug Yule, were quieter, more intimate affairs, the playing and songwriting reflecting a kinder, gentler Lou Reed.

Cale's restless nature and avant-garde classical sensibilities led him into a variety of recording situations after he left the Velvets. He made an album with fellow La Monte Young associate Terry Riley, whose own late-sixties LPs for Columbia Masterworks had introduced the new minimalist classical music to the world at large. As it developed, Cale's solo career

1967

Nico's first solo LP *Chelsea Girl,* is released, with backing by three quarters of the VU. Subsequent Nico LPs *The Marble Index* (1969) and *Desertshore* (1971) are arranged by John Cale, who later produces debut LPs for the Stooges, Jonathan Richman and the Modern Lovers, and Patti Smith.

proved as eclectic and unpredictable as the man himself, ranging from the neoclassical *Paris 1919* to the hard-edged, abrasively rocking mid-seventies albums *Fear* and *Guts.* But perhaps his greatest impact on rock and roll was as a producer. In time, he would produce debut albums for two of the most important punk-rock precursors, Jonathan Richman and the Modern Lovers and Patti Smith. But already, in the late sixties, he was anticipating the shape of punk to come with his production for a new band out of Detroit, Michigan: Iggy (Pop) and the Stooges.

Raised in a Michigan trailer park, James Osterberg acquired his "Iggy" nickname when he played drums for an r&b-oriented garage band, the Iguanas. The groups that had come clambering out of America's suburban garages in the wake of the British Invasion were an inspiration during Iggy's high school years: "The Kingsmen's 'Louie Louie,' Cannibal and the Headhunters, who were an East L.A. street gang, 'Farmer John' by the Premieres—I just flipped when I heard those things, it was a transcendental experience. These songs sounded like they were recorded in gymnasiums, they had such a big, ringing sound. What I loved was the distortion, the overtones, the sound of the universe that I was hearing in these little records. Phil Spector records, too, and the Motown stuff, which always had a big, powerful sound to it. And there was always a friction in the beat, something that rubs against you like a little itch that you have to scratch: the sexual thing."

Having heard the "sound of the universe," Iggy was determined to make that sound his own. He did not find it an insurmountable problem that the musicians he was able to infect with his vision were high school dropouts who were barely competent on their instruments, "juvenile delinquent kids who were running wild in America, basically supported by their parents but completely out of control. They'd sleep all day and then party

Iggy Pop, left, and the Stooges; "in those days, Iggy was scary," recalls manager Danny Fields.

1967

As a teenager in Detroit, Iggy Pop hangs out in nearby Ann Arbor with friends whose parents' scene attracts major exponents of the American art world, including Andy Warhol and Robert Rauschenberg; Iggy later works with both men.

1967

Jim Morrison and the Doors' eponymous debut album includes the sex 'n' drugs anthem "Light My Fire."

Judith Malina and Julian Beck, artist-provocateurs, behind bars after another outrage by their Living Theater.

all night, and they just wanted to be rock stars." Bassist Dave Alexander was the most experienced player in the band; the brothers Ron and Scott Asheton (guitar and drums, respectively) had a bit more woodshedding to do, but at least they were able to do it at home while their mother was away at work. Iggy would show up with their daily ration of marijuana: "Every day I would wake 'em up and get 'em stoned and then I would play them the following records: I'd play 'em Ravi Shankar, John Coltrane, some Harry Partch—the American avant-garde composer—and then maybe a little Stones, Hendrix, Who, that sort of thing. But then I'd play 'em some Lebanese belly-dance music, or one record that I particularly like called *Bedouin Music of the Southern Sinai.* And then we'd go down in the basement where we played and just go wild. By the time we got kicked out of rehearsing at their mother's house, we had a band." Having learned to appreciate everything from Arabic and avant-garde music to jazz to hard rock while they were still working out how to play their instruments, with all of their influences filtered through "the attitude of juvenile delinquency and general mental grievance," this band was bound to be different.

The Stooges were signed to Elektra records in 1968 largely because the company had sent Danny Fields to check out the burgeoning "underground" scene in Detroit and nearby Ann Arbor. Elektra, a company originally identified with the coffeehouse folk-music boom, had become perhaps America's hippest rock label. Among Elektra's mid-sixties signings was the Paul Butterfield Blues Band, featuring incendiary guitarist Michael Bloomfield. The guitarist and the band's rhythm section had backed Bob Dylan on his earliest electric gig at the Newport Folk Festival. Butterfield and crew then recorded the experimental, heavily raga-influenced *East-West* (1966), perhaps the first "rock" album to feature extended modal improvising.

1967

The Doors quickly follow up their successful debut with *Strange Days*.

1968

During the Democratic National Convention in Chicago, the MC5 from Detroit play for demonstrators.

In 1967, Elektra released the debut album by a band from Los Angeles, the Doors. Fronted by former UCLA film student and self-styled poet Jim Morrison, the Doors opposed the "peace, love, and flowers" strain of sixties solipsism with darkly droning tales of death and transcendence, murky Freudian freak-outs, and ecstatic derangement of the senses as practiced by the late-nineteenth-century French poet Rimbaud, whose luminous imagery is an evident influence in songs like "The Crystal Ship" and "Moonlight Ride." The Doors spoke to the shadow side of rock and roll's Dionysian impulse, reveling in a psychosexual theatricality and an aesthetic of direct audience confrontation at least partly inspired by the in-your-face revolutionary fervor of Julian Beck and Judith Malina's Living Theater troupe. Fired from the Whiskey A Go Go for performing their ten-minutes-plus Oedipal epic "The End," the Doors found more sympathetic ears at Elektra. To almost everyone's surprise, their 1967 debut album *The Doors* included a song that became one of the year's biggest hits and an enduring rock anthem: "Light My Fire." If the Doors could be dark, weird, and commercially successful, perhaps other "revolutionary rock" would fare as well.

So Elektra sent Danny Fields to Michigan, not to hear the Stooges, whom he hadn't yet heard of, but to attend a show by the MC5. Detroit was and remains a hard-rock town, having nurtured the likes of Mitch Ryder and the Detroit Wheels and Alice Cooper. The Motor City Five, already shortened to MC5 when the band played its earliest gigs, were a supremely tight and hard-hitting example of this Detroit sensibility, but like the Stooges, they kept their ears wide open. Poet and activist John Sinclair, who wrote about the free jazz of John Coltrane, Sun Ra, Ornette Coleman, and their cohorts for *Downbeat,* encouraged the Five's jazz listening and became their manager. He also enlisted their services for the revolution; his White Panther party was a Yippie-like association of radicals and artists whose

Beck and Malina's confrontational strategies left a lasting impression on the Doors, especially their lead singer, Jim Morrison. L to R, drummer John Densmore, guitarist Robby Krieger, Morrison, and organist Ray Manzarek.

1968

White Light White Heat,
which features the
seventeen-minute "Sister
Ray," is the Velvet Underground's second album.

1968

As a consequence of ego
clashes with Lou Reed
over the band's direction,
John Cale departs from the
Velvets in September.

program called for "revolution, dope, and fucking in the streets." The MC5 initially attracted media attention when they played in Chicago's Grant Park for the demonstrators protesting the nearby 1968 Democratic National Convention, volleying their huge twin-guitar sound against the tear gas and billy clubs of Mayor Richard Daley's police. The venue was rough—their fellow rockers stayed home, perhaps to write protest songs—but it was not entirely unsuitable to the Five's volatile rhetoric and high-energy performing style. When Fields saw them whip a capacity crowd at Detroit's Grande Ballroom into near-hysteria, they were opening their show with the invitation—or was it a command?—to "kick out the jams, motherfuckers."

It was the MC5 who convinced Fields to attend a show by the scene's other musical radicals, the Stooges. The band Fields saw was nowhere near as technically accomplished as the MC5, who boasted two distinctive guitar stylists in Wayne Kramer and Fred "Sonic" Smith, and a flexible, jazz-aware rhythm section. But if anything, the Stooges were more rabidly confrontational. "You had rowdy elements in the audiences in Michigan, and also resistant elements," says Iggy Pop. "So I started mixing it up with the crowds, and if they wouldn't give me what I wanted I would go out and take the show to them."

Elektra signed the MC5 forthwith, but Danny Fields found the Stooges even more fascinating and made sure they got a recording contract as well. "In those days," he says, "Iggy was scary. I became his manager, and I was terrified every time he went out onstage that he would cause death and/or mayhem, that he would smash someone over the head with a bench, say, or eviscerate himself onstage. It was very, very powerful; I never saw anything like it. And for me, the Stooges were by far the most musically interesting band since the Velvet Underground." John Cale was an appro-

1969

Minus John Cale, *The Velvet Underground* is released, followed by *Loaded* (1970). Reed quits before the fourth album is issued.

1969

The Stooges release their debut, produced by John Cale, whose one-note piano propels the proto-punk anthem "I Wanna Be Your Dog."

priate choice to produce their first album, *The Stooges* (1969). When he added his minimalist one-note piano to the immortal "I Wanna Be Your Dog" and a sawing electric viola drone to the ten-minute free-improv workout "We Will Fall," it fit right in with the corrosive churning of Ron Asheton's wah-wah guitar and the whacking, trudge-tempo grooves of bassist Dave Alexander and drummer Scott Asheton. The second Stooges album, *Funhouse* (1970), was even better, with Steven Mackay's Albert Ayler–ish tenor saxophone thickening the already sludgy grooves and bringing the improvisational freak-outs to a frothing pitch of intensity. "T.V. Eye" and "Down on the Street" provided prototypes for much subsequent punk songwriting. "L.A. Blues" prefigured the noisy "no wave" of the early 1980s. And the heavy, hulking crawl tempo and hypnotic plagal cadences of "Dirt" offered a virtually complete blueprint for the Goth-rock/death-rock stylings of postpunk icons such as Bauhaus, the Birthday Party, and Joy Division.

Without the Velvet Underground and the Stooges (and to a lesser extent, the Doors and the MC5), one has to wonder where the first wave of American punk rockers would have found their inspiration. In 1972–73, however, New York's immediate punk precursors, the New York Dolls, were just getting started. The burgeoning rock media, the tastemakers, the crowds, and the money were elsewhere, and both the Velvets' Lou Reed and the Stooges' Iggy Pop were floundering. Reed's eponymous solo album, released in 1972, was not a critical success, and commercially it wasn't even in the ballpark. The Stooges had broken up in June 1971, with the MC5 calling it quits some six months later. The standard-bearer for Detroit hard rock was now Alice Cooper, née Vincent Furnier, who had (predictably) streamlined the Stooges' grungier style while becoming the first successful American rocker to adopt a glam look. Cooper also had a penchant for

Detroit's MC5, whose hard-rocking twin-guitar assault has inspired subsequent generations of hard-core musicians. L to R, standing: drummer Dennis Thompson, guitarist Wayne Kramer; front row: vocalist Rob Tyner, guitarist Fred "Sonic" Smith, bassist Michael Davis.

185

1969
At a concert in Miami, a drunk Jim Morrison is arrested on the charge of exposing himself *songus interruptus*—the beginning of the end for the Doors.

1970
The Stooges' second LP, *Funhouse,* features enough new music templates to inspire later punk, post-punk, no-wave, and death rock for years to come.

cheesy horror-movie imagery, expressed in songs like "Dead Babies" and in an ever-more-elaborate stage show, featuring, at various junctures, live snakes and a working guillotine. In time, the horror put the androgyny to flight. "Alice Cooper had to stop wearing ladies' sling-back shoes and false eyelashes and dresses and get more into horror," asserts former Warhol "creature" and punk bandleader Wayne (now Jayne) County, "because people in America could understand horror and blood and dead babies, but they couldn't understand male/female sexuality, androgyny, or . . . as little American boys would say, fag music."

Alice Cooper, keeper of the Detroit hard-rock flame, says he thought of his band as "a dagger in the heart of the love generation."

One listener who did appreciate the likes of the Velvets and the Stooges was Britain's David Bowie, finally hitting his commercial stride in early 1972 in the guise of the possibly hermaphroditic extraterrestrial Ziggy Stardust, and backed by a diamond-hard, stripped-down guitar band, the Spiders from Mars. "The Velvet Underground became very important to me," says Bowie. "There was this mixture of Cale's avant-garde influence and Lou Reed's very fine pop tunesmithism, and the combination was so brutal. For me, Lou and Iggy Pop represented the wild side of existentialist America; they were the personification of the next generation after Kerouac and Ferlinghetti and Ginsberg. It was that side of the underbelly of American culture that they represented, everything I thought we should have in England. At that time one was borrowing heavily from the American influence, but of course being filtered through the British system, it came out more vaudeville than MC5."

In 1972 Bowie met Reed and Iggy amid the fabled rock-star excess in the "back room" at Max's Kansas City, the New York club, restaurant, and hangout. "I think nothing of import passed across the table that night," says Bowie. "We didn't want to break face. Still, it was quite a serious, concrete-feeling kind of meeting, and I got to know both of them very well." It didn't take long for Bowie to realize that both his friends were seriously in need of

1971

The Stooges break up for the first time; the MC5 disbands for good. Detroit now rocks and (writhes) to native son Alice Cooper.

1971

Jim Morrison, 27, is found dead July 3 of a heart attack in the bathtub of his room in Paris.

a career boost, and that he now had it in his power to do something about it. Subsequently, he co-produced Reed's breakthrough solo album, *Transformer* (1972), which contains what is still Reed's best-known song, "Walk on the Wild Side," a chronicle of Andy Warhol's Factory crew. By Reed's previous standards, the album was slickly produced, but the songwriting sparkled and there were indelible guitar riffs from coproducer Mick Ronson, Bowie's onstage foil in the Spiders from Mars. "The whole glam thing was great for me," says Reed, who toured with a new androgynous look and a Detroit-style hard-rock band built around the road-tested guitar team of Dick Wagner and Steve Hunter. "This was something I had already seen with Warhol, but I hadn't *done* that thing. The seventies was a chance for me to get in on it, and since no one knew me from Adam particularly, I could say I was anything. I had learned that from Andy: Nobody knows. You could be anything."

Bowie also helped Iggy Pop reassemble the Stooges (who now featured a more technically accomplished hard-rock guitarist, James Williamson) and produced their 1973 album *Raw Power*. This time the Bowie touch resulted in an album that was simply more conventional than *The Stooges* and *Funhouse*, though some hard-rock fans preferred it to the band's more anarchic earlier work. In any event, the album failed to spark the sort of Pygmalion-like rebirth Bowie had helped engineer for Lou Reed. Iggy's career continued to languish, though he and Bowie remained fast friends.

Between 1972 and 1976, Bowie went through a dizzying series of personas like so many suits of clothes. Ziggy Stardust and the Spiders from Mars became a sensation, especially in Britain; after Ziggy's memorable farewell concert, Bowie made *Aladdin Sane* (1973), whose title character had a streak of lightning painted down half his face. *Diamond Dogs* (1974) was an attempt to write a stage musical around themes from George Orwell's *1984* and the William Burroughs's oeuvre; in the cover painting, Bowie was both ambisexual and half-canine. His most elaborately mounted tour followed. Then came the "plastic soul" of *Young Americans* (1975), cut at Philadelphia's legendary Sigma Sound with some of the same session musicians who backed the O'Jays and Harold Melvin and the Blue Notes. John Lennon limbered up his rarely displayed chops as an r&b-oriented rhythm guitarist on a funky tune he wrote with Bowie, "Fame." There was altogether too much of that around.

Finally, on the *Station to Station* album and tour, Bowie rejected the sheer theatrical spectacle of his earlier shows, appearing on an almost bare stage in stark expressionist/*noir* lighting as "the Thin White Duke, throwing darts in lovers' eyes." Another name for the Duke was cocaine, which was as omnipresent as fame in Bowie's world. Cruising the L.A. freeways late at night in a limo, wired and paranoid, Bowie asked himself the same question the critics had been asking all along: Who is David Bowie? *Is* there a David Bowie behind the glitz and the glamor and the passing parade of disposable identities?

"In Los Angeles at the time I knew nobody but bad people and I was doing nothing but bad stuff," Bowie says. "My own self-inflicted pressures had got to the point where they were quite obviously breaking me up. I think you would only have to take fifteen seconds from 'Cracked Actor' to see the state of mind that I was in. So I changed location and put myself in a very anonymous situation in a quiet working-class part of Berlin, a Turkish area, just to distance myself from the very drug-oriented lifestyle that I'd been leading."

Iggy Pop, who'd been hanging out for much of Bowie's last tour, joined him in Berlin. "We were excited to be there even before we got there," Iggy remembers. "Both of us had been living in L.A., where everybody wants to kiss your ass for the wrong reasons, and Berlin was directly the opposite of that. This is a no-man's land, a very egalitarian city, and men-

Spiders from Mars guitarist Mick Ronson, left, gets down with main man David Bowie.

1972

David Bowie produces
Lou Reed's breakthrough
solo album, *Transformer,*
as well as Iggy and a
reassembled Stooges'
Raw Power (1973).

All three immerse them-
selves in personae of
excess, to emerge several
years later with reconfig-
ured identities and art.

tally tough. When we moved there David got a flat and I lived there for a
while. And the first thing we did was we each bought a couple of flannel
shirts, workers' type shirts. Because we weren't going to be these West Coast
kinda people anymore, we were going to be a different kind of people. We
got tougher minded and the music got tougher minded and much more
daring, and it had more to say—his music, I think, as well as mine."

In Berlin, Bowie and Iggy Pop claimed for themselves something few
rock and roll musicians are able to achieve once they get on the album-
tour-album-tour treadmill: the opportunity to rethink their art from top to
bottom and start afresh. Bowie, working with the composer/producer and
Roxy Music alumnus Brian Eno on his 1976 albums *Low* and *Heroes,* was
finally able to incorporate the avant-garde minimalism that had earlier
inspired the Velvets into a musical idiom that was indisputably his own. He
also found the time to produce Iggy Pop's most gripping and original
albums since 1970's *Funhouse*—*The Idiot* (1976) and *Lust for Life* (1977).
When Iggy returned to the U.S. to tour, Bowie joined the group as an
"anonymous" sideman in form-fitting black leather, playing basic, work-
manlike electric piano. For the first time in a long time, he looked like he
was having fun.

As the punk era dawned, every sensational new band seemed to be
affirming its debt to the Velvet Underground, the Stooges, and the garage-
band credo "Keep it simple, stupid." The punks were trashing sixties icons
right and left, but David Bowie, Iggy Pop, and Lou Reed continued to hold
their attention, and to earn their (often grudging) respect. The "trash" of
the sixties was back with a vengeance, just in time to help save rock and roll
from its big, bad, bloated self.

Lou Reed, transformed by
glam: "This was something I
had already seen with
Warhol, but I hadn't *done*
that thing. The seventies
was a chance for me to get
in on it."

The Church of the Sonic Guitar

The Church of the Sonic Guitar

"Accept that music is not sealed to passion, nor to piety, nor to feelings; accept that it can blossom in spaces so wide that your image cannot project itself within them, that it must make you melt within its unique light!"

Louis Dandrel

"Current cosmology (the study of the universe as an ordered whole) considers that there was an original moment of creation. I propose to call that moment the Big Ring since the old term is modeled on the noisy violence of our own culture. At the time of the Big Ring, unknown forces brought the universe into being. The sounding itself, the ringing of that first note is creation, which ever since has been expanding, dividing, and echoing. It is reverberating even now."

David Hykes

"I had a hot blues out, man. I'd be driving my truck . . . and pretty soon I'd hear it [his first electric blues hit] walking along the street, I'd hear it driving along the street. . . . I would be driving home from playing, two or three o'clock in the morning, and I had a convertible, with the top back 'cause it was warm. I could hear people all upstairs playing that record. It would be rolling up there, man. I heard it all over. One time I heard it coming from way upstairs somewhere, and it scared me. I thought I had died."

Muddy Waters

"Guitar Slim . . . was gettin' a fuzz-tone distortion way before anyone else. You didn't hear it again until people like Jimi Hendrix came along. Believe it or not, Slim never used an amplifier. He always used a P.A. set, never an amplifier. He was an overtone fanatic, and he had these tiny iron cone speakers and the sound would run through them speakers and I guess any vibration would create that sound, because Slim always played at peak volume. . . . If Slim was playing, you could hear him a mile away."

Guitarist Earl King

" 'Scuse me while I kiss the sky."

Jimi Hendrix

Pages 190–191:

❶ T-Bone Walker: blues-based, electric lead guitar begins here, though Walker's roots were in an earlier era. Blind Lemon Jefferson was a primary inspiration.

❷ Lonnie Johnson, raised in New Orleans's melting pot of musical influences, recorded blues, jazz, and even country ballads in a career spanning decades.

❸ Guitarist Les Paul, left, invented the solid-body electric guitar; with recording and marital partner Mary Ford, right, he brought overdubbed electric guitars to the pop charts, beginning in 1951 with "How High the Moon."

❹ Eddie Durham, whose twangy, almost rockabilly-style electric guitar solos with small groups led by Count Basie and Lester Young in the mid-thirties are among the first on record.

Since the 1960s, rock and roll fanatics have been, ipso facto, guitar fanatics. Their ideal of rock and roll heaven might be Eric Clapton's blues feel, melodic invention, and tonal purity; Jimi Hendrix's vocalizing of the instrument's expressive capabilities in the course of turning its sound into an elemental force; the tonal elegance, long-lined lyricism, and coherent thematic development of Duane Allman's marathon improvisations; the gritty crunch and bite, and highly personal, close-to-the-bone timbres of Keith Richards; the heavy riffcraft and screaming leads of heavy-metal bands; or the aggressive, rapid-fire chording of punk. Whatever their chosen denomination, post-1960s rockers have almost invariably been worshippers in the Church of the Sonic Guitar.

Postmodern rock has strengthened and solidified the electric guitar's vatic supremacy as the music's most recognizable sonic and visual icon. When listening to the from-the-gut riff-thrash of Metallica, Slayer, or Danzig, one visualizes banners emblazoned with the inverted cross, audiences saluting the stage with the Dionysian sign of the horns—and a line of guitarists, heads bent, long hair flailing as they thrash in unison. In what might be termed the punk-art wing of contemporary rock, the sonorous resonating properties of feedback-sustained guitar textures have been celebrated like the mysteries of the ancients by bands and performers such as Lou Reed and the Velvet Underground, Tom Verlaine and Television, and more recently, Sonic Youth. To attend a show by one of these groups is to immerse oneself in a clanging, droning sensurround of guitar harmonics within a precisely demarcated, ritually invoked sonic space. This is the movable Church of the Sonic Guitar, a vast and vaulted cathedral vibrating with the patterns and proportions of sound-ratios tuned precisely enough to have pleased Pythagoras. Listening to these bands at sufficiently high volume must be something like experiencing the "Big Ring" from inside the sound box of a truly humongous electric guitar.

This is a far from idle comparison. The *acoustic* guitar's flexibility in terms of tuning made it the ideal instrumental vehicle for the nontempered, microtonal melodic language of the blues, in which key intervals such as the third, fifth, and seventh are not *flatted,* as a black key flats the tone of the adjacent white key on a piano, but *flattened,* with the degree of the flattening bearing a direct relationship to the level of emotional intensity. (In the blues, as among the Akan of Ghana and other tribal groups speaking pitch-tone languages, falling pitch corresponds to intensifying emotion.) The *electric* guitar can merely make the instrument's single-note lines a little louder, so that the musician can solo like a saxophonist or brass player. But once a certain volume threshold has been passed, the electric guitar becomes another instrument entirely. Its tuning flexibility can now be used to set up sympathetic resonances between the strings, so that techniques such as open tunings and barre chords can get the entire instrument humming sonorously, sustained by amplification until it becomes a representation in sound of the wonder of creation itself.

A piano, whose strings are tuned to the fractional, rationalized intervals of so-called equal temperament (the tuning standard for most post-Bach classical music), cannot achieve this effect without being radically retuned. The modern composer La Monte Young, whose early sixties performing group included John Cale and other original members of the Velvet Underground, has done just that in his epic composition "The Well-Tuned Piano." (Hit any key on Young's retuned piano, and every string in the piano sounds a sympathetic resonance.) An electric guitar, like Young's piano, can be made to resonate with a hall's acoustics, or with the underlying sixty-cycle hum of the city's electrical grid, forming massive sound textures according to harmonic relationships that *already exist* in nature. Compare this to the arbitrary equal-temperament system, which produces acoustically irrational interference patterns and dissonances when certain tones are allowed to ring together. (Try playing a major triad, C-E-G, on a piano with the sustain pedal depressed, and listen to the chaotic acoustical turbulence as the combined tones reverberate, clash, and then raggedly decay.)

The electric guitar, once the volume has surpassed the sustain threshold, doesn't just "ring." It also produces overtones, sum and difference tones, interference patterns, and other acoustical phenomena. Variant tunings bring particular aspects of these phenomena to the fore, as in the music of Sonic Youth and similar bands, who have learned to write melodious, memorable pop tunes without recourse to conventional harmony. In rock of this sort, acoustical effects can become so pronounced that they seem to "eat," or cancel out, the original tones whose interactions produced them. But underlying all of these more or less unstable tonal relationships is an unchanging mathematics of resonance and vibration, a system of ratios or tonal proportions that not only exists independently in nature but may underlie reality itself. The idea that "nature is vibration" is the basis of ancient Indian and Chinese metaphysics, has been an underground tradition in Western thought since Pythagoras, and seems to be supported by some of the theoretical and experimental findings of postrelativity physics. La Monte Young proposes that when we hear these mathematical proportions manifested in sound, we intuitively recognize that profound information on "fundamental vibrational structure" is being revealed. This is the intuition that we feel, as a kind of religious awe, when we worship in the Church of the Sonic Guitar.

Play That Guitar 'Til It Smoke

All electric guitarists owe a debt to Red Hot Red, also known as Rhubarb Red during his early years as a country-swing guitarist but best known by his subsequent stage name: Les Paul. The man originally named Lester William Polsfuss, born in Waukesha, Wisconsin, in 1915, was still a teenager when he amplified his Sears Roebuck acoustic guitar with a phonograph needle wired into his family's radio. He made his first recordings in the mid-1930s, playing jazz-savvy country music as Rhubarb Red and backing blues singer Georgia White as Les Paul. He went on to establish a reputation as an accomplished jazz guitarist before turning to pop music and inventing, in his home recording lab, techniques that are still fundamental to rock and pop record making. During the 1940s he pioneered multitrack recording, overdubbing guitar parts to create the sound of a one-man guitar orchestra. He also innovated close-miking techniques that gave him better control of his instrument's sound, and toward these same ends he developed the first solid-body electric guitar. When Gibson finally began manufacturing Paul's solid-body guitar in the early fifties, ten years after he built the first prototype, the company dubbed it the Gibson Les Paul. The instrument is still a favorite among guitarists, including the likes of Jimmy Page and Eric Clapton. Page is an outstanding example of a studio-friendly guitarist and record producer who uses different guitar models, amplifiers, and miking and overdubbing techniques to "paint" in sounds, deploying combinations

195

of guitar sonorities and part-layering much as a painter works with textures and hues. When visiting New York, Page has often made it a point to take in one of Paul's regular jazz-club gigs.

Guitarists as disparate as Page, rockabilly doyen James Burton, and jazzman Wes Montgomery have testified to Paul's enduring influence. But Les Paul was no rocker. His chord voicings were unfailingly tasteful and sophisticated, and he showed little interest in sonic exploration beyond the volume threshold at which harmonic overtones become clearly audible. He also favored an almost antiseptically clean guitar tone, disdaining the sort of deliberate distortion rock guitarists have traditionally referred to as grunge. Paul's pop music, exemplified by the overdubbed guitars and voices of his chirpy 1951 hit with singer Mary Ford, "How High the Moon," was tastefully Apollonian. The pioneers of *Dionysian* electric guitar playing— rock and roll guitar playing—are to be found elsewhere, most notably among the guitarists of Texas and Oklahoma, heartland of both western swing and the earliest electric blues. Some of these guitarists seem to have rigged their own electric guitars before hearing of Les Paul, and the rough-edged sonorities inherent in their homemade amplification remained a part of their presentation even after they began using more orthodox equipment.

T-Bone Walker, the bluesman who helped popularize the electric guitar during the late thirties and early forties while playing in the Les Hite big band, originally recorded in Dallas in 1929 as Oak Cliff T-Bone. His move into amplification in the mid-1930s hardly seems to have affected the style heard on the 1929 disc, at least at first. The picking on his early- and mid-1940s sides for the Black and White label was clean, with a terse, dry tone, and minimal vibrato and sustain. Of the other guitarists who first plugged in during the years 1935–37, Eddie Durham, who tripled as arranger, trombonist, and guitarist with Count Basie, contributed some bluesy solos to 1930s sides by Basie small groups featuring Lester Young. With their suggestions of country twang and their aggressively rhythmic chording, Durham's solos sound in retrospect like early models for rock and roll guitar solos. But again, these solos could have been conceived on an acoustic guitar. Players such as Lonnie Johnson and Eddie Lang had been soloing in a similar style, on acoustic guitars, since the 1920s; for their featured spots, they'd simply move their instrument closer to the recording mike. For Eddie Durham, and even for T-Bone Walker, amplification basically enabled them to solo on live gigs the way they soloed on records and still be heard, even with full-band backing.

The most experimental of the early electric guitarists, as far as we can judge from the recorded evidence, was Bob Dunn, who built a pickup and patched together an amp for his lap-steel guitar while working with one of the jazziest and most musicianly of the Southwest's white western-swing bands, Milton Brown and his Musical Brownies. Dunn's solos on Brown's mid-1930s discs are startlingly futuristic. Using his slide bar to sculpt and color hornlike melodic phrases that were apparently influenced by the leading jazz horn men of the day, Dunn created a revolutionary electric-guitar sound so utterly idiosyncratic that he seems to have inspired few, if any, imitators. The work of Bob Wills's steel-guitar man, Leon McAuliffe, was much more conservative and stolidly country-swing-rooted, though McAuliffe was responsible for one electric guitar showpiece that became popular with black and white performers near the end of the big-band era, "Steel Guitar Rag." The tune proved so durable that Ike Turner was able to revive it as an effective electric-guitar showpiece on the 1961 album *Dance with Ike and Tina Turner's Kings of Rhythm.*

In *San Antonio Rose,* his exhaustive study of the life and music of western-swing kingpin Bob Wills and his Texas Playboys, Charles Townshend offers fragmentary but suggestive evidence that T-Bone Walker and Charlie Christian, the front-runners in the first generation of black electric guitarists, were inspired, at least in part, by the early amplified playing of white musicians such as Dunn and McAuliffe. Walker, who was born in 1910, and Christian, six years his junior, were friends and musical partners during the early 1930s, playing together on Texas street corners for tips, trading licks and chord voicings. Walker's heritage was that of a classic Texas bluesman; as a child, he guided Blind Lemon Jefferson around Dallas from street corner to tavern, picking up on Jefferson's discursive, hornlike single-string melody lines at the same time. Christian, who like Walker was from Dallas, also spent several years working out of Oklahoma City with popular territory bands like Alphonso Trent's.

Though Walker has found his niche in history as the father of elec-

"Take it away, Leon," western swing bandleader Bob Wills would shout before launching electric steel guitarist Leon McAuliffe on "hot jazz" showpieces.

tric blues guitar and Christian is revered as the first great electric guitarist in jazz, their backgrounds and teenage friendship would have outweighed any considerations of genre in their own minds; for a time they even studied with the same teacher, the otherwise obscure Chuck Richardson. In the Southwest Territory, blues and jazz had been intimately related from the beginning. Country bluesmen recorded with jazz-band backing and learned chord voicings from more harmonically advanced jazzmen. Jazz bands regularly featured shouting blues singers like Joe Turner, and, after the mid-1930s, blues-singing guitarists such as T-Bone Walker. Western-swing and jazz present a similar continuum on the white side of the tracks, with men like McAuliffe representing a jazzy but heavily country-inflected style, while mavericks like Dunn played a kind of pure, futuristic jazz all their own. Every one of these players was solidly grounded in the blues. Black and white guitarists freely traded ideas and techniques, including the skills of fashioning some of the earliest homemade amplifiers and pickups. Differences in race were keenly felt in other ways. White musicians usually got the better-paying jobs, and social custom prevented race mixing on public bandstands. During the 1930s heyday of the swing bands, black territory outfits like Count Basie's early Kansas City combo did make radio broadcasts, but white musicians got the lion's share of radio exposure.

How loudly did the early electric guitarists play? Here, alas, the recorded evidence is practically useless. Certainly by the late 1940s, guitar bluesmen in the South and Southwest were blasting away. Sam Phillips's early 1950s recording policy at Sun, which involved capturing bluesmen playing on the equipment and at the volume they were accustomed to, leaves little doubt that in boisterous southern juke joints, amps were frequently turned up to ten, an impression further strengthened by some of Elmore James's early 1950s Flair and Meteor sides, recorded in Mississippi clubs and home studios with Ike Turner at the controls. Houston guitarist Goree Carter was playing jacked-up, hell-for-leather jump figures, identical to licks later popularized by Chuck Berry but originally derived from T-Bone Walker, on his rampaging 1949 single "Rock Awhile." If one is inclined to search out "the first rock and roll record"—a dubious pursuit at best, since it all depends on how you define rock and roll—Carter's "Rock Awhile" seems a reasonable choice. The clarion guitar intro differs hardly at all from some of the intros Chuck Berry would unleash on his own records after 1955; the guitar solo crackles through an overdriven amplifier, and the boogie-based rhythm charges right along. The subject matter, too, is appropriate—the record announces that it's time to "rock awhile" and proceeds to illustrate how it's done. To my way of thinking, Carter's "Rock Awhile" is a much more appropriate candidate for "first rock and roll record" than the more frequently cited "Rocket '88,'" recorded for Sam Phillips almost two years later by Ike Turner's Kings of Rhythm, hiding behind the pseudonym of Jackie Brenston (the lead vocalist) and his Delta Cats. (The respective dates as given in discographies are "circa April 1949" for "Rock Awhile" and March 5, 1951, for "Rocket '88,'" but the issue is of more interest to record collectors than to anyone else—one might as well call the first rock and roll record Trixie Smith's "My Man Rocks Me [With One Steady Roll]" from 1922, citing its unmistakable lyric intent, and be done with the whole thing.)

But we were talking about electric guitars, *loud* electric guitars, and when they first appeared on record. If recording had simply documented the music of the juke joints and taverns, we would have plenty of examples of jacked-up guitar from the 1940s—the noisier the gig, the louder an electric bluesman like Muddy Waters would play, just to cut through the din. The problem was studio recording technology. Imagine a hyperamplified electric guitar blazing away in the tiny J&M studio where Fats Domino and Little Richard recorded their hits. The precise instrumental balance and exact microphone placement that engineer Cosimo Matassa and the musicians had worked long and hard to perfect would have been blown away by a single guitar chord, the VU meter on the studio's primitive tape recorder would have red-lined, and a welter of distortion—not controlled distortion, but noisy, cacophonous, runaway distortion—would have been the recorded result. There are, in fact, guitar solos on some of the discs cut at J&M in the late 1940s and the early 1950s, but the guitarists, team players to a man, simply edged up their volume controls a bit, according to a prearranged plan, and fitted their solos neatly into the ensemble textures the way saxophone soloists like Lee Allen did. Occasionally there is a notable exception to prevailing trends: Billy Tate's "You Told Me," recorded at J&M in 1955 with Fats Domino on piano, builds up to a gloriously dirty, snarling guitar solo.

There were other, more deliberate exceptions, and here Chess in Chicago and Sun in Memphis led the way. Muddy Waters's recording career at Chess is one of the earliest examples of a producer, engineer, and musician working together to create an electric-guitar sound suitable to the idiom—a sound that consciously creates the illusion of a juke-joint guitar cranked up to ten but is actually recorded at a lower volume, with effects created through judicious manipulation of room acoustics and recording technology. When Waters came to Chess in 1947, he initially recorded backed up by piano and bass, giving his records a sound not dissimilar to the pre–World War II discs of Chicago bluesmen such as Tampa Red. But Leonard Chess was an experimenter. And besides, he was a businessman—those early Waters records didn't sell. So in April 1948 he recorded Muddy playing electric guitar with only Big Crawford's bass to back it up. The resulting record, "I Can't Be Satisfied"/"I Feel like Going Home," was the most traditional record Waters had made since arriving in Chicago five years earlier, as far as its basic musical materials were concerned—this was Delta blues the way Son House or Robert Johnson might have played it. Yet this record was something entirely new. The reactions of the record-buying public told Chess that much. The initial pressing was sold out in a matter of hours, and enterprising railroad porters riding the Illinois Central down south from Chicago did brisk business carrying copies of the record and selling them in southern cities and towns at vastly inflated prices. The difference, the novelty, was Chess's ingenious new way of recording voice and electric guitar and bass, and blending them together into a sound so powerful, so vibrant with presence, it was *scary*—scary enough for Waters himself, driving home alone after work, to hear "people all upstairs playing that record. . . . One time I heard it coming from way upstairs somewhere, and it scared me. I thought I had died."

The Chess repertory of idiosyncratic recording techniques grew to include using the studio's tile bathroom as a resonating chamber for guitar amps, mixing the sound of a directly miked amplifier with room ambience, and recording both guitar and lead vocal "hot"—so close to distortion on the VU meter that the very loudest notes push the needle just a shade into the red. The records created in this way jumped out at you. They were scary enough as *songs,* with their tales of hoodoo hexes and gypsy fortune-tellers.

Everything about the production amplified and focused that scariness, the archetypal blues scariness of standing at a pitch black Delta crossroads in the middle of the night, waiting for the devil—or Legba, the Yoruba/hoodoo god of the crossroads, the opener of paths between worlds—and feeling your blood run cold with every susurration of the roadside weeds.

Muddy Waters was already working in the Chicago taverns with a full electric band when he made those records, but Leonard Chess built up his studio sound instrument by instrument, adding Little Walter's harmonica in the summer of 1950, but not allowing him to bring his amplifier (which he'd been playing through since the 1940s) until July 1951; Jimmy Rogers's second electric guitar was added by the end of that year. By perfecting his single electric guitar sound first and then adding to the ensemble instrument by instrument, Leonard Chess methodically created a recorded simulacrum of the raw, live sound an electric band makes playing loudly in a room.

Down in Memphis, Sam Phillips's approach was also methodical, though in a different way. According to Phillips, his motivation for recording the black and hillbilly combos that came trouping into his studio as soon as he opened its doors in 1950 was "giving the influence to the people to be free in their expression." This motivation, or method, had certain corollaries that were part of the actual recording process: "I didn't want to get these people in some stupid-assed studio and lead them astray from what they had been used to doing. To put it another way, I didn't try to take them uptown and dress them up. If they had broken-down equipment or their instruments were ragged, I didn't want them to feel ashamed. I wanted them to go ahead and play the way they were used to playing. Because the *expression* was the thing. I never listened to the sound of one instrument. I listened for the effect, the total effect."

An early instance of Phillips's philosophy in action was the March 1951 recording of "Rocket '88.'" Ike Turner and his band had driven up to Memphis from the Delta town of Clarksdale to audition, and on the way, guitarist Willie Kizart's amplifier had fallen from the top of the car. When the band set up in the studio and Kizart plugged in, the amp began emitting fuzz and crackling with static. Phillips recalls that "when it fell, that burst the speaker cone. We had no way of getting it fixed. . . . It would

201

probably have taken a couple of days, so we started playing around with the damn thing. I stuffed a little paper in there where the speaker cone was ruptured, and it sounded good. It sounded like a saxophone. And we decided to go ahead and record." What Phillips fails to add is that this jury-rigged fuzztone guitar sounded good to *him*—an engineer at another label, even Chess, probably would have thrown the band out of the studio.

Certainly Phillips was proficient enough to have engineered national network radio feeds for big bands broadcasting from the posh rooftop club at Memphis's Hotel Peabody before he opened his studio. Once he secured the studio location at 706 Union—a small storefront, bigger than Cosimo Matassa's J&M in New Orleans but not by much—he began by gutting the insides and rebuilding according to his acute ear for acoustics. The studio's ceiling had a peculiar slope to it; Phillips maximized its quality as a sound resonator by installing corrugated tiles in a wavy pattern of ridges and valleys. The shape of the ceiling and the setup of the studio were augmented by an ingenious and entirely original system of "slap-back" tape echo that involved feeding the original signal from one tape machine through a second machine with an infinitesimal delay. This artificial ambience, and Phillips's exceptional ear for balancing instruments and voices, enabled him to give his artists "the influence . . . to be free in their expression" while actually recording an idealized representation of their customary live sound.

Phillips hadn't started his own Sun label when he recorded "Rocket '88,'" which was booted along by Kizart's fuzztone guitar booming out a distorted boogie-bass figure. Little Richard thought enough of "Rocket '88,'" some five years later to appropriate its signature riff as a lead-in to "Good Golly Miss Molly." Of more immediate interest to Phillips was the original record's commercial performance. He leased it to Chess, and it became one of the biggest r&b hits of the year, reaching number one on the r&b charts and remaining on the charts for seventeen weeks. It was a catchy, rocking tune, but that fuzzed-out guitar boogie was clearly one of its chief selling points. In other respects, it did not differ significantly from the other rocking automobile blues that were becoming popular around the same time.

From then on, when Phillips was recording a blues combo, he let the guitarist wail. B. B. King's earliest recordings for Phillips have an exciting, dirty guitar tone that was smoothed out considerably for his later record-ings. Howling Wolf and his combo, whom Phillips heard broadcasting live on West Memphis radio station KWEM and sought out, recorded a series of blues classics at Sun. On every one of them, guitarist Willie Johnson's slashing rhythm licks and jazzy fill-in runs cut through the band sound like a hot knife through butter. When Johnson really let loose—turning up his amp until it crackled, slamming out dense and distorted power chords—he kicked the band into savage overdrive. With Wolf moaning, growling, and howling his traditional Delta lyrics and punctuating the rough combo sound with harmonica wails, they sounded bigger than life and twice as raunchy. Their first single, "Moaning at Midnight"/"How Many More Years," has all the eerie hoodoo of Muddy Waters's early discs and then some. On "How Many More Years," Johnson's slamming power chords crashed like thunder. On a slightly later Sun studio side, "House Rockers," Wolf catapulted Johnson into his guitar solo by hollering, "Play that gui-tar, Willie Johnson, till it smoke . . . blow your top, blow your top, blow your TOP!"

Still without a label of his own, Phillips leased these first Wolf record-ings to Chess, who recognized a winner when they heard one and promptly spirited Wolf away to Chicago and an exclusive Chess contract. For Phillips, losing Jackie Brenston and Wolf to Chess, and Rosco Gordon and B. B. King to Modern/R.P.M., was devastating. Short on funds, still dependent on location recordings of weddings and funerals for his livelihood, Sam never-theless started a label of his own. His first venture, the Phillips label, issued only one known release, and it was one of the loudest, most overdriven and distorted guitar stomps ever recorded: "Boogie in the Park" by Memphis one-man-band Joe Hill Louis, who cranked his guitar while blowing a rack harmonica and banging at a rudimentary drum kit. Finally, in 1953, Phillips launched Sun.

Among the talents attracted by Sun were two harmonica-playing singers from the West Memphis area, James Cotton and Junior Parker. Both recorded with Auburn (Pat) Hare, an Arkansas-born guitarist Phillips had been using on various recording sessions since a June 1952 date with blues singer Walter Bradford's combo. Hare was a Memphis-area guitarist cut from the same bolt of cloth as Willie Johnson. Both men were blues players to the core but had some familiarity with jazzy chord voicings. Both played single-note lines in fills and solos, a staple among electric guitarists since the mid-1940s success of T-Bone Walker ushered in the era of electric blues guitar. But they were also slicing, savage rhythm players. Other guitarists in other towns may have developed similar ideas at the same time or even earlier, but on the basis of recorded evidence (which is just about all we have to go on), Johnson and Hare were originators of one of the most basic gambits in the rock and roll guitarist's arsenal, the power chord.

A chord is several notes harmonized and sounded simultaneously. The melodies of pop songs are supported by a succession of such chords—in musicians' parlance, a "chord progression." A *power* chord has its harmonic dimension, but its purpose is fundamentally rhythmic. Usually, a power chord is accented for maximum impact. As it has become a more and more venerable device in the rock and roll guitar lexicon, its uses have become more various. Riff figures and, in heavy metal, entire songs are built around power chords, which follow one another in quick succession. If you're still not entirely sure what I'm talking about, go listen to Keith Richards's definitive guitar figures on "Jumpin' Jack Flash." Richards once commented that he got ideas for some of the most celebrated power-chord figures on Rolling Stones records from the *acoustic* power chords that propel 1950s Everly Brothers singles like "Bye Bye Love" and "Wake Up, Little Susie." Robbie Robertson of the Band says he picked up the practice from hearing Willie Johnson's work on the early Howling Wolf discs being broadcast over Nashville's WLAC.

But back in the Sun studios, in the years 1952–54, Pat Hare was the power-chord king. One of the most gripping examples of his style was "Cotton Crop Blues," released in 1954 under vocalist James Cotton's name. Whatever equipment Hare was playing through, there must have been more wrong with it than a burst speaker cone. (Sam Phillips suggests mismatched impedance between guitar and amplifier.) Rarely has a grittier, nastier, more ferocious electric-guitar sound been captured on record, before or since, and Hare's repeated use of a rapid series of two downward-modulating power chords, the second of which is allowed to hang menacingly in the air, is the record's "hook" or structural glue. This figure turns what could have been a merely good blues record about the indignities of a life spent picking cotton—an explanation (as if one were really needed) for the then-ongoing mass exodus of black southerners north to Chicago—into something extraordinary and unforgettable. The first heavy-metal record? I'd say yes, with tongue only slightly in cheek.

At the same session, or the day after (the dates are May 13 and/or May 14, 1954), Hare cut a single of his own, and all the pent-up violence and emotional intensity that had been evident in his playing from the beginning came pouring out. Speaking of scary records, Hare's "I'm Gonna Murder My Baby" is *The Texas Chainsaw Massacre* on a three-minute vinyl disc. Again, Hare used a hard-slammed power-chord as a recurring instrumental "hook" throughout his half-spoken, half-sung, entirely threatening performance. (His spoken asides are along the lines of "I'm gonna kill 'er tomorrow.") Some years later, after playing on Junior Parker's Sun and Duke sides and then moving to Chicago, Hare joined the Muddy Waters band and was reunited with his longtime partner James Cotton. Hare played on one spectacular Waters record after another between 1957 and 1960, from "She's 19 Years Old" and "Walking through the Park" (the latter has a classic Hare solo) to the *Muddy Waters at Newport* album of 1960, which introduced a new generation of young white rockers to electric blues and was especially influential in England among groups such as the Rolling Stones and the Yardbirds. And then life caught up with art: Hare was arrested, tried, and sent to prison for allegedly murdering his girlfriend. Although he was occasionally let out to play a local gig, he never finished his sentence; he died behind bars.

Meanwhile, electric blues-based guitarists were barnstorming across the South, sometimes meeting in large big-city clubs for "battles of the blues" that inspired them to pull out all the stops. Of the Texas guitarists most directly influenced by T-Bone Walker, Clarence "Gatemouth" Brown was one of the flashiest, and perhaps the most resourceful explorer of the electric guitar's sonic resources. His early- and mid-1950s singles abound in volume and sustain effects, deliberate amplifier overloading, wildly stuttering scrambles up the neck, screaming high-note sustain, and other proto-rock-and-roll devices. "Dirty Work at the Crossroads" is probably the most inclusive single representation of these effects.

In the annals of early- and mid-1950s electric-guitar flash, Guitar

Clarence "Gatemouth" Brown came blasting through an overdriven amplifier with screaming high notes and harmonic sustain on early-fifties recordings.

Slim's legend looms large indeed. Earl King related a typical story to interviewer Jeff Hannusch: Gatemouth Brown, T-Bone Walker, Lowell Fulson, and Guitar Slim were all performing one night at the White Eagle in Opelousas, Louisiana. Slim was headlining because "The Things I Used to Do" [his 1954 r&b smash with piano and arrangement by Ray Charles] was a scorcher. They were all sitting in the dressing room and Guitar Slim walked up to 'em and said, 'Gentlemen, we got the greatest guitar players in the country assembled right here. But when I leave here tonight, ain't nobody gonna realize you even been here.' Well, they all laughed but that's exactly what happened. Slim come out with his hair dyed blue, blue suit, blue pair of shoes. He had three hundred and fifty feet of mike wire connected to his guitar, and a valet carrying him on his shoulders all through the crowd and out into the parking lot. Man, he was stopping cars driving down the highway. No one could outperform Slim."

Eyewitnesses also agree that nobody could out*blast* Slim when it came to volume. Earl King's story about Slim disdaining amplifiers and playing directly through a P.A., whose iron cone speakers would further enrich the harmonic overtones of his ringing guitar strings, means in effect that he had a setup offering him virtually unlimited feedback and sustain, all of which he could rigorously control with the volume and tonal settings on the guitar itself once the P.A. was properly adjusted. "He had a lot of melodic overtones in his solos," King confirms. "Slim tuned standard, but he used that capo to get the effect of open strings. . . . I've seen Slim play many a time without it. He just used it for effect." And what an effect it must have been. Early- and mid-1950s r&b audiences were still accustomed to bands that featured honking saxophones as their primary solo voice, fronted by blues singers who kept their guitar work subordinate to the impact of the vocals. Slim reversed the priorities. He was a bluesman by birthright; born Eddie Jones in the Mississippi Delta town of Greenwood (or possibly Hollandale), he combined early training in gospel singing with a beginning guitar style that led early commentators to dismiss him as an imitator of T-Bone Walker and, especially, the flashier Gatemouth Brown. The blue suits, shoes, and hair, the 350-foot guitar cords, and the Jimi Hendrix–like sonic effects soon made it clear that he was an original.

Consider the following Earl King story, from Jeff Hannusch's invaluable *I Hear You Knockin': The Sound of New Orleans Rhythm and Blues.* "You knew Slim was back in town [New Orleans] 'cause early in the morning, around seven-eight o'clock, if he was tanked up, you'd hear them amps and P.A. going off. People'd be calling the police, 'cause you could hear Slim three blocks away! And here's Slim up in his room with his shorts on, goin' through his stage routine. . . . If you went up there, there'd always be about seven or eight different women up there. He'd have his songs written with eyebrow pencil on pieces of paper tacked to the wall."

When solid-body Les Pauls appeared on the market, Slim immediately realized that with a solid-body guitar he could more easily control the feedback and sustain than with the electric hollow-body he had been using. According to Slim's bandleader, Lloyd Lambert, he would also turn the bass controls on his guitar and P.A. as low as they would go and crank the treble up to ten. Lambert realized that standing in the middle of this sonic firestorm every night wasn't helping his hearing, but he couldn't tell Slim anything, either about the volume he played at or the pace at which he lived his life. By 1958, his drinking had reached a debilitating stage that made it more and more difficult for him to travel.

"I wouldn't say he was a pretty good drinker," Lambert told Hannusch. "He was the best! Slim just wouldn't take care of himself. He lived fast, different women every night. I'd try and tell him to eat good and get his rest, but he'd say, 'Lloyd, I live three days to y'all's one. The world don't owe me a thing when I'm gone.'" He died in New York in February 1959 at the age of thirty-two, from bronchial pneumonia complicated by alcoholism.

If Slim was one of rock and roll's original kings of excess and a high-and-mighty saint in the Church of the Sonic Guitar, he was also, during his lifetime, a nightmare to record. One of the most hauntingly beautiful of his sides, the 1952 "Feeling Sad," has no guitar on it at all, but the purity and passion of its down-home gospel vocal, the plaint of a soldier in Korea that "I was sending you my money, baby, and all the time you was doin' me wrong," make listening to it an experience not likely to be forgotten. Slim began recording for Specialty in 1953, scoring almost immediately with the biggest hit of his career and one of the top r&b records of 1954, "The Things I Used to Do," arranged by up-and-coming pianist Ray Charles. But Specialty's Art Rupe and his man in New Orleans, Johnny Vincent,

1 Charlie Christian revolutionized jazz guitar, becoming the instrument's first great *electric* stylist before his early death in 1942.

2 Muddy Waters, Delta bluesman supreme, gets his mojo working; his Chicago band of the early fifties was perhaps the first great *electric* band.

3 Albert King, playing upside down and left-handed, revolutionized lead guitar stylings with his much-imitated sides for Stax in the mid-sixties.

4 Earl King, blues guitarist and master of New Orleans "fonk," learned his craft from Guitar Slim.

5 Musicians gathering for a chitlin circuit tour take time to pose for a snapshot, among them Bobby "Blue" Bland (left, kneeling); Junior Parker (left, standing); and gonzo guitarist Pat Hare (standing, right).

later the colorful proprietor of his own Ace label, had little patience for a guitarist who would remain cooperative while studio balances were carefully adjusted, wait for the count-off, and then jack his amplifier right on up to ten. There is little doubt that Slim would have turned it up to eleven if it had been possible.

Earl King was not simply Slim's traveling companion and posthumous keeper of the flame. He was, and is, a formidably talented singer, songwriter, and guitarist in his own right; his New Orleans–made singles of the late 1950s and early 1960s are themselves solid links in the rock-into-soul chain. And like many talented performers of the time, King paid his dues by sometimes being called in at the last minute to impersonate an indisposed star at an already booked engagement. In one case, the star was Guitar Slim, and King reportedly was every bit as convincing being Slim as James Brown or Otis Redding were impersonating Little Richard. But King has also left us a recorded legacy that helps put Slim's true contribution to the music in perspective. His 1960–62 sessions for the Imperial label, which include some of his most accomplished and enduring compositions in "Trick Bag" and "Mama and Papa," also include a modern reinterpretation of Slim's "The Things I Used to Do." More important, these sessions yielded a classic two-part single that is, in effect, the missing link between Slim and modern rock guitar, "Come On," an irresistibly funky dance tune highlighted by a riveting, extended guitar solo. King begins playing bluesy lines, more like the Slim we know from records, but he soon begins to stretch up to screaming, liquid high-note phrases that are uncannily reminiscent of Jimi Hendrix solos recorded more than five years later. There can be little doubt that Hendrix, a veteran of the r&b circuit with stints backing Little Richard and the Isley Brothers to his credit, heard "Come On" and took its lessons to heart. Not only did Hendrix build a certain aspect of his style from King's screaming high-note melisma, he recorded his own versions of Guitar Slim's "The Things I Used to Do" and Earl King's "Come On," explicitly laying bare the roots of his art as they extend back through King to Guitar Slim to the likes of Gatemouth Brown to the father of electric blues guitar, T-Bone Walker. Working the other way from the watershed of Hendrix's brief but brilliant career, we can follow this influence into the work of every accomplished rock guitarist playing today. This is what we mean when we call rock and roll a *living* tradition.

If Guitar Slim is the patron saint of our Church of the Sonic Guitar, Ike Turner can only be its fallen angel, the dark prince, who is also Lucifer, the "light-bringer."

Apparently, Turner was a young man of more than average intelligence, resourcefulness, and musical acumen. Born in Clarksdale, Mississippi (the Delta town that gave us John Lee Hooker, Sam Cooke, and from its immediate outskirts, the likes of Muddy Waters), on November 5, 1932, Ike easily could have grown up a conventional bluesman, learning from his elders and forging his own style from traditional elements in the time-honored tradition. He did seek out teachers, taking early piano lessons from musicians such as King Biscuit Time ivory-tickler Pinetop Perkins, and gleaning advice from the formidable Sonny Boy Williamson. But when he was in high school, the fast-talking, smooth-dressing Turner landed a regular disc-jockey slot on Clarksdale radio station WROX. On his show he played the latest jumping r&b discs from Los Angeles and New York, as well as from Chicago and closer to home, listening carefully and developing a musical orientation more influenced by the energy and ferment of the late 1940s national r&b scene than by Delta doings. He also learned to run the station's mixing board; engineering live broadcasts by both blues and hillbilly artists provided enough hands-on experience to enable him to engineer his own sessions in later years.

While in high school, Turner also played with the Tophatters, a student big band drawn together by their love of modern jazz. But there was little money to be made playing modern jazz—especially in Clarksdale, Mississippi. So Ike and a few of his closest musical cohorts from the Tophatters broke off and formed the Kings of Rhythm. All of them were capable interpreters of deep Delta blues, but being younger and having been at work assiduously expanding their musical horizons and slicking up their image, they preferred playing jump blues with a rocking boogie beat and a section of riffing saxophones. Ike himself played piano; his guitarist, Willie Kizart, was the son of a well-known Delta blues pianist, Lee Kizart, and the guitar pupil of one of the blues culture's singular musical modernists, Earl Hooker.

With this band, Turner recorded a number of sides for Sam Phillips, including the 1951 number one r&b hit "Rocket '88'" that Little Richard was to find so inspiring five years later. During the next four years, he recorded B. B. King, Elmore James, Howling Wolf, and other future blues giants in a studio he'd rigged up in his own house in Clarksdale. Then, in mid-1954, he reformed the temporarily dormant Kings of Rhythm and moved the entire group to St. Louis.

Like Memphis, St. Louis was a mecca for black southerners who'd hoed one too many rows of cotton; the city had boasted a vital and diverse black music scene since the 1920s, embracing both country blues and sophisticated jazz. By 1955, two St. Louis bands were running neck and neck as local favorites—the Kings of Rhythm and Chuck Berry's trio. Possibly their closest competition was another transplanted Mississippian who was to become one of the most durable and influential blues guitarists of the 1960s, Albert King. But King, whose fluid phrases moved like oil oozing over stone, appealed mostly to a somewhat older blues crowd. Turner and Berry were playing for a younger audience that liked to dance. They'd do early gigs in St. Louis, then cross the Mississippi River into wide-open East St. Louis, where the clubs and dives kept rocking into the morning hours. Turner and Berry were also in competition for the growing white audience then beginning to embrace rocking black r&b, and were great favorites with the white teen crowd at spots like George Edrick's Club Imperial.

At first, Turner and his band lived together in a big house. The all-night partying never seemed to keep him from waking everyone up in the morning and organizing highly efficient rehearsals, with a single-minded authority that probably makes James Brown his only real rival as a band-leader/martinet. But everyone agreed that the rehearsals were worth it—the band was *tight,* as can be heard on a series of recordings made between 1955 and 1959. By this time, with the help of lessons from Willie Kizart and, undoubtedly, a great deal of practice, Turner had transformed himself from a pianist into a gonzo guitarist. Sam Phillips's memories of his early 1950s Sun sessions, not surprisingly, reveal that already "Ike had the best-prepared band that ever came in and asked me to work with them. And," he added, "Ike! What a piano player he was! People don't know that Ike Turner was the first stand-up piano player. Man, he could tear a piano apart and put it back together again on the same song." But this was nothing compared to the over-the-top ravings Turner unleashed on electric guitar when the Kings of Rhythm traveled to Cincinnati to record for Federal in August and September of 1956.

After absorbing the basics of blues-guitar technique, Turner became fascinated by the "whammy bar," a new technological innovation on certain solid-body electric guitars. The player struck a note or chord with his right hand, then quickly reached down and gave the curved metal bar sticking out of the sound box near the bridge a nice energetic shake. The device shivered the note or chord with a vibratolike quaver, the degree of vibrato and distortion depending on how violently the guitarist yanked the bar, and how energetically he bent and abraded his strings. Turner manhandled his instrument, whammy bar and all, with what sounded like maniacal abandon.

On Federal sides like "I'm Tore Up," featuring vocalist Billy Gayles, and the steamroller rockers "Sad as a Man Can Be" and "Gonna Wait for My Chance," with singing by Jackie Brenston of "Rocket '88'" fame, Turner unleashed his full power, wresting twisted, tortured, bent, and shattered blue notes and chords out of his guitar, not just for emphasis but in practically every bar of every solo. This was a wildness that simply hadn't been heard before and was well ahead of its time—the whammy bar's heyday in the late 1950s and early 1960s never produced another player with such savage urgency. Overtones rang out bell-like, only to be shattered by violent manipulations of the whammy bar, giving way to lines of screaming high notes that began sounding bluesy and then bent and distorted themselves until the guitar sounded, for a moment, like a primitive synthesizer.

Several additional examples of Turner's playing from this period are, if anything, even more gonzo. Tommy Louis's furiously rocking "Wail Baby Wail," a shouter in the Little Richard mode, sets up a guitar solo that seamlessly blends the then-popular Chuck Berry intro-and-break style with all the furious string bending and whammy-barring of which Turner was capable, suggesting at least some stylistic connection between the two champs of mid-1950s St. Louis guitar, Berry and Turner; Ike also tried his hand at Berry's characteristic blues/hillbilly fusion on instrumentals like "Steel Guitar Rag." In 1958, Turner and at least some members of his band were in Chicago, doing session work as well as their own records for the somewhat shady Cobra/Artistic operation, whose owner reportedly lost the company in a poker game. Turner played one of two electric lead guitars on "Double Trouble," the first recorded masterpiece by one of the greatest of all modern blues guitarists, Otis Rush. Rush's eerie moan of hard times and hoodoo paranoia is punctuated by his own crying, fluid phrases; periodically, the mood escalates from dread to pure terror as Turner inserts a quivering shard of a glassy blues chord. ("Double Trouble" is the single most striking performance in a series of Otis Rush Cobra sides that later played a key role in inspiring the British blues revival. A comparison of Rush's Cobra single "All Your Love" with the John Mayall/Eric Clapton version reveals the latter as a nearly literal homage, and Led Zeppelin was only marginally more creative in their remake of "I Can't Quit You Baby.")

By 1958, Ike Turner had discovered Annie May Bullock, a.k.a. Tina Turner, and from that time on he became the Svengali behind her, directing the band with his usual iron-fisted methods. His guitar playing largely receded into the background. There is one fascinating album of guitar instrumentals by Turner on the Crown label, and he plays a mean blues solo on a live Ike and Tina performance in Africa captured in the film *Soul to Soul*. "The New Breed," an instrumental from 1965, features guitar as sonically daring as the groundbreaking work Jeff Beck was then doing with the Yardbirds. "Takin' Back My Name," a single from 1970, finds Ike copping a Keith Richards attitude on guitar, and outrocking the Stones on their own musical turf.

Since then, there's been a well-publicized split, accusations, arrests. It's too bad, because Ike Turner deserves a prominent place in rock and roll history, and not just as a guitarist whose wild-man strategies were rarely heard again until the advent of the Velvet Underground and later punk groups like Richard Hell and the Voidoids, with resourceful gonzo-guitar inheritor Robert Quine. Turner's remarkable accomplishments as a talent scout; the classic blues records he produced in the early 1950s for the Modern label; his bands; Ike and Tina albums; spin-off projects—all added up to a rich and varied career.

Wildcat Tamers

Bluesmen were not the only black guitarists pioneering techniques most rock fans credit to white rockers of a later generation. One indelible strain of electric-guitar playing was rooted more in gospel music than in blues, and first came to the fore as popular music on certain black-vocal-group records. One figure stands out among this latter breed as a guitarist, songwriter, and arranger—a rock and roll auteur—of uncommon gifts and substantial, though largely unsung, influence: Lowman Pauling. The brother of early Motown writer-producer Clarence Paul, Lowman made his mark as the musical director of one of the most accomplished and consistently innovative of fifties vocal groups, the "5" Royales.

Pauling and future Royales lead singer Johnny Tanner grew up together singing in church and laboring in the tobacco fields around Winston-Salem, North Carolina. Harmonizing in church led to informal street-corner singing, but when they formed their first group in high school, in 1942, it was purely a gospel group, the Royal Sons. By 1951, the Royal Sons' growing regional reputation and undeniable expertise won them a contract with New York's Apollo label, which had been enjoying some commercial success with recent gospel recordings by Mahalia Jackson (the New Orleans gospel firebrand named by Little Richard as an important early influence and the source of his falsetto whoops) and the Roberta Martin singers. The Sons' first records were hard-core southern gospel songs with titles such as "Bedside of a Neighbor" and "So God Can Use Me." But Apollo was an expanding company, having also recorded some of the earliest bebop jazz discs and some r&b hits. Reportedly, the Royales' recording contract gave Apollo the option of mandating changes in their style. When they returned to New York in mid-1952 for their second Apollo session, the company's Carl LeBow, encouraged by at least some of the group members, suggested a move into r&b. Pauling, who had apparently been the group's arranger, guitarist, bass singer, and driving force from the first, was ready with several r&b songs he had written himself. His "You Know I Know" was a southeastern regional hit, followed by "Baby, Don't Do It," a national r&b smash. The latter record is jazzy, with a richly harmonized piano intro, New Orleans–influenced saxophone riffs, artful, deliberate stammering from

215

churchy lead singer Johnny Tanner, and one of Pauling's little arranging devices, an unexpected but effective stop-time break. With lines like "If you leave me, pretty baby, I'll have bread without no meat," the song was guaranteed to offend gospel loyalists.

The follow-up, "Help Me Somebody," also topped the r&b charts. This was the most dynamic and arresting Royales record yet. It begins with Tanner testifying solo and then slides into a medium-slow shuffle groove, the gorgeously voiced chorus (reminiscent at times of the sonorities of a Duke Ellington reed section) adding force to Tanner's repeated plea, "Somebody help me get back in there again." Then, at the bridge, the tempo changes abruptly from the chugging shuffle to a double-time, straight-ahead swing-jazz feel, carried by walking string bass. The vocalist testifies in gospel tongues, halfway between song and speech, as this swing section builds, then breaks just in time for Tanner to wail, unaccompanied, "You know I didn't miss my water till my well ran dry," later the popular refrain of an early-sixties Memphis soul hit by William Bell. The swing break segues seamlessly back into the original shuffle groove, and the lead singer and "congregation" testify with mounting passion through the song's ride-out chorus. Pauling's guitar is virtually inaudible on these early discs, probably because few recording engineers were as willing to risk sonic overloading as Sam Phillips and the crew at Chess. But as a composer-arranger, Pauling was already finding his own voice.

During the early fifties, the "5" Royales toured tirelessly on the southern "chitlin circuit," wailing in theaters, clubs, and that peculiarly southeastern version of the traditional roadhouse, the converted tobacco barn. Apollo's publicity releases boasted that they were playing for audiences totaling around a million people a year, and the company issued a "5" Royales album, an unusual move for a black vocal group in those days, when the name of the r&b recording game was singles. By the spring of 1954, Carl LeBow had graduated from being Apollo's A&R man to serving as a manager/adviser for the Royales. As such, he engineered their move to King records, a Cincinnati company that had been among the most successful and imitated r&b and hillbilly indie labels, building acts such as Bullmoose Jackson, Billy Ward and the Dominos (in both their original incarnations, with Clyde McPhatter, then Jackie Wilson as lead singer), a group called the Royals, led by Hank Ballard, and, after 1955, James Brown.

So powerful was the "5" Royales' reputation as performers that the Royals were persuaded by the company and their own management to change their name to Hank Ballard and the Midnighters. With the Royales and the Midnighters both on their roster, King had the two powerhouse groups then touring the southeastern theater-and-tobacco-barn circuit. Both groups were also in demand for lucrative, often Bacchanalian frat-party gigs at all-white southern schools. The Midnighters' songs about sex and its consequences—the "Work with Me Annie"/"Annie Had a Baby"/"Sexy Ways" series that stirred much controversy when mid-fifties white teenagers were exposed to it via radio—endeared them to the frat crowd. But the "5" Royales had been making their own salacious, less-than-double-entendre records since their early Apollo hit "Laundromat Blues," and with their musical strengths and killer showmanship, they more than held their own.

It was a dirty job, sweating out all-night dances where the performers often were forbidden by law from using the public restrooms, delivering surrogate come-ons for all the fraternity jocks. It was also the chief training ground for many of the future soul stars and session players of the sixties. The Midnighters and Royales were kings of the circuit until the arrival, around the beginning of the 1960s, of Doug Clark and his Hot Nuts. Here was an act literally tailor-made for the frat parties—"Hot nuts," they advertised in their theme song, adding, "you get 'em from the peanut man/you get 'em anywhere you can. . . ." During my own college days in early-sixties Arkansas, the story making the rounds was that Clark and the Hot Nuts offered a choice of three different shows, each of which had its own set fee. There was the regular show, at the regular fee. For an additional fee, the Hot Nuts did their show clad only in jockstraps. For the third and most expensive show, they performed nude. I have no idea whether this story is actually true, but it does shed interesting light on the psychosexual dynamics of the white frat-party circuit.

But back to the "5" Royales. Like so many of the labels recording r&b before and during the rock and roll explosion, King maintained a stable of session musicians who were primarily jazzmen by training and inclination.

217

1 B. B. King, the most polished and precisely virtuosic of guitar bluesmen, with one of the guitars he calls "Lucille."

2 Lowman Pauling, guitarist and songwriter for the "5" Royales and the idol of sixties soul guitarists such as Steve Cropper, indulging in a bit of deliberate feedback onstage at Harlem's Apollo Theater.

3 Ike Turner, dark prince of the sonic guitar, all by his bad self.

4 Cropper, whose stinging fills and terse, stuttering solos helped define the Memphis sound, was above all an incomparable *rhythm* guitarist, and as such an inspiration for rockers like John Fogerty and John Lennon.

Singers could indulge in all the twists and turns of the gospel singer's art, but prior to 1955 the Royales' King singles were gospel-style vocal-group rave-ups backed by jazzers playing in swing time. Gradually, session by session, a sound began to emerge that more closely approximated the guitar-heavy drive and rocking shout rhythms of the group's live performances. According to r&b historian Jonas Bernholm, Pauling "was perhaps the least well-known of the greatest r&b guitarists of this era that include Chuck Berry, Bo Diddley, and [New York sessionman supreme] Mickey Baker. . . . As the only instrumentalist behind the group during their gospel days, he had developed a very strong sense of rhythmic drive, and this was particularly evident on songs such as 'The Real Thing' [1959]. The overwhelming audience response to his gimmicks—playing his Gibson Les Paul Signature behind his head or using feedback with the strings facing the amplifier—encouraged him to include even more playing onstage and on the group's records." In an interview, Johnny Tanner told Bernholm, "He was a showman. He could play the guitar behind his back, he could kick it with his feet. He was a showman *plus he could play*." Steve Cropper, whose work with Booker T. and the MGs backing Otis Redding, Wilson Pickett, and others made him the most imitated soul guitarist of the sixties, names Pauling as his primary influence. Mac Rebennack, a.k.a. Dr. John, is another Pauling booster, claiming the "5" Royales were so good they didn't need to indulge in showmanship; they could devastate a crowd with vocal power alone.

During the mid-fifties, while his guitar slowly worked its way toward the foreground of the mixes on the Royales' singles, Pauling was also developing his talents as a songwriter. Between 1955 and 1958 he was responsible for a string of classic songs that were for the most part destined to achieve their greatest popularity a few years later, via other artists' cover versions. His "Think" was the record that put the "5" Royales back on the r&b charts in 1957, after a temporary sales slump, but the song is more closely associated with James Brown, whose cover version eclipsed the sales of the Royales' original in the early sixties. In 1957 the Royales released their original rendition of Pauling's "Dedicated to the One I Love," which sold well in Atlanta and New Orleans, among other cities, but didn't become a national hit until its 1961 revival by the Shirelles. Their version was a million-seller, and the song went to the top of the pop charts again in 1967 in a version by the Mamas and the Papas.

In some of his best songs from this period, Pauling made a concerted attempt, bravely utopian in retrospect, to reconcile the sacred and profane philosophies of gospel and rhythm and blues. He became a rock and roll philosopher. His 1956 "Get Something Out of It," for example, abandoned the "let's rock/have fun/live now/pay later" motif of much fifties rock with a cautionary message more typical of the gospel circuit, warning, "You're goin' too fast" and "the faster you go, the quicker you will get to the end." In 1958 the Royales recorded his "Tell the Truth," an injunction to veracity, but once again it failed to become a hit until a few years later, when Ray Charles rerecorded it, using a close approximation of Pauling's original arrangement.

On these records, Pauling's stinging, slinky lead-guitar work can finally be heard in all its glory. "Think" is built on a stop-time arrangement that pits chorus and lead singer against terse, astringent, yet somehow elegant, electric guitar fills; soul guitar playing starts here. On "Tell the Truth," the guitar has finally taken its place in the mix as a driving rhythm instrument. Pauling's playing alternates staccato single-note riffs, hard-pumping 8th-note chordal figures, and slamming double-time power-strums on the turnarounds. It is a virtual one-record textbook for future rock and roll rhythm guitarists. Perhaps its purest British Invasion reincarnation is in John Lennon's rhythm playing during the Beatles' early days—compare it, for example, to Lennon's guitar on the Beatles' "Twist and Shout." The line of transmission from Pauling to Lennon isn't terribly difficult to intuit. When I met Lennon shortly before his death, he was keeping only a few old 45 singles around to play on the vintage jukebox at his Dakota apartment; around half of his 45's were early-sixties soul discs by Arthur Alexander. The musicians on the Alexander records were white southern r&b freaks who'd received their early baptism by fire on the same southeastern frat-party circuit worked by the black groups and who, like their contemporary Steve Cropper, idolized Lowman Pauling.

Pauling and the Royales reached their rock and roll apogee on records in 1958–59 with the double-whammy of "The Real Thing" and "The Slummer the Slum." The former is one of the most joyously kinetic frat-party ravers in all of rock and roll, and once again it is Pauling's guitar, pumping out an unrelenting 8th-note drive-pattern, that spurs the groove over the top. This is one of the few Pauling guitar performances that bear some resemblance to an already-established style, in this case, the rhythm playing of Chuck Berry.

"The Slummer the Slum," from 1958, is Pauling's masterpiece. This time there is no mystery as to why the record failed to become a hit. It's an outspoken social commentary that directly addresses racial inequities, but in a lyric form usually reserved for records that teach you how to do a new dance. In fact, "The Slummer the Slum" *is* a new dance, but the record's tone is so aggressive and bitterly ironic, it's not a dance you'd really want to do.

"The Slummer the Slum" begins with Pauling unleashing some of the most ferocious lead-guitar riffs heard on record up to that time, accompanied by a very minimal stop-time backing. (Stop-time arrangements, also a staple of Ray Charles's fifties recordings, probably derived from swing-era jazz; they are, in turn, the origin of what rappers call "the breaks.") Lead singer Johnny Tanner enters with a warning about making judgments on the basis of appearance: "Don't try to figure out/Where I come from/I could be a slick cat from Wall Street/Or I could be the Purple People Eater's son/But I can do the Slummer the Slum!" After a guitar break that comes in sudden, angry, coruscating bursts, the lyric gets even more explicit: "There's just one difference/Between me and you/You've got money in your pocket/And I've got a hole in my shoe/All from doin' the Slummer the Slum" (chang!), etc.

The vast difference between this record's mood and message and Little Richard's utopian come-together exhortations of just a few years earlier is yet another example of black rock and roll's ability to reflect, and often prefigure, attitudinal shifts in the American body politic. Richard in 1955 was a down-home, freaky-and-proud-of-it black man celebrating the penetration of his brand of music into white-controlled media that had always excluded it, from white radio shows and sock hops and the pop charts to celluloid immortality playing opposite Jayne Mansfield in *The Girl Can't Help It*. By 1958–59, the major record labels were successfully beginning to wrest the pop charts away from the upstart indie labels and "vulgar animalistic nigger rock and roll bop" that had made such an upsetting, anarchic breakthrough in the mid-fifties. The day of the white-plastic teen idol was dawning, and the term "rhythm and blues," which had begun to seem outdated as harder and harder black sounds invaded the pop charts, was once again applied to the great majority of black records, which once again failed to make the pop crossover.

James Brown, whose earliest King singles had been equal parts Little Richard and "5" Royales, with plenty of soul but a shortage of originality, was consolidating his strengths by the early sixties. A disagreement between Brown and his people and the Royales and theirs is said to have contributed to the Royales' leaving King at the beginning of the sixties. It wasn't just that the two acts were similar, though they were—there is a lot of Johnny Tanner in James Brown's early vocals, and the Famous Flames' original guitarist, Cleveland Lowe, had borrowed a number of Lowman Pauling's tricks. Even the Famous Flames' vocal harmonies sounded at times surprisingly close to the Royales'. The same month the Royales left the label, Brown scored with his cover of Pauling's "Think." The Royales moved to Memphis's Home of the Blues label, where they worked with Willie Mitchell, a former jazz bandleader who would achieve his greatest success in the seventies producing Al Green. One of the Royales' first Home of the Blues singles attempted to beat Brown at his own game by covering his first King hit, "Please Please Please." The record went nowhere, and although Pauling went on to make several early-sixties singles that helped define the direction of the next decade's funkiest soul music, the Royales had broken up and faded from view. Pauling died in January 1974, unappreciated, unheralded. Recognition for his achievements has long been overdue.

Pauling was not the only vocal-group-associated guitarist whose middle- and late-fifties recordings bridged rock and roll and soul music. Another important transitional figure, guitarist/singer/writer/arranger Alden Bunn, was also a North Carolina native; he actually played guitar on several early "5" Royales singles. Bunn, who called himself Tarheel Slim, grew up near Rocky Mount and was influenced as a child by his mother's Blind Boy Fuller 78's. Fuller was a widely popular blues artist of the thirties whose complex fingerpicking, ragtime melodies and turnarounds, serpentine single-string melodic interpolations, and choppy rhythm playing shaped the early styles of future East Coast rock and roll studio guitarists such as Brownie McGhee. The southeastern country-blues tradition, with its emphasis on non-blues song forms and chord progressions and its rich vocabulary of rhythmic, harmonic, and textural effects, seems to have been a particularly fertile breeding ground for gospel guitarists (Rev. Gary Davis was another Fuller disciple), including many who later crossed over with their singing groups from sacred to secular music.

Tarheel Slim followed this pattern. Thurman Ruth, leader of the Selah Jubilee Singers, heard him playing and singing one night near Wilson, North Carolina, and immediately asked him to join the group. "When the tobacco season is over," Slim responded, and he was as good as his word. He traveled and recorded with the Selahs until the beginning of the fifties, when they decided to try their luck at r&b, changing their name to the Larks. By 1952, Slim was making electric blues records as Allen Bunn. On his 1952 single "The Guy with the 45," the clean, smooth tone and legato phrasing of his single-note blues guitar intro and fills differ strikingly from the contemporary sound of both the Memphis and Delta school (rough-toned, superamplified, "heavy") and the more percussive picking, jazzier phrasing, and drier tone of T-Bone Walker and his southwestern and West Coast disciples.

Tarheel Slim made his own blues records, appeared as a sideman on vocal-group discs, and did varied session work around New York. In 1957, Slim and his wife began making vocal-duet records as Tarheel Slim and Little Ann. They cut some memorable ballads, forerunners of the earliest soul-ballad styles, but on the 1958 "Lock Me in Your Heart (And Throw Away the Key)" Slim takes a solo that combines fluid single-note picking and rapidly strummed chordal clangs in a manner that suggests country and rockabilly guitar as much as it does East Coast blues stylings.

This black blues-rockabilly hybrid reached a new level of freshness and invention when Slim joined forces with another southeastern-born, country-bred guitarist living in New York City, the redoubtable Wild Jimmy Spruill. In 1959, Slim and Spruill locked guitars on the cataclysmic two-sided nonhit single "Wildcat Tamer"/"Number 9 Train," recorded for Harlem record-store entrepreneur Bobby Robinson's Fire label around the time Robinson was making some of the most thunderous electric-guitar records of the decade with Mississippi bluesman Elmore James. "Wildcat Tamer" and "Number 9 Train" are among the first records to define the two-guitar small combo sound that would flower in the wake of the British Invasion. Both players mix tremolo, twang, slamming runs, and crazed lead playing on the macho "Wildcat Tamer." "Number 9 Train" is a deeper piece of work, with Slim and Spruill blending their hyperactive but always supportive playing at peak intensity behind Slim's impassioned complaint about the train that "took my baby down the line." The leads and finger-picking, clean runs and tremolo shimmer, are so tightly integrated that lead and rhythm distinctions are only intermittently relevant. This was a thoroughly modern record, anticipating the twin-guitar attack of the early Rolling Stones.

Tarheel Slim and Wild Jimmy Spruill were not the only black guitarists to integrate country and rockabilly picking into their styles during the 1950s. The black rockabilly subgenre seems to have been a nationwide phenomenon. In the midwest, black r&b pianist and singer Big Al Downing cut a memorable mid-fifties country-flavored single, "Down on the Farm," backed by a white rockabilly combo under the leadership of one Bobby Poe. It was Little Richard-meets-Carl Perkins in flavor. Mississippi-born, Chicago-based bluesman Magic Sam, whose mid-fifties recordings for the Cobra label are among the toughest blues discs of the period, made one outstanding rockabilly raver, the lyrically scarifying "21 Days in Jail," on which he introduced a telegraphic style of rhythm-guitar fingerpicking and raucous, declamatory solo breaks. The closest thing on record to Magic Sam's picking on "21 Days in Jail" is white Mississippi guitarist Al Hopson's wrangling, barbed-wire guitar bursts behind Sun records rockabilly Warren Smith on one of the fifties' best white blues performances, "Miss Froggie." On the West Coast, bluesman Johnny Fuller put plenty of country twang into his "Haunted House," covered a few years later by another white Memphis rockabilly, Gene Simmons, for the Hi label.

Chuck Berry, beginning with "Maybelline," was undoubtedly the original inspiration for this electric-guitar miscegenation, which continued through the fifties. Berry himself has traced some of these ideas to Louis Jordan's guitarist, Carl Hogan, and the overriding influence of T-Bone Walker cannot be gainsaid. The dialogue continued, with young white guitarist and future Rick Nelson and Elvis Presley sideman James Burton contributing some swampy, Lowman Pauling–like picking to Dale Hawkins's Chess hit "Suzie Q." and Pauling himself showing some c&w influences on "5" Royales discs such as the 1955 "Mohawk Squaw." In the late fifties, black Chicago guitarist Eddie Clearwater, recording for the obscure Atomic-H label, which was then housed in the basement of a church, took the more countrified side of Chuck Berry's picking to its inevitable extreme on a record that stands as definitive black rockabilly despite its near-total obscurity, "Hillbilly Blues." Several country-bred white guitarists also made important contributions to the blues/hillbilly guitar crossover, most notably Merle Travis and Arthur "Guitar Boogie" Smith, though West Coast pickers like Joe Maphis and Jimmy Bryant were also exceptional.

The 'billy-tinged mode of electric guitar playing also figured in the musical development of two groups whose overall style and history make them definitive precursors of sixties soul, the Falcons and Nolan Strong and the Diablos. Both groups were from Detroit. Strong is held in near-reverence by vocal-group aficionados for ballad performances such as "The Wind," one of the most hushed, ethereal, and magical-sounding group plaints of the fifties. But hits like the charging, up-tempo "Mind over Matter," with Bob Edwards's driving guitar and a soaring vocal melody that perfectly matches the lyric's suprasensory theme, was more redolent of things to come.

The Falcons would be notable in the mid-fifties-to-early-sixties changeover from rock and roll to soul if only for their personnel. The principal lead singer, Joe Stubbs, had a brother named Levi, who later became lead singer of one of Motown's most enduring vocal groups, the Four Tops. The Falcons' second lead was Eddie Floyd, who already had considerable gospel experience and went on to make some of the most emblematic soul records of the sixties for Memphis's Stax label, most notably "Knock On Wood" and the sublime gospel-soul ballad "Got to Make a Comeback." The baritone singer was Mack (later Sir Mack) Rice, who achieved fame during the mid-sixties soul boom as a songwriter with tunes like "Mustang Sally." That song turned out to be a mid-sixties hit for the singer who replaced Joe Stubbs as the Falcons' lead in the early sixties, Wilson Pickett. The Wicked Pickett's finest hour as a Falcon was the emotion-drenched lead on "I Found a Love" that landed him his solo contract with Atlantic Records.

If any fifties vocal group was a school for future soul stars, it was the Falcons. Like the "5" Royales, Nolan Strong and the Diablos, and other gospel-soul vocal groups, they also contributed to the development of the electric rhythm guitar. The Falcons' axman, Lance Finnie, developed the sort of gospel group rhythm-guitar figures that would become a black pop-music staple during the sixties, especially at Motown, where similar playing by the likes of Robert White and Eddie Willis powered so many of the label's early hits. Finnie got to strut his kinetic rhythm-guitar moxie on the Falcons' transcendent late-fifties hits "You're So Fine" and "Just for Your Love," and his bell-toned lead work enlivened "(When) You're in Love," "Sent Up," and "No Time for Fun." The latter introduced a funky scratch-rhythm guitar figure, used not as a continuing ostinato but as an unexpected addition to the already-full group sound, coming in just before the end of the song.

Following the Falcons from their fifties beginnings through the early sixties is a lot like following the recordings of the "5" Royales or the Diablos in chronological order. The dominant saxophone and piano and swing-jazz feel of the earlier sides gradually gives way to a simpler, more guitar-dominated sound. We are in the habit of calling the earlier music r&b, the later music soul, and the more guitar-dominated music rock and roll. But they are all one music, changing to keep abreast of developments in both recording technology and popular tastes while retaining traditional song forms and modes of vocal expression. The guitar was featured more and more prominently, gradually replacing the saxophone as rock and roll's most important instrumental solo voice. But the singer and the song were still preeminent. During the late fifties and early sixties, guitarists as volatile but otherwise varied as surf-music originator Dick Dale, young Hawks firebrand Robbie Robertson, even instrumental hit-maker Link Wray, were still fighting battles with producers and engineers over the setting of their amplifiers' volume knobs.

The Falcons, a fifties vocal group full of future soul stars, with guitarist Lance Finnie in the foreground.

Shapes of Things

The guitarists who came of age in the mid-sixties were the first rock generation to challenge effectively the hegemony of singer and song. Even among these younger guitarists, a considerable amount of experimentation and innovation took place within the context of the traditional song-centered three-minute pop single. The Yardbirds' mid-sixties singles, for example, were the medium for some extraordinary advances in guitar sound and technique, with Jeff Beck and, a bit later, Jimmy Page as the featured guitarists. The Byrds' Roger McGuinn fashioned a highly individual guitar language playing his electric 12-string on mid-sixties singles by the Byrds; his inspirations included the Indian ragas of Ravi Shankar and the raga-like modal jazz of saxophonist John Coltrane. Between them, the Yardbirds' "Shapes of Things" and "Happenings Ten Years' Time Ago" and the Byrds' "Eight Miles High" and "5D (Fifth Dimension)," all from 1965–66, opened enough new sonic territory to keep guitarists woodshedding into the next decade.

In Jimi Hendrix's work, the guitar explorations that had challenged the constraints of song form and singles length on the Yardbirds' and Byrds' discs took their place stage center. Hendrix could get away with performing evergreens like "Rock Me Baby," "Wild Thing," and "Hey Joe" because, like Jerry Lee Lewis before him, he projected such unmistakable originality, and innovated with such energy and zeal, that he could make any song he tackled his own. But while with Lewis an incendiary personal dynamism became the dominant mode of expression, the no-less-incendiary Hendrix put the focus squarely on his guitar. Lewis had reputedly poured lighter fluid into a piano and set it afire at the end of one of his shows in order to upstage Chuck Berry. At the Monterey Pop Festival, Hendrix smashed and burned his guitar, and kept his amps on full-throttle. The sound of guitar strings vibrating and uncoiling as the instrument crumpled and went up in flames wasn't just showmanship, as in the Who's instrument-smashing rampages; it was *music*. Hendrix at Woodstock played a "Star-Spangled Banner" that similarly made *musical* use of noise elements—evocations of bombs falling and exploding, the screaming of sirens, the howls of the victims as the guitarist whipped up an entirely sonic conflagration.

The Jimi Hendrix Experience was to provide the principal model for power trios in particular and the development of heavy metal in general. Of the period's other guitar-centered protometal trios, Cream offered a somewhat different direction. Guitarist Eric Clapton was testing the limits of his blues-based musical vocabulary in marathon improvisations, goaded by the mercurial, jazz-trained rhythm section of bassist Jack Bruce and drummer Ginger Baker. Cream's popular success ushered in a vogue for epic guitar solos, but even Clapton feels that Cream's performances were hit-or-miss. So were the improvisational efforts of most other rockers, despite the example of Miles Davis and John Coltrane, whose classic album collaboration *Kind of Blue* showed rockers how to use alternate modes and scales, generating considerable melodic variety from the blues and just one or two chords. Hendrix wisely avoided soloing too long on the same tune. When it came to sustaining melodic invention and listener interest with guitar solos a half hour or more in length, the period's reigning master was Duane Allman. An avid fan of Miles and Trane, Allman soared on flights of astonishing creativity and imagination with the Allman Brothers Band. Had he lived, he might have at least partly redeemed rock as an improvising soloist's idiom. But Allman was killed in a 1971 motorcycle accident, and rock, probably for the best, remains more a song-oriented ensemble music than a soloist's launching pad.

The Velvet Underground created some of the most enduring group music of the sixties. At the time, the band was widely reviled for crashing and trashing the peace-and-love party with songs about copping heroin ("I'm Waiting for the Man"), shooting speed ("White Light White Heat"), sadomasochistic sex ("Venus in Furs"), and orgies involving sailors and transvestites ("Sister Ray"). Their first album, *The Velvet Underground and Nico,* released within a few months of the Beatles' reassuring trip companion *Sgt. Pepper,* was the first example of what would become a postpunk rock staple, the bad-trip album. More than twenty-five years later, the two albums sound like the products of different eras as well as different sensibilities. *Sgt. Pepper* remains tied to its time, as quaint and dated as a Fillmore poster and a pair of granny glasses; the era *The Velvet Underground and Nico* calls up is our present one. This is partly a function of its unflinching song lyrics—activities that then belonged to a marginalized subculture

1. Jeff Beck, feeding back; with the mid-sixties Yardbirds, he was the reigning king of the sonic stun.

2. Lou Reed, whose feedback-riddled soloing on the first two Velvet Underground LPs embraced noise and anarchy to a degree unprecedented in earlier rock and roll.

3. Guitar Slim, saint of the sonic guitar; "Slim always played at peak volume," remembers Earl King, "you could hear him a mile away."

4. Jimi Hendrix, who synthesized blues guitar traditions from Guitar Slim to B. B. King, added textural experimentation and tonal modifiers, and emerged with one of the most distinctive and virtuosic guitar styles rock has known.

are now mass-culture concerns—but mostly it is a tribute to music so radical it scarcely seems to have aged at all.

Since its earliest days, rock and roll has benefited greatly from a continuing dialogue between players with conventional musical training and unschooled musicians adept in vernacular idioms. One could argue that the process of formally schooled jazz musicians learning to accompany street-schooled singers and players is where rock comes from in the first place—Dave Bartholomew's New Orleans studio band learning to follow Fats Domino and Professor Longhair, for example, or Scotty Moore and Bill Black covering for Elvis Presley when he dropped a bar or a beat or abruptly changed tempo. The Velvet Underground was powered by a similar dynamic. Singer-songwriter-guitarist Lou Reed had played bar band r&b and was working as a pop tunesmith when he met a group of musicians who were rehearsing and occasionally performing with the avant-garde composer La Monte Young's group, the Theater of Eternal Music, a.k.a. the Dream Syndicate. Tony Conrad, Angus MacLise, and conservatory-trained violist-composer John Cale were all members of Young's group as well as early V.U. personnel. When Reed met them, he had recently written and recorded a would-be dance hit, "The Ostrich," which involved tuning all the strings of his guitar to the same note in order to get a harmonics-rich drone sound. Young, pursuing the loftier goal of a drone music with pure Pythagorean mathematics underlying its tuning, had been directing Conrad and Cale to tune all the strings of their respective instruments, the electric violin and electric viola, to one note. Clearly it was an idea whose time had come.

Cale elected to continue working with Reed, and by late 1965 or early 1966 the astonishing music captured on the Velvet Underground's debut album was fully mature. Young's impact on the group's music was facilitated by his own influences, which he shared with many of the rock musicians of the Velvets' generation: the drone and shimmering harmonics of Indian music; the distinctive melodic language of the blues; the classical avant-garde of Webern, Stockhausen, and Cage; and an affinity for volume levels surpassing anything previously heard in rock, let alone "classical" concert music. There was also an "industrial" influence; Young speaks fondly of his early years, when he listened to the hum of high-tension electrical lines and stepdown transformers and sang along with the clamor and clang of a machine shop. Rock and roll was amenable to all these influences, and the Velvet Underground disseminated them more widely than anyone can have suspected at the time. The cliché about the band is that not many people bought their records, but everyone who did started a band that became influential in its own right. Like many clichés, this one contains more than a grain of truth.

Back in the fifties, Guitar Slim's use of a public address system with iron speaker cones as a guitar amplifier created sonic effects previously undreamed of. In the mid-sixties, John Cale put heavy-gauge guitar strings on his electric viola, played it through an amplifier stack, and achieved a sound he favorably compared to that of a jet taking off. Cale would find a single tone that was common to all the chords in one of Reed's songs— technically known as a pedal-point or drone—and saw away at it on all four strings, while guitarists Lou Reed and Sterling Morrison added to the immense, droning mass of sound, and drummer Maureen Tucker supported them with thunderous tribal rhythms. Sixties listeners were sometimes confused to hear such mystical, spiritual-sounding music framing tales of low-life extremity, but that was the whole point. One way of looking at rock like the Velvet Underground's is that the lyrics deal with the world as it is, while the music makes all the pain and suffering a little more bearable by manifesting the sacred geometry of an imaginal sonic paradise.

The Velvet Underground's influence was keenly felt first in Germany, where late-sixties bands such as Can and Faust picked up on V.U.'s heavily amplified drones and harmonic shimmer. Iggy Pop and his Stooges got the message earlier than most American bands; David Bowie almost single-handedly brought the sonic guitar sound (and the influence of the cross-dressing New York demimonde hymned by the Velvets) into British rock. When the punk rebellion began taking shape in the mid-seventies, primarily in the Bowery dive CBGB (truly a Church of the Sonic Guitar), Television in particular carried on the Velvets' legacy of street-real lyrics and harmonic clang-and-drone, with appropriate nods to John Coltrane's modal jazz and the Byrds' resonating raga-rock from lead guitarist Tom Verlaine. Then, in the early 1980s, just when it was beginning to seem that the rich vein mined by the Velvets and their successors had been

Television's Tom Verlaine, poet and sonic illuminist; "when I see the glory," he sang on Television's second album, *Adventure,* "I ain't gotta worry."

233

exhausted, Sonic Youth arrived with enough new tunings and fresh ways of making guitar tones shimmer, shatter, sustain, and resonate to keep "alternative" guitar bands busy experimenting for the next decade—yet another generation of worshippers for the Church of the Sonic Guitar.

William "Bootsy" Collins,
a.k.a. Bootzilla, funk
bassist supreme, back-
bone of the late-sixties
J.B.'s, P-Funk, and
Bootsy's Rubber Band,
bumpin' on-the-one in his
best funk finery.

Brand New Bag

8

"Give the drummer some!"

    James Brown to drummer Clyde Stubblefield, "Cold Sweat" (1967)

*"When you talk about James Brown and his music you're almost automatically talking about drums. Like all great classical black music, it's built around rhythm first. James as a result attracted and was attracted to great drummers throughout his career. And when he was looking for a drummer, he would not seek a drummer to replicate the previous drummer. He was willing to build a style around a new drummer rather than find a drummer to plug into a style that he already had; he was always open-minded to new drummers and new ideas. He loved the challenge that each drummer would bring him musically, and that had as much to do with keeping his music fresh as anything else that was going on. And James **sang like a drummer.** He was playing drums with his larynx, okay?"*

    Alan Leeds, former James Brown road manager

"Thinking ain't illegal yet. . . . Free your mind and your ass will follow."

    George Clinton, a.k.a. Dr. Funkenstein of P-Funk

"Earth, Wind and Fire was doing clean dirt, and we [P-Funk] was doing dirty dirt, the kind you sweep under the rug."
Bootsy Collins of P-Funk and Bootsy's Rubber Band

"Where do I think funk goes from here? Funk ain't going nowhere, funk is forever coming: It don't go, it comes."
George Clinton

Rhythmic innovation in rock and roll, as in black music generally, is a collaborative process, worked out night by night, gig by gig, between musicians, singers, songwriters, arrangers, and audiences. All the participants have a part to play. A musician will pick up a rhythmic idea, a syncopation, a fresh kind of swing and sway from watching people dance—or, as we've seen in cases as disparate as Motown bassist James Jamerson and Delta blues patriarch Sonny Boy Williamson, by watching the way people walk, or listening to their intonation when they speak. A singer will improvise a line or spontaneously sing a rhythmic figure in the heat of call-and-response with a concert audience, remember it, and eventually develop it into a song. An arranger may hear something in a different kind of music—jazz, say, or European classical music—and bring that to the table. This continuing search for the new groove, stretching across the years, becomes an evolutionary chain of rhythmic praxis, linking the music's earliest and deepest wellsprings to the mainstream of the rock and roll tradition, and on to the latest developments in that tradition. In the seventies, the new groove was called funk.

In black vernacular, the word "funk" originally referred to an odor—an impolite odor. Funk was the smell of sweat, the smell of sex, the smell of . . . Well, in turn-of-the-century New Orleans they sang, "Funky butt,

1933

(alternate date: 1928)
James Brown is born into
poverty in South Carolina.

1939

Jelly Roll Morton's
Commodore recording of
his "I Thought I Heard
Buddy Bolden Say" con-
tributes the word *funky* to
the popular lexicon.

funky butt, take it away," a refrain Jelly Roll Morton incorporated into his
song about the earliest known jazzman, "I Thought I Heard Buddy Bolden
Say." In the jazz of the late fifties and early sixties, black musicians referred
to music with a gospel-derived backbeat as "funky jazz" or "soul jazz." You
didn't just sit and listen to funky jazz, you snapped your fingers, clapped
your hands, "got into it."

African arts scholar Robert Farris Thompson suggests that "funky"
may derive from the Ki-Kongo *lu-fuki,* defined as "positive sweat." This is
very close to the contemporary American usage, and Thompson notes that
in present-day Africa, Ba-Kongo people use *lu-fuki* and the American
"funky" synonymously—"to praise persons for the integrity of their art."
Thus James Brown's celebrated admonition to "Make it funky now!"
Certainly no one in rock or r&b has put more sweat into his performances
than Soul Brother Number One. Add to this Ki-Kongo concept of "positive
sweat" the Yoruba concept of *ashé,* or "cool" ("This is character," writes
Thompson in *Flash of the Spirit,* "This is mystic coolness") and what have
you got? "Cold Sweat"!

"'Cold Sweat' was one of the first projects Pee Wee Ellis worked on
after he became James Brown's bandleader and arranger in 1967," says longtime Brown associate Alan Leeds. "To hear him tell it, James came to him
with an idea, with some kind of rhythm or riff, and said, 'When you're on
the bus tonight after the gig, why don't you fiddle around with this idea and
see if you can turn it into something?' James was able to work this way
because he traveled, performed, and recorded with the same band, and it
was a band of a higher caliber than most r&b bands. That was his advantage. The musicians were in the studio contributing to this music, and
thinking about it on the bus every night, talking about the riffs. The whole
thing was very much an evolution, and records like 'Cold Sweat' were the

1949–52

Incarcerated for petty theft, young James Brown starts singing gospel with the Byrd family while on parole.

1955

James Brown impersonates Little Richard on a regional tour when Richard leaves Macon, Georgia, for national fame.

result. With 'Cold Sweat,' people were buying the album to get the whole seven-minute version, which had that spontaneity that was something unique to James Brown. 'Cold Sweat' was one of those moments where a whole segment of the community discovered a song at the same time and for that period of time, their whole life was dancing to this song."

James Brown, at the piano, taking his band through a "head" (spontaneous, unwritten) arrangement.

James Brown was born poorer than poor in a piney-woods shack outside Barnwell, South Carolina, and raised in an Augusta, Georgia, bordello. His birth year is generally given as 1933, though some sources say 1928; either way, he belongs chronologically to the generation of rock and roll's founding fathers. His education was spotty at best, and from 1949 to 1952 he was incarcerated for petty theft. On parole, he began singing gospel music in Toccoa, Georgia, with various members of the Byrd family; Bobby Byrd went on to serve as Brown's chief backing vocalist and onstage foil for much of the next quarter-century. In the mid-fifties, Brown and Byrd were still young men, and there were new worlds to conquer: "When we saw all the girls screaming for groups like Hank Ballard and the Midnighters," Bobby Byrd has recalled, "We thought, 'Oh, so *this* is what we want to do!'"

First they were a hard-working r&b cover band, a traveling jukebox; Byrd would emulate shouter Joe Turner, the other singers covered Lowell Fulson and Clyde McPhatter, and James Brown was a small, skinny approximation of Roy Brown—the originator of "Good Rockin Tonight" and, significantly, the first popular blues wailer to emphasize his gospel roots. But Roy Brown didn't move much onstage. As for James, "the dancing ya'll seen later on ain't nothing to what he used to do back then," according to Bobby Byrd. "James could stand flat-footed and flip over into a split. He'd tumble, too, over and over like in gymnastics."

When Little Richard left his home in Macon, Georgia, for the big time, in 1955, Brown and his group, now called the Flames, played the

1956

James Brown and his Flames do the gospel moan: "Please Please Please," on King Records' subsidiary label Federal, hits #5 on the r&b charts.

remainder of the dates Richard had booked on the regional touring circuit. Byrd: "This is when he really started hollering and screaming and dancing fit to burst. He just had to outdo Richard." That fall, James and the Flames worked up a raw gospel moan, "Please Please Please," which they went on to record for King Records in February 1956. It eventually rose to number five on the r&b charts. Although nine subsequent singles were commercial failures, another gospelish soul ballad, "Try Me," topped the r&b charts and made it into the pop top-fifty in 1958, proving that "Please Please Please" was no fluke.

The chart success of "Try Me" enabled Brown and his (now) Famous Flames vocal group to hire their first regular touring band. Soon they were good enough to carry the first half of the show on their own, playing churning instrumentals while teenagers indulged in their latest dance sensation, the Mashed Potatoes. King Records' owner, an old-school indie mogul named Syd Nathan who had made a fortune from country music and r&b, didn't take Brown's request that he record the band seriously. So Brown took his musicians into a Miami studio and recorded "(Do the) Mashed Potatoes" on his own. Issued by the tiny Dade label under the name Nat Kendrick (Brown's drummer) and the Swans, but with Brown's characteristic screams of encouragement abundantly audible, the record placed in the r&b top ten, building partly on the momentum of a once-localized dance craze that was now sweeping the country.

Syd Nathan should have learned his lesson, but when Brown wanted to release an album of his popular and incendiary stage show, recorded live at Harlem's Apollo Theater, the label head quietly put the project on the back burner. Only after Brown had recorded the string-drenched ballad "Prisoner of Love" (which went on to become a top-twenty *pop* hit) did Nathan reluctantly agree to release *Live at the Apollo*, which surprised

1958

Nine singles after his "beginner's luck" with "Please Please Please," James Brown releases the #1 r&b/#48 pop hit "Try Me."

1960

When King Records nixes Brown's idea to record with his touring band, the musicians cop a pseudonym to cut the dance hit "(Do the) Mashed Potatoes."

everyone by rising all the way to number two on the pop-album charts. With Motown gearing up its pop-crossover campaign to become "the Sound of Young America" and the grittier sound of southern soul just beginning to find its groove, Brown's brand of gospel-style excitement was the rawest sound around. His commercial breakthrough at this time suggests that a considerable number of white teenagers still craved the sort of no-holds-barred Dionysian frenzy that had been in short supply in the pop world since the heyday of Little Richard. On the pop charts of 1962–63, only the Isley Brothers' "Twist and Shout" and the Contours' "Do You Love Me" exuded a comparable ferocity.

It was at this point that Brown began to distance himself from the rest of the pack by embarking on the quest for the ultimate groove. His own outstanding abilities as a dancer, not to mention an early stint as the Flames' singing drummer, had given him a special feel for the music's rhythmic character, leading to early experiments with Latin rhythms ("Good Good Lovin'") and unusually accented shuffle-rhythm variations ("Night Train"). In 1964, King and Mercury Records' Smash subsidiary duked it out for the right to issue Brown's now self-produced recordings. Meanwhile, Brown worked with his band, including newcomers such as jazz-schooled arranger/saxophonist Nat Jones and the Parker brothers, Maceo (alto, tenor, and baritone sax) and Melvin (drums), on something more than a new groove—a new direction, a whole new ballgame. The popping "Out of Sight" was the prototype, with its sparsely textured cross-rhythms and emphatically repeated one-note horn riff. The full-fledged breakthrough came in early 1965, with "Papa's Got a Brand New Bag."

Like many other James Brown songs, "Bag" was fashioned out of an onstage improvisation involving singer and audience, and recorded in under an hour on the way to another show. But there was a new guitar

1964

Still struggling with the King company, Brown forms his own Fair Deal Productions and gives his next set of singles to the Mercury subsidiary Smash.

1965

King Records lose their year-long suit against Brown. The Godfather of Soul emerges from the fracas with complete artistic control of his career.

sound, a kind of metallic one-chord break figure similar to the horns' reiteration on "Out of Sight," played by a significant new recruit, the experienced blues guitarist Jimmy Nolen. It sounded something like "chanka-chanka-chank" and soon both Nolen and the percussive guitar style he developed with Brown acquired an onomatopoetic nickname: Chank. Nominally a lead guitarist, with a style rooted in T-Bone Walker and the Texas brand of blues, Nolen was actually playing a rhythm pattern—and so were the horns, the drums, and even the singer, "playing drums with his larynx," as Alan Leeds called it.

"Out of Sight" had been a hybrid, a song with (minimal) chord changes that gave way to a long one-chord vamp in the latter half of the record, like a Cuban band playing the song proper and then stretching out on a one-chord *son montuno.* "Suddenly," notes Leeds, "instead of the vamp being the tag or the end to the song, with 'Papa's Got a Brand New Bag' the vamp became the song itself, the whole song. What James and [arranger] Nat Jones did was throw away the traditional song structure, whether it was the Tin Pan Alley–song or the blues- or gospel-song structure, in order to focus on the rhythms. The bass, instead of doing a traditional kind of 'walking' accompaniment just to give the record bottom, it stayed in one place and became a focal point, a pulse, so it was acting more like a drum than a bass guitar. They got the guitarists doing the same thing, playing repetitive patterns. So the magic became something like putting a quilt together—taking all the rhythm patterns and weaving them together in such a magical way as to create this wonderful *feel* that's going to drive audiences crazy."

Audiences did "go crazy," making "Bag" one of Brown's biggest hits so far. Musicians were stunned. Alan Leeds remembers some of them complaining, "What is this? This isn't a real song, it's just this weird kind of vamp." Even Brown was surprised by what he had created. "It's a little

James Brown, executing some fancy steps with the Famous Flames, creating "this wonderful *feel* that's going to drive audiences crazy."

1964

"Papa's Got a Brand New Bag" reveals Brown's breakthrough to a new sound with the vinyl debut of guitarist Jimmy Nolen's metallic "chank."

1967

James Brown's landmark "Cold Sweat" electrifies the musical community.

beyond me right now," he told Leeds, then a disc jockey, when the song was still climbing the charts. "It's just *out there!* If you're thinking, 'Well, maybe this guy is crazy,' take any record off your stack and put it on your box, even a James Brown record, and you won't find one that sounds like this one. It's a new bag, just like I sang."

Now in a position to hire more and better musicians, Brown beefed up his horn section with jazz pros like trumpeter Waymon Reed and saxophonist Pee Wee Ellis. And he revamped his rhythm section, hiring no-nonsense rhythm guitarist Alphonso "Country" Kellum to chop away behind "Chank," plus *two* formidable drummers, John "Jabo" Starks and Clyde Stubblefield. "James was really tough on drummers and would wear them out," says Leeds. "Every few months you'd look and there'd be a different combination of drummers up there, each one as great as the next, but each with a different feel, a different flavor. He would have two or three different drummers on the road and in the studio, and their roles would change. There would be a lead drummer for each song who was basically playing the song as if he were the only drummer in the band. Then there would be a second drummer, who would be there for accents. Whoever had that secondary role on a given song watched James's feet or his hands, and every hand signal, every move of the foot demanded a rim shot or a kick-drum accent. The drummers were like the quarterbacks of this football team. And there was very little scripted. On a given night James might decide to move this way, move that way, and all of this demanded that the drummer *be on it.* In the mid-sixties, beginning with records like 'Out of Sight' and 'Papa's Got a Brand New Bag,' he started to take this kind of spontaneity that made him special onstage and translate that into the recording studio. He wanted to push the envelope, and thankfully he was in a recording situation that enabled him to do that."

1967–68

Meanwhile, back in Detroit: Norman Whitfield emerges as front-runner from Berry Gordy's pack of Motown writer-producers with not one, but two versions of his classic "I Heard It Through the Grapevine," by Gladys Knight and the Pips (1967) and Marvin Gaye (1968).

1967

Mixed-race/gender band Sly and The Family Stone, reinforces psychedelia's utopianism with James Brown's funk. Amen.

The next landmark recording was 1967's "Cold Sweat," which went even further than its predecessors in duplicating the vitality of Brown's live performances, and in making the play of razor-sharp polyrhythms the substance of the song. It was also the first of Brown's hits to include a brief drum solo, by the original "Funky Drummer," Clyde Stubblefield. Like most of Brown's hits, it was a first or second take. Like "Bag," it electrified the musical community. "'Cold Sweat' deeply affected the musicians I knew," says Jerry Wexler, who was then producing the likes of Aretha Franklin and Wilson Pickett. "It just freaked them out. For a time, no one could get a handle on what to do next."

What came next was the high tide of psychedelia and the counterculture, and a number of attempts to reconcile the hippie/head/anti-war sensibility with the feel of James Brown's funk. Out of San Francisco and nearby Oakland came Sly and the Family Stone, led by a former disc jockey and record producer (of the outstanding Bay Area folk-rock band the Beau Brummels, among others). His name was Sylvester Stewart, but the "superbad" character he played in his band's music, and eventually to his detriment in real life, was the name everyone knew him by: Sly Stone.

With the astonishing self-taught bassist Larry Graham contributing a busier, more percussive, and more heavily amplified version of the ostinato style developed by James Brown's bass man Bernard Odum, Sly and the Family Stone moved the bass even further into the foreground. Sly seemed to construe Brown's demolition of conventional song structures as a challenge to build fresh structures of his own amid the ruins. His songs incorporated sing-along chants, pop-style melodic hooks, and modular lyric sequences that scrambled the verse/chorus distinctions of traditional pop. His ingenious, mercurial arrangements played with constantly shifting voicings and instrumentation; in the course of a single song you were

Sylvester Stewart or Sly Stone? Whichever persona the multitalented guitarist-organist-writer-arranger-bandleader assumed, his music stretched rock and funk into fresh new grooves.

1968

"No matter how hard you try, you can't stop me now" is the point of "Message From a Black Man" and other upfront, topical gems like "Cloud Nine" and 1969's "War" and "Runaway Child, Running Wild," all crafted by Motown's Norman Whitfield for the Temptations.

likely to hear solo vocals, group harmonizing, voices without instruments, instruments without voices, rhythms shifting, dropping out, and returning with renewed emphasis, a sax-and-trumpet break, a guitar solo—almost anything. The plainspoken lyrics mixed it up with various social unmentionables—"Don't call me nigger, whitey/Don't call me whitey, nigger"—and often presented the band, which included whites and blacks, men and women, as a kind of microcosm of the ideal society—a society free of racism, sexism, and all other isms plaguing an acutely divisive age.

Rhythmically and in terms of "weaving" the groove, Sly and the Family Stone took their cues from Godfather James, though they soon perfected their own crisp, nervous, sometimes extravagantly syncopated variant. Meanwhile, at Motown, aggressive young producer Norman Whitfield was making rapid strides after producing both the Gladys Knight and Marvin Gaye versions of his soul classic "I Heard It Through the Grapevine." Given the supremely polished and popular Temptations to produce when Smokey Robinson moved on to other projects, Whitfield crafted a series of revolutionary singles that synthesized both the James Brown and Sly Stone versions of the funk.

For Motown, still essentially a pop label purveying the "Sound of Young America," the Whitfield/Temptations records were shockers. The 1968 "Cloud Nine" was a tale of inner-city drug addiction told, without moralizing, from the doper's point of view. "Runaway Child, Running Wild" deployed massive blocks of sound with sharply delineated polyrhythmic economy; as Whitfield later admitted, he was trying to "out-Sly Sly"—and it was working. "Don't Let the Joneses Get You Down" was a rolling, vicious tidal wave of guitar clang, chiming orchestra bells and Fender-Rhodes electric piano, hard cymbal smashes, and, at bottom, a *massive* funk groove. "Message from a Black Man," another hit from 1968, was message

The Temptations were sophisticated, high-stepping kings of the concert stage, as indicated by these shots of the "Temptation Walk" from a Motown publicity release (above and opposite).

1969

Look magazine hails James Brown as possibly "the most important black man in America."

1970

A strict disciplinarian as a bandleader, James Brown lets go most of his large, experienced band and hires a younger, hungrier crew he calls the J.B.'s.

funk that didn't mince words: "No matter how hard you try," went the determined refrain, "you can't stop me now." In 1969 and 1970 the Temptations protested "War" (a later version by Edwin Starr was the bigger hit) and partied down at the "Psychedelic Shack," even though the world outside seemed to be nothing but a "Ball of Confusion." The fragmentation of the black family was addressed in "Papa Was a Rolling Stone," but there was still time for bittersweet romance in "Just My Imagination (Running Away with Me)," an indelible ballad with Eddie Kendricks's warm and tender falsetto front and center. The Whitfield/Temptations collaborations of 1967–72 are among rock and roll's most consistently creative and adventuresome bodies of work. If they are not widely accepted as such, it's partly because critics and fans have generally found it easier to relate to individual singer-songwriters than to vocal groups and producers— individuals such as the Temptations' fellow Motown artists Stevie Wonder and Marvin Gaye.

The winds of change were blowing at Motown. In 1971, both Wonder and Gaye went to the wall with company founder Berry Gordy and emerged with their artistic freedom. No longer would they be subject to the dictates and whims of Motown's staff producers, writers, and arrangers; now they would chart their own courses. Wonder, who turned twenty-one in 1971, renegotiated his recording contract and immediately plowed most of his advance into a state-of-the-art home studio. Though he had been making hit records since 1963, Wonder belonged to a younger generation than the other Motown singers. He enjoyed keeping abreast of the latest wrinkles in jazz, in rock, and in recording techniques and electronics. He began working at home with engineers and coproducers Robert Margouleff and Malcolm Cecil, whose special expertise was in electronically generated sounds and in programming that dauntingly complex new instrument, the

The Temps were also major players in the funk revolution of the seventies, largely thanks to their writer-producer, Norman Whitfield.

247

1971

Two of the J.B.'s, the Collins brothers, Phelps (a.k.a. Catfish) and William (a.k.a. Bootsy) exit the James Brown band after helping forge "the new super-heavy funk," heard in classics such as "Get Up (I Feel Like Being a) Sex Machine."

Stevie Wonder, no longer "Little" Stevie, reinvented himself and his music in the early seventies, combining the latest in synthesizer and studio technology with lyrics of the spirit and the street.

synthesizer. His aim was to make all the music himself, principally with drums and percussion, which he played more than adequately, and an ever-growing array of keyboards and electronics. Rhythmically, his music was shaped by funk, which by the early seventies was a way of dealing with rhythm that no popular artist could ignore. At the same time, he was anticipating a pop-music future in which "one-man bands" would become as common as more traditional lineups—the world of electro-funk and electro-pop in which we now live. Many listeners first encountered this world by way of Wonder's albums *Music of My Mind, Talking Book* (both 1972), and most strikingly, *Innervisions* (1973), which addressed both spiritual values ("Higher Ground") and street realities ("Living for the City").

Wonder's labelmate Marvin Gaye had long possessed one of music's most supple and sophisticated voices. In 1970, he listened with a mounting sense of anger and outrage to his brother's war stories from Vietnam, and took a long, hard look around at the crumbling buildings, splintering families, drug addiction, and desolation in Detroit's riot-scarred inner city. When Al Cleveland and Renaldo "Obie" Benson of the Four Tops brought him a partly completed new topical song, something clicked for Marvin Gaye, who had grown increasingly dissatisfied with Motown's emphasis on teenage love songs but was feeling creatively blocked in terms of his own direction. The song was "What's Going On," and it was taking Gaye where he wanted to go, into fresh musical territory, while remaining firmly anchored in the community and compassion of the black church, the fervor of the preacher, the participation of the congregation. This was a world Gaye knew well, the world of his preacher father and his church upbringing.

While Berry Gordy, Smokey Robinson, and much of the Motown staff were leaving grimy, dangerous Detroit behind for what they hoped

1971

Funkmeister George Clinton snaps up the Collins brothers and pursues a mission of "saving dance music from the blahs."

1971

A Motown star since age ten, Stevie Wonder turns twenty-one and gains control of his $1 million trust·fund, investing in a state- of-the-art home recording studio and founding Taurus Productions.

would be fun in the southern California sun, Gaye prepared to paint his masterpiece, gathering some of the most practiced exponents of the "Motown sound" to help him create the last great Motown music made in Detroit. As tenor saxophone soloist, weaving gritty, rasping exclamations into the music's richly layered textures, Gaye chose Wild Bill Moore, whose "We're Gonna Rock, We're Gonna Roll" had foretold the rocking future back in 1947. The other horns, guitars, vibes, and percussion were all handled by Motown stalwarts, and on bass was the great James Jamerson, playing with astonishing invention and feeling. Gordy was afraid to release the album, but Gaye insisted, and once it hit the streets, there could be no doubt that he had an enormous hit on his hands, as well as a thematically coherent "concept album" the critics would never tire of praising.

What's Going On draws elements of funk rhythm, jazz improvisation, gospel feel, and a sense of smoldering passion into its intricate, compelling skein. Just when white rockers in droves were turning away from the dance floor to make "art" music, designed for serious listening, Gaye came up with a record that made you think, feel, and *move*—on the dance floor, in the streets, between the sheets. Vietnam, dangers nuclear and ecological, unemployment, drugs, poverty, and spirituality were the subjects; the message was love. It wasn't until *Let's Get It On* (1973) that Gaye would turn to the sexual revolution, a subject he addressed with his customary outspokenness. Like James Brown, Norman Whitfield, Sly Stone, and Stevie Wonder, Marvin Gaye saw "pushing the envelope" as both a privilege and a duty: This was what being an artist was all about.

Back in the James Brown camp, the coming of the seventies had been a time of turmoil. His "classic sixties band" knew they were the best in the business—"When these guys took the stage at the Apollo, they just looked like major leaguers," says Alan Leeds. "They carried themselves with that

Marvin Gaye pioneered the funk concept album and opened black pop to social protest with his groundbreaking *What's Going On*, but he was a love man at heart, as his subsequent albums *Let's Get It On* and *I Want You* reaffirmed.

1971

Stevie Wonder negotiates
a precedent-shattering new
contract with Motown;
while the company contin-
ues to distribute his
records, Wonder now
controls his publishing
and enjoys artistic auto-
nomy as well as a far
higher royalty rate.

strut somebody has when they're on a championship team." But Brown was still a stern disciplinarian, fining individual musicians for missing a cue, playing a wrong note, or showing up for the gig with unshined shoes, and his champs were growing resentful—especially when, as they saw it, he was tight-fisted about paying them. They organized, rebelled, delivered an ulti-matum, and in March 1970, Brown called their bluff. He sent Bobby Byrd to Cincinnati in his Lear jet to fetch a group of younger musicians, many of them still teenagers, who had been playing the occasional recording session and backing various Brown-produced performers on the road. When his regular band showed up for work that night, demanding action on their ultimatum, Brown called in his replacements, and most of the veterans walked. Only Byrd and drummer "Jabo" Starks remained loyal.

Among the teenage musicians who suddenly found themselves play-ing behind the Godfather of Soul were the two Collins brothers, Phelps (a.k.a. Catfish), a guitarist, and William (a.k.a. Bootsy), a bassist. The two slotted easily into the rhythm section, with Byrd on organ and Starks on drums, and on April 25 they were in the studio together, no longer the James Brown Orchestra but simply the J.B.'s.

"James had sensed their strengths and their weaknesses and had begun to rearrange his music accordingly," Leeds recalls. "The old band had been like the horn band of all time, and the weakest part of the new band was the horn players. So unlike his previous bands, where the horns had been very prominent, the new band focused almost entirely on the rhythm section. The horns were almost like an afterthought, playing simplified ver-sions of some of the old band's riffs. Well, about a month into the tenure of Bootsy and the others, I heard them doing one of the older tunes, 'Give It Up or Turnit a Loose,' and I was stunned because the arrangement was so radically different—there were new guitar licks, and the overall feel had

Despite Motown's initial fears for *What's Going On,* three of the lp's nine songs—"What's Going On," "Mercy Mercy Me," and "Inner City Blues"— hit the top 10 on the r&b *and* pop charts.

changed. After the show James said, 'Oh, that's my new song. Just wait until we go to Nashville tomorrow, you'll see.'

"The next night, after the show in Nashville, there was a recording session scheduled, and these kids were *hyped!* They were doing a record with the Godfather, this was their goal in life. James and Bobby Byrd had written out some lyrics in the dressing room, using the back of one of the window cards that advertised the shows and a felt-tip pen. I looked, and it said something about sex this, sex that. It was obvious that lyrically this was a spontaneous idea, and once the band started warming up, what I was hearing was 'Give It Up or Turnit a Loose' the way they'd played it the night before. That's how a lot of the songs evolved. They might change a song's guitar riff one week, change the horn riffs a month later, get a different feel from a different drummer, so that it turned into this whole other thing. Once you put new words to it, you had a new hit record."

"Get Up I Feel like Being a Sex Machine" was more than "Give It Up" with a face-lift. This was a new, superheavy funk, and the key player was Bootsy, whose goofy grin and what-me-worry impishness were among the coping mechanisms of a powerfully original musical mind. Funk bass playing, as exemplified by James Jamerson and the busier, more showy Larry Graham was a virtuoso style, given to driving but fluid lines as melodic as those of any lead guitarist. Bootsy Collins took the bass back to the basement, filling out the music's bottom with a resonant sonic boom and dropping devastating bass-drumlike accents in all the right places. Bootsy had truly taken to heart Brown's practice of accenting "on the one," which reversed the rhythmic priorities that had long been standard in jazz, rock, and r&b—traditionally music with accents on the backbeat, on two and four. For Bootsy, as for his future employer and collaborator George Clinton, "the one" was not just where the accent went but a concept with

1971

Kenny Gamble and Leon Huff form their own record label, Philadelphia International. Within months, the black-owned independent sells over ten million records, with such crossover hits as Billy Paul's "Me and Mrs. Jones" and the O'Jays' "Backstabbers."

spiritual, perhaps metaphysical, dimensions. Cuban musicians had developed similar ideas about the *clave* pattern. For Bootsy, the inner subtleties of the "one" were best appreciated under the influence of LSD, though he did become momentarily discomfited on at least one such occasion when the bass he was playing seemed to be turning into a snake—or was it just melting a bit?

While with James Brown, Bootsy, Catfish, and company played on a series of singles that once again had the effect of virtually redefining the funk: "Super Bad," "Talking Loud and Saying Nothing," "Get Up, Get into It, Get Involved," "Soul Power." Brown seemed to be relaxing; he dropped his system of fines and moderated his insistence on spit and polish. But the Collins brothers in particular were young, spirited, and sometimes spaced, and after a spring 1971 European tour, the Godfather came to a parting of the ways with Bootsy and Phelps. They were snapped up by a bandleader who had been around the block a few times himself, singing doo-wop in New Jersey, recording with the Parliaments ("a poor man's Temptations") at Motown. His name was George Clinton, and while his ambition and leadership qualities were perhaps comparable to James Brown's, his personal style was something else. If Bootsy was taking some weird new drug, George didn't necessarily want him to stop; he wanted to try some himself.

And so, stumbling out of middle America in mile-high Afros, platform shoes, glam-rock glitter, and oversized sunglasses came Parliament-Funkadelic, on a mission ringleader George Clinton described, perhaps ingenuously, as "saving dance music from the blahs." Building on the Collins brothers' heavy-funk base, Clinton added screaming lead guitar in the Jimi Hendrix mode (most notably by Eddie "Maggot Brain" Hazel and Michael Hampton), the Horny Horns (more ex-J.B.'s mainstays, often including trombonist Fred Wesley and funk saxophone's reigning master,

Parliament-Funkadelic's mastermind George Clinton urges his fans, the Funkateers, to "tear the roof off the sucker!"

1972

"Blaxploitation" cinema transposes the badlands of the Old West for the streets of the inner city and provides a new forum—the soundtrack album—for some highly significant music; e.g., Curtis Mayfield's *Superfly,* Isaac Hayes's *Shaft,* and Marvin Gaye's *Trouble Man.*

Maceo Parker), backup singers, dancers—and lots of amplifiers. Touring with white rock groups, including the Stooges, in their early years, P-Funk incorporated all the volume a Marshall stack could crank out, all the onstage brinksmanship an Iggy Pop could muster, and all the drugs in the rocker's pharmacopoeia. A brief dalliance with the mysterious and sinister Process Church of the Final Judgment, a group author Ed Sanders linked circumstantially to the Manson murders, helped inspire such Funkadelic dystopias as *Maggot Brain* and *America Eats Its Young.* Gradually, Clinton developed a more positive mythology involving outer space, black tribalism, and the whole-system integrity of the funk itself. "If you *fake* the funk," warned Clinton, "your nose will grow."

P-Funk never quite realized Clinton's ambition to become "the black Beatles." Their closest rivals in what we might call arena funk were Earth, Wind and Fire, another powerful, big band but one more often concerned with being uplifting than with getting down. To many observers, E.W.F. were playing the "black Beatles" to P-Funk's black Rolling Stones. But while black radio stations jumped all over E.W.F.'s finely crafted pop singles, they largely ignored P-Funk because their songs were too long, their use of rock guitars and their concept albums too "white." White radio wouldn't play them for the usual reason: They were black. Nevertheless, by 1976, P-Funk had hired a top stage designer and put together an elaborate world tour, the Mothership Connection, highlighted by the landing of a most impressive flying saucer from which Clinton would emerge, sometimes dressed to the nines, sometimes stark naked. The show would end, several hours later, with the audience wrung dry by the relentlessly churning grooves but still alive enough to shout along with the band's chants of "Shit! Goddam! Get off your ass and jam!"; "Tear the roof off the sucker!"; and "We're gonna turn this mother out!" Amid the general revelry, Clinton's

1976
Afro wigs and platform
shoes go into orbit with
George Clinton and P-
Funk's elaborate world
tour, the Mothership
Connection.

1977
NYC's Studio 54, on the
site of an abandoned
opera house on West 54th
Street in Manhattan, is the
apogee of seventies disco
display.

messages of self-determination and resistance to the political and cultural status quo were getting through. "Free your mind," he prophesied, "and your ass will follow."

Hard funk such as James Brown or P-Funk was inherently radical: It transformed a music that had *emphasized* the groove and the message into a music that was *all* groove and message. Many black musicians and entertainers were unwilling to go that far musically, but in the seventies even the black pop mainstream was influenced by funk's exaltation of message. Motown, and especially Norman Whitfield's productions, had shown the way. They were heavily orchestrated, with strings, brass, voices, and large rhythm sections, but if you stripped all that away, the grooves were strong, incisive, and funky. They favored songs with memorable melodic "hooks" and rich, pretty harmonies; the lyrics might be inspirational or despairing, but they addressed real issues and didn't pull their punches.

Beginning around 1972, there was a new and unexpected outlet for music of this kind in the "blaxploitation" cinema. Though many of these films had conventional gangster or even western plot lines, they offered a forum for some highly significant music. Curtis Mayfield, whose songwriting and recordings with the Impressions had both chronicled and cheered on the civil rights activism of the sixties, applied his keen eye, warmth, and empathy to the tale of an inner-city cocaine dealer known as *Superfly;* his soundtrack album is one of the masterworks of seventies funk, comparable to *What's Going On* and to Sly's *There's a Riot Goin' On* in both impact and influence. Isaac Hayes's *Shaft* was no match for *Superfly* in the lyric department but was equally original and perhaps equally influential musically. The sophisticated orchestral funk of Marvin Gaye's *Trouble Man,* the supple rhythms and endearingly cheesy wah-wah guitars on Bobby Womack's *Across 110th Street,* and the funk cooked up by James Brown and Fred

Curtis Mayfield, who per-
fected an influential chop-
rhythm guitar style in his
sixties work with the
Impressions, stayed in the
forefront of seventies funk
with hits like *Superfly*.

1977

Singer/drummer Earl Young of Philadelphia International's rhythm section, M.F.S.B., doubles as frontman for the Trammps, who reach #1 with their blistering "Disco Inferno." The Philly Sound and Young's drumming figure as original sources for a number of disco dance grooves.

Wesley for *Black Caesar* and *Slaughter's Big Rip-Off* are additional testaments to the fecundity of the blaxploitation genre. At the other end of the spectrum, and in a class by themselves, are the profane, violent, streetwise, and frequently hilarious films of Rudy Ray Moore, who brought black tale telling and insult games from the street corner and the prison to the screen as the indestructible pimp/hero *Dolemite*. Moore has been showing up in rap and hip-hop videos in the 1990s, a recognition that his prison-style "toasting" (a tradition of imaginatively obscene rhyming and tale telling) was one of the principal sources for the rap tradition, especially in its "gangsta" manifestations. And, of course, seventies funk in general has been sampled to death in rap, with James Brown and George Clinton locked in a race to become the most-sampled recording artists of all time.

Message and groove also played a central role in the music of Kenny Gamble and Leon Huff's Philadelphia International Records, a black-owned company that came close to matching Motown's success during its seventies heyday. Hits produced by Gamble, Huff, and/or their frequent associate Thom Bell could be light and sugary, like the Intruders, Delfonics, and Stylistics. Or they could have a touch more grit, like Billy Paul's slipping-around opus "Me and Mrs. Jones" or Harold Melvin and the Blue Notes' "Bad Luck," featuring churchy lead singer Teddy Pendergrass. Drawing on an exceptionally diverse pool of musicians—jazzmen, soul men, classical violinists, big-band brass players—and deploying instruments seldom heard in black pop—French horn, flügelhorn, bass trombone, harp, timpani—Gamble and Huff and their arrangers fashioned a lush, glossy, almost symphonic brand of funk-based dance music. When they worked with the O'Jays, however, their priorities shifted somewhat.

The O'Jays had started as a fifties doo-wop group out of Canton, Ohio, and recorded for a variety of labels before everything came together

The O'Jays, spokesmen for songwriter-producers Gamble and Huff, put the grit in the Philadelphia sound with "Back Stabbers" and "Love Train."

1983

After a bitter divorce, depression, bankruptcy, a lawsuit brought by the IRS, suicide attempts, and European exile, Marvin Gaye reaches a provisional settlement with the feds for $2 million and comes back home to tour behind the success of his "come-back" hit "Sexual Healing."

for them at Philly International in 1972. Their voices were heavier, grainier, more hard-edged than those of the other P.I. singers, and their lead, Eddie Levert, was a gospel-shouter turned soul man who really knew how to drive a lyric home. Gamble and Huff entrusted their most heartfelt message songs to the O'Jays, some of them pleas for peace and brotherhood ("Love Train," "Put Your Hands Together"), others depictions and analyses of family and community concerns ("Survival," "For the Love of Money," "Livin' for the Weekend"). There were full-blown concept albums, most notably *Ship Ahoy,* which followed a group of Africans across the Atlantic in the hold of a slave ship and into servitude in the American South. But the *pièce de résistance* was *Back Stabbers.*

Thom Bell, who usually worked with sweet, high voices, displayed all his brilliance as an arranger on "Back Stabbers" and the thematically related "992 Arguments," both furious blasts of driving dance music with angry, outspoken lyrics and instrumental passages that seamlessly shifted their focus, from the chopping rhythm and lead guitars to the percussion section, from the strings and horns to the explosive, house-rocking piano glissandos of Leon Huff, formerly a session man for Leiber and Stoller and Phil Spector. On these and other up-tempo workouts, the P.I. rhythm section was anchored by bassist Ronnie Baker, and by drummer Earl Young, who doubled as vocalist and leader of the Trammps—yes, the perpetrators of "Disco Inferno." In fact, many of the Philadelphia musicians credit Young's drumming on tracks like "Back Stabbers" as the original source of the particular dance grooves popularized, and repeated *ad nauseam,* during the era of "Disco Fever."

"For us, the songs dictated the beat," says Kenny Gamble. "Earl knew how to work with producers, he let them get the best out of him creatively, and the basic beat we came up with was a kind of gospel/blues/jazz feel on

1984

Beset with tour problems ranging from stage fright, sore throats, and chemical excess to a rash of mysterious death threats, Marvin Gaye is fatally shot by his father, the Reverend Marvin Gaye, Sr., on April Fool's Day.

the sock cymbal and a straight 4/4 feel on the drum. We never set out consciously to do a disco record, but we set out to do funky dance records." To which Leon Huff adds, "We did hang out in the discos sometimes; we loved to see those people dance off of our music. The music had to be up music. Energy, people wanted energy." Gamble: "And at Philly International, the music did have a lot of energy, a *lot*." Huff: "Yeah, there's a house on fire in those records."

Let it burn, baby, let it burn!

The New York Dolls on tour, dressed for the night and blinded by the light; L to R, vocalist David Johansen, guitarist Johnny Thunders, guitarist Sylvain Sylvain, drummer Jerry Nolan, and bassist Arthur Kane.

Blank
Generation

"*Garage bands became more important in the early seventies because rock and roll had gotten very complicated. Progressive rock was an adult medium; instrumental prowess and musicianship were the driving force. Even though I like a lot of that stuff, something was lacking: the fact that you could learn to play three chords and get up onstage within a week. That spark, that desire, that's the kind of thing that makes rock and roll tick. I think that's why it began in the first place: It's a music for the person who needs to make music.*"

Lenny Kaye, Patti Smith Group

"*History is a form of sentimentality. Like the content of television shows. Television is abstract. It's a joke. History is a joke. Television and history are the centers of nothing. They are auras, like hair, available for styling twenty-four hours a day.*"

Richard Hell, from "The Voidoid" (1973)

"*It was maybe a sheer love of sound that was behind it all . . . a particular sound, yes, when blending guitars together, mostly knowing the effect we wanted to have on ourselves and thus hopefully on an audience, without caring to name that effect . . . just a certain sound which could be dense or sparse, but the tone would be the same. The intention was not so intentional if you catch my drift. . . . my elbow's getting itchy, let's talk about something else.*"

Tom Verlaine, Television

Guitarists Tom Verlaine, center, and Richard Lloyd of Television, who unwittingly helped launch the post-Dolls wave of New York underground rock when they began gigging at CBGB early in 1974.

"That line about 'no future,' it's prophetic: You will have no future if you don't make one for yourself, it's as simple as that. If you accept the forms that be, then you're doomed to your own ultimate blandness. . . . Anyone can be nice and sing pleasant ditties, and there's much more to life than that, there's the other side. Some call it the darker side; I don't think so. I think it's more fun than that."

John Lydon, a.k.a. Johnny Rotten, the Sex Pistols

"A lot of people get it completely wrong. They say, 'Okay, we're going to do a Sex Pistols song.' And they play it three times faster than the actual song was. But that's where the power is—when it's slowed down, when it's paced. Everyone thinks punk has got to be fast and stupid. They get it all wrong."

Steve Jones, the Sex Pistols

"The successful implementation of a revolution requires two things: thinkers and thugs. Individually, these groups are powerless. But put them together, and you've got a mighty fighting machine: The thinkers set the agenda and the thugs put in the boot." These words come not from a treatise on political insurgency but from an article devoted to punk rock in the January 1995 *Guitar World* magazine. "Luckily," author Alan di Perna continues, "the primordial New York punk scene was blessed with its share of both species." Included among the former are Patti Smith, Television, Richard Hell, and maverick Ohioans Pere Ubu. Among the latter: the Ramones, Johnny Thunders's Heartbreakers, and Cleveland's Dead Boys. All these performers and bands anticipated and influenced the more flamboyant (and commercially successful) British punk movement exemplified by the Sex Pistols and the Clash.

1967
Tom Miller and Richard
Meyers move to New York
to become poets; as Tom
Verlaine and Richard Hell,
they become the vanguard
of NYC punk rock.

1967
Like fellow punks-to-be
Tom Verlaine and Richard
Hell, Patti Smith arrives
in New York City as an
aspiring poet.

Rock and roll has always had a "punk" underground of sorts. In the fifties, there were rockabilly wild men who played hard and fast, leaving a trail of pandemonium and wreckage behind them; their crazed, almost anarchic recordings made "Heartbreak Hotel" sound like Mozart—well, maybe not quite *that* bad. Memphis's Sun label had Billy Lee Riley, who literally used to hang from the rafters, screaming into a microphone while his band, the Little Green Men (later the backbone of the Sun session crew), pounded out that jungle beat. And Sun had Sonny Burgess, who wore flaming red suits, socks, and shoes, with guitar and hair to match. Burgess fronted a band so drunkenly fractious that they made even Riley's crew sound polished; a lone trumpeter cut through the sizzling, manic guitars with bugle calls and similar non sequiturs while Burgess howled about his "red-headed woman, meanest thing I know." Gene Vincent, with his black leather jacket, his sneer, and his frenzied, amphetamine-stoked stage shows, was a fifties punk who greatly influenced the wilder side of John Lennon. Another was Eddie Cochran, whose "Summertime Blues" and "C'mon Everybody" were teenage anthems that demanded only rudimentary guitar skills, and were widely covered by both garage bands and pros like the Who in subsequent decades.

We have already met most of punk's sixties antecedents: the Velvet Underground, the MC5, and especially Iggy Pop and the Stooges. "There was a superhigh energy with the Stooges," says guitarist Johnny Ramone. "You could see that they were able to play true rock and roll without having to play like Jimmy Page or Jeff Beck. People started overindulging with long guitar solos in the late sixties, and when you watched somebody like Beck or Hendrix, you felt like you'd have to practice for twenty years to be able to play those songs. We needed people like that, but we also needed people who were able to just play and be song-oriented and sound great,

1969

The Wailers begin a three-year association with the visionary Jamaican producer Lee Perry, who emphasizes Bob Marley's lead vocals and introduces

the Wailers vocal group to their definitive rhythm section—brothers Aston ("Family Man") and drummer Carlton Barrett.

1971

Jonathan Richman assembles Modern Lovers, with future Talking Head Jerry Harrison, future Cars drummer David Robinson, and Ernie Brooks.

people who play real rock and roll." Adds Richard Hell, "With the Stooges, and with those kind of bands like the Seeds, the Standells, and ? and the Mysterians, it was just this noisy rage and anger that didn't have anything to do with finesse. It was about energy, and fuck the adults."

In the late sixties, the entire *middle* had dropped out of the American rock and roll economy. Bands that had been playing dance-concerts in movie-theater-size venues like San Francisco's Fillmore ballroom and New York's Fillmore East were becoming so popular in the period immediately following the massive Woodstock festival that ballrooms and theaters were no longer big enough to accommodate their fans. They began demanding bigger and bigger fees, and moved on to the arenas and stadiums when the smaller halls could no longer afford them. Within a year or two, rampant closings reduced what had been a coast-to-coast network of halls to a few proud survivors such as the original Fillmore—and even that hall's days were numbered. More experimental bands that had acquired invaluable experience and exposure opening for bigger names in the ballrooms and theaters went back to the small clubs, if they could find any. "Name-brand" rock settled into the arena and stadium circuit; in order to reach the fans in the cheap seats, concert presentations grew more and more elaborate. The band members might look like ants from back there, the sound might be tinny and harsh or a distant, distorted rumble, but with smoke bombs going off, spotlights raking the audience, laser displays, immense stage sets, and outsized props at least there was something to see. Meanwhile, the musicians themselves grew increasingly wealthy, with lifestyles far removed from that of the average rock and roll fan.

"We were all pretty disgusted with what was going on in rock and roll when we started the band in 1974," says lead singer Joey of the Ramones. "What was real popular in those days was disco and corporate rock. We

Lead vocalist Joey encourages the Ramones' idealized audience of mutants, mental cases, pinheads, and punk rockers in a buzz saw–style sing-along at demolition-derby tempo.

1972

Jonathan Richman and the Modern Lovers record demos in California with Velvet Underground cofounder John Cale producing.

1972

The New York Dolls, dressed to kill in lipstick and combat boots, begin playing their scrappy glam-punk at Manhattan's Mercer Arts Center.

were disenchanted with the state of radio, which had also become very corporate; nothing was how it used to be. There was no excitement in the music anymore, no fun or color or character or personality. Everything was totally superficial, prefabricated. Spirit was a thing of the past." Rock, it seems, was having an identity crisis.

It was time for somebody with guts to reassert the primacy of feel and heart over technique and spectacle. The Stooges had pointed the way: acquiring "chops," the musician's term for instrumental technique, was not the point. "Usually we got up there and jammed one riff and built into an energy freak-out," says Stooges guitarist Ron Asheton, "until finally we'd broken a guitar, or one of my hands would be twice as big as the other and my guitar would be covered in blood." As for Iggy himself, MC5 manager John Sinclair had witnessed an early Stooges performance and reflected, "Wow, this guy will stop at nothing! This isn't just a show—he's out of his mind! . . . Iggy had gone beyond performance—to the point where it really was some kind of psychodrama. It exceeded conventional theater. He might do *anything*."

Already, by the early seventies, harbingers of punk to come were beginning to surface here and there. In Boston, a fanatical follower of the Velvet Underground and the Stooges, Jonathan Richman, would "stalk through the parks of Cambridge, declaiming his songs to anyone within earshot, yelling things like, 'I'm not a hippie! I'm not stoned!'" according to observer Peter Laughner. In 1971, Richman started the Modern Lovers with organist Jerry Harrison (later a Talking Head), drummer Dave Robinson (later a Car), and bassist Ernie Brooks (who would play with several subsequent groups, among them New York's adventurous Necessaries). Richman wore his hair short and was outspokenly opposed to the drugs and hedonism of the period; one of his early songs was the declaration "I'm Straight."

1973

The New York Dolls sign
with Mercury and record
their first and only official
albums, *The New York
Dolls* and *Too Much
Too Soon.*

1973

The Dolls perform in
London, lose their original
drummer Billy Murcia, and
attract the gimlet-eyed
attention of bondage-
clothier Malcolm McLaren.

The music was not so straight; Richman loved the Velvets and the Stooges for their music, if not their lifestyles, and the Modern Lovers drew on the work of both these groups, to the extent that Richman would write, in the album notes for *The Original Modern Lovers,* "If it weren't for [Iggy] and Lou Reed this record wouldn't have existed." When they set out for California in order to cut demos for the album, in 1972, Richman's first choice as producer was former Velvet John Cale. The resulting recordings boasted compressed, ingenious songs like "Roadrunner" and "Pablo Picasso" ("nobody ever called Pablo Picasso an asshole") and droning, stripped-down arrangements with abundant fuzz and distortion. The time was not right; the original band broke up in 1974, some two years before their Cale-produced demos finally surfaced in album form.

Cleveland seems an unlikely hotspot for early protopunk activity, but the Velvets and the Stooges played there frequently, and left a lasting impact. (It's tempting to see these two bands as a self-contained revolution, with the Velvets the thinkers and the Stooges the thugs. But there was method, and an eclectic musical vision, behind the Stooges' madness, and the Velvets could sound supremely thuggish when they chose to.) Cleveland's early-seventies rock avant-garde included the Electric Eels, the Mirrors (with future *Psychotronic* magazine trash-film theorist Michael Weldon on drums), and Rocket from the Tombs. None of these groups got far enough to make albums at the time, but Cleveland's early purveyors of "semipopular music" (Robert Christgau's term) were among the first to adopt the punk D.I.Y. ethos—Do It Yourself. Two of the principals in Rocket from the Tombs, guitarist Peter Laughner and vocalist David Thomas, went on to form Pere Ubu, injecting a healthy dose of Captain Beefheart's mutant blues strains into their Velvets/Stooges/glitter influences. (Beefheart is another sixties renegade whose influence can be

1973

Ten years after his earliest recordings with the Wailers, Bob Marley skims the best of his song catalog for the stellar one-two punch of *Catch a Fire* and *Burnin',* albums programmed by Marley and producer Chris Blackwell with the international rock audience in mind.

1973

Original Wailers Peter Tosh and Bunny Wailer (née Livingston) leave the group to Bob Marley in order to pursue solo careers.

detected in a broad range of punk and new-wave rock from the seventies and eighties.)

Pere Ubu started their own Hearthan label in 1975 and issued a series of self-produced singles that were to have immense appeal among some of the more experimental British punkers, such as Wire and Magazine. Ubu itself would grow increasingly challenging and abstract after guitarist/vocalist Laughner's departure in spring 1976. (Laughner's subsequent activities included briefly replacing second guitarist Richard Lloyd in Television; he died of liver failure in 1977.) But the Ubu lineup that made the Hearthan singles of 1975–76 achieved an admirable balancing act between punk's cerebral and brutalist extremes. "Final Solution," for example, superimposed whirring chopper-blade synthesizer and a noisy, raggedly majestic Laughner guitar lead over a stop-time tune freely "adapted" from Eddie Cochran's "Summertime Blues." The lyrics were cleverly twisted teenage-wasteland psychodrama: "The girls won't touch me 'cause I got a misdirection/And livin' at night isn't helping my complexion." Ironically, some of the most striking songs Laughner and David Thomas had a hand in during the mid-seventies—"Sonic Reducer," "Ain't It Fun" ("... when you *know* that you're gonna die young")—surfaced in 1977–78 on records by the Dead Boys (whose guitarist had played alongside the two Ubu main men in Rocket from the Tombs). The Dead Boys are often credited/blamed with turning the New York punk sound more toward heavy metal and the unrelenting "loud fast rules" of hard core; their role in "popularizing" lyrics by Laughner and Thomas, who were certainly thinkers rather than thugs, should warn us against taking such reductionist theories too seriously. Making a useful distinction is not the same thing as telling the whole story.

And the punk-rock story begins, for all practical purposes, in New York City. There, in scruffy downtown venues such as the Mercer Arts

Vocalist-songwriters David Thomas, left, and Peter Laughner were founders of Pere Ubu, Cleveland, Ohio's protopunk trailblazers: "Buy me a ticket to the Sonic Reduction."

1973

Tom Verlaine teaches his poet buddy Richard Hell to play bass, rounds out the trio with drummer Billy Ficca; they record demos as the Neon Boys.

1974

The Neon Boys add Richard Lloyd to their line-up and begin residency at CBGB, a seedy bar on New York's Bowery; they adopt a new moniker, Television.

Center and the Bowery bar CBGB, enough musicians found common ground in their dissatisfaction with the state of rock and roll to do something about it, transforming a gaggle of alienated individuals into a full-blown movement. Of course, that isn't how it seemed at the time; in rock and roll, movements that announce their intentions beforehand tend to be manufactured, "hypes" in biz-speak, rather than musical situations that develop organically, in response to genuine needs. What's different about New York is that the music business and the music press are centered there. Even the "underground" draws attention from these quarters, sometimes to its advantage, sometimes not.

The New York Dolls were mostly former teenage gang members from Brooklyn who chose guitars over zip guns but carried some of their gang-bred values—banding together to oppose social regimentation, us against the world, baby, D.T.K. (Down To Kill)—to rock and roll. Their Staten Island–bred singer, David Johansen, did not share this background, but he had more musical experience than the others, having sung in various r&b-oriented cover bands since age fifteen. That background was just fine with Dolls lead guitarist Johnny Thunders (formerly Johnny Volume, originally John Anthony Gezale Jr.), whose taste ran to sixties garage-rock, early Stones and Yardbirds, and gritty r&b and doo-wop singles by the likes of Bo Diddley, Screaming Jay Hawkins, the Contours, and the Jayhawks/Cadets of "Stranded in the Jungle" fame. The Dolls rehearsed nights in a bicycle shop on Manhattan's Upper West Side; their first gig was filling in for a no-show band at a Christmas party in the welfare hotel across the street. For their first *official* gig, at Times Square's seedy Hotel Diplomat the following March, they decided to dress up—in lipstick and powder, cellophane tutus, feather boas, and fishnet stockings, with or without combat boots.

This affectation of gender-bending—for none of the Dolls claimed

CBGB, birthplace of punk rock and Holy Shrine of the Big Beat, the Bad Attitude, and the Sonic Guitar.

1974

Four dropout musicians in Queens, New York, form a band and adopt a common surname, becoming the Ramones.

1974

The Modern Lovers disband, several years before their Velvet Underground-inspired protopunk begins to attract an audience.

to be gay—constituted an early American response to the British glam-rock movement. In Britain at the time, glam was largely considered teeny-bopper music, disposable trash. Its leading practitioners—David Bowie, Slade, Marc Bolan's T. Rex—favored short, basic, raunchy songs built around incisive rhythm guitar riffs; solos, elaborate arrangements, jamming, and other "progressive" rock standbys were not to be tolerated. The glam-rockers were giving rock and roll back to the kids, though not everyone understood why they had to wear dresses and lipstick to do it.

In spring 1972, the Dolls began playing regularly at the Mercer Arts Center, a downtown theater complex on the boundary between the Lower East Side and the West Village that had resorted to booking unsigned local rock bands to help pay for its off-off-Broadway theatrical endeavors. The Dolls built up a substantial, largely teenage following at the Mercer, attracted a manager and a booking agent, and by midyear were off to London, where they had secured a slot opening for the Faces at Wembley Arena. The British press and record companies were buzzing around them like flies, but it all fell apart that November when drummer Billy Murcia died at a London party from an unfortunate combination of pills and alcohol. Back in New York, the Dolls acquired a considerably more powerful and accomplished drummer (and another former Brooklyn gang member) in Jerry Nolan, who played his first Dolls gig at the Mercer just before Christmas. Unfortunately, the record companies that had been courting them stopped short before actually signing them to a contract, put off as much by the band's look and attitude as by Murcia's untimely death. Only Mercury A&R man Paul Nelson kept after them.

Signing with Mercury in 1973, the Dolls made two albums, *The New York Dolls* and *Too Much Too Soon.* The records went nowhere commercially, the band failed to connect with middle American audiences, and by 1975

267

1975
Pere Ubu inaugurate the American indie-rock underground, releasing their debut single "30 Seconds Over Tokyo" on their own Hearthan label.

1975
The New York Dolls implode; Johnny Thunders and Jerry Nolan stick together, recruiting Richard Hell and Walter Lure to form the Heartbreakers.

1975
Hell leaves the Heartbreakers to put together his own avant-punk sonic assault team, the Voidoids.

several members were so heavily into alcohol and/or drugs that they collectively decided to call it quits. But the Dolls had accomplished much, despite what it must have felt like at the time. They had provided a beacon for the New York underground that would come together in their wake, showing that it was possible to go against dominant trends and create your own audience, your own scene. And the two Dolls around whom most of the drug rumors collected, Johnny Thunders and Jerry Nolan, would be heard from again, as key players in the punk revolution kindled at CBGB.

Hilly Kristal, a bearish, bearded man given to flannel shirts and work boots, had christened his dark, long, narrow bar C.B.G.B. and OMFUG, a mouthful that stood for Country, Blue Grass, Blues, and Other Music For Uplifting Gourmandisers. It was not to be, not the way Hilly intended. Early in 1974, guitarists Tom Verlaine and Richard Lloyd were looking for a place where their new band, Television, could perform regularly, develop their sound, perhaps begin to attract a following. The Dolls' lengthy residency at the Mercer Arts Center had shown them the way, but the Mercer was no longer an option. It had collapsed—not financially, but literally, in a pile of bricks, plaster, and rubble—in August 1973. CBGB's, as it was soon being called by habitués, was destined to take up the slack.

Hilly Kristal, left, outside his Bowery bar.

Television's two founders, Tom Verlaine (née Miller) and Richard Hell (née Meyers), had met at a Delaware boarding school. Verlaine was playing piano and saxophone at the time; it was the mid-sixties, and while he appreciated groups like the Rolling Stones, the tall, thin teenager was more interested in the bristling, clamorous, high-energy free jazz of John Coltrane, Eric Dolphy—and especially Albert Ayler, whose artistic credo was "sounds, not notes; feelings, not phrases." The typical Ayler performance began with simple hymn- or folk-song-like theme statements and then caromed into the sonic stratosphere, with drums flailing, brass bray-

1975

Londoner Malcolm
McLaren spends several
months in the U.S., man-
aging the New York Dolls,
taking note of Richard
Hell's torn T-shirts, safety-

pin fetishism, and
chopped, spiked hair, and
returns to London to
assemble a punk band of
his own, the Sex Pistols.

ing and stuttering, and Ayler's tenor saxophone testifying in unknown
tongues, drawn-out screams, and violent, wrenching honks. The music was
radically abrasive and, for aficionados, a thing of awesome sonic beauty.
Ayler's influence on early punk was as pervasive as the impact of Coltrane's
Eastern/modal phase on the sixties' improvisational rock and psychedelia.
Ayler's punk-rocker fan club included, in addition to Verlaine and Hell,
Iggy Pop, the MC5, Lou Reed, Peter Laughner of Pere Ubu, Alan Vega of
Suicide, Lenny Kaye of the Patti Smith Group, and later Greg Ginn and
Henry Rollins of Black Flag—and that's the short list.

When Hell and Verlaine moved to New York City in 1967, they
worked in a bookstore and wrote poetry, some of which they published privately under the joint pen name Theresa Stern. Their literary influences, in
addition to Burroughs, the beats, and surrealism, were primarily nineteenth-century French "décadents" such as Baudelaire, Lautreamont,
Rimbaud, Huysmans, and, from the early twentieth century, Cendrars and
Céline. It's not difficult to detect traces of Baudelaire's "Flowers of Evil,"
Lautreamont's clinical catalog of horrors in "Maldoror," Rimbaud's advo-
cacy of "systematic and total derangement of the senses," Huysmans's
romance with diabolism in "La Bas," and even titles like Céline's "Journey
to the End of the Night" in the songs of Verlaine and Hell. Many of their literary interests were shared by another young poet who arrived in New York
City in 1967, Patti Smith.

By the early seventies, Smith was giving live poetry readings/perfor-
mances, accompanied on electric guitar by Lenny Kaye. Verlaine and Hell,
having concluded that self-published poetry was getting them nowhere,
decided to start a band. Verlaine had set aside the saxophone and taken up
guitar in high school. He had even met a resourceful drummer, Billy Ficca,
who agreed to come to New York and lend his talents to the project. Hell

**Poetess Patti Smith with
her Rickenbacker electric
guitar, ready to rock.**

1975

Patti Smith's *Horses,* the first album to emerge from the punk-rock cauldron that was CBGB, is produced by John Cale and released by Arista.

1975

Talking Heads play their first gig at CBGB in June.

1976

The Ramones record their eponymously titled debut album; in July they take their learn-three-chords-and-start-a-band punk ethos to London.

had never played a musical instrument, so Verlaine decided to teach him bass, or more precisely, to teach him the bass *parts* for songs the two were writing. After a brief, inconclusive attempt to play as a three-piece, christened the Neon Boys, the band found a compatible second guitarist, Richard Lloyd. With CBGB providing a weekly gig, they were soon attracting attention under their new moniker, Television.

They were an adventurous and cheeky group, determined to explore the outer limits of guitar-band sonics and group and solo improvisation without regard for the limitations of their mostly garage-level chops. Like the Velvet Underground before them, they were sonic illuminists—devotees of those elusive moments when an electric guitar's silvery harmonics seem to shimmer and swell, straining to burst the sonic envelope and *blaze forth* like light, like fire. Verlaine's lyrics were visionary, sometimes skewed sideways: "I remember/How the darkness doubled/I recall/Lightning struck itself" begins their epic "Marquee Moon."

In August 1974, some six months after Television's Bowery debut, another new band began making regular appearances at CBGB—the Ramones, from middle-class Forest Hills in Queens. They were not the same sort of band as Television—not at all. Their songs rarely exceeded two-and-a-half minutes in length, rarely used more than two or three rudimentary major chords, rarely strayed from the same (speedy) tempo. Bassist Dee Dee Ramone—all four musicians had adopted the Ramone surname—counted off every song in the same drill-sergeant's bark because, explains guitarist Johnny Ramone, "It just came natural to him; he counted to four really well." When barstool pundits accused them of writing nothing but "negative" songs—some early titles were "I Don't Wanna Get Involved with You," "I Don't Wanna Walk Around with You," and "I Don't Care"—they obligingly accentuated the "positive" with straightfor-

1976

The Sex Pistols jack up
rock and roll's energy and
tempo a notch or three
with their debut single,
"Anarchy in the U.K."

1976

The Sex Pistols contribute
their #1 U.K. hit "God
Save the Queen" to
the British monarch's
Silver Jubilee.

ward declarations such as "Now I Wanna Sniff Some Glue," "You're Gonna Kill That Girl," "Beat on the Brat (With a Baseball Bat)," and "I Wanna Be Sedated." As all these titles suggest, subtlety was not exactly the Ramones' forte, but at first they didn't think of themselves as "punks." When pressed to characterize their chosen idiom, vocalist Joey Ramone dubbed it "sick bubblegum music." The Ramones' music and Television's could have originated on different planets. The fact that the two bands developed in the same Bowery bar almost simultaneously, and were both saddled with the unwanted and substantially off-putting "punk rock" label, may be evidence that, in the words of Sun Ra, "the Creator of the Universe got a sense of humor."

As word got around about the dingy Bowery bar with great acoustics and a willingness to hire raw, unsigned rock bands, it became a magnet for musicians united in their disaffection with the musical status quo. Enter Blondie, with their passion for the Brill Building/girl-group sound and their striking singer, Debbie Harry; Talking Heads, with their art-school weirdness and fractured funk rhythms; Suicide, two leather-jacketed art terrorists whom some remembered from the old Mercer Arts Center; and Patti Smith, whose collaboration with Lenny Kaye had evolved into a full-tilt rock and roll band. When Tom Verlaine's insistence on writing and singing virtually every song led to Richard Hell's departure from Television, the bassist/poet joined forces with ex-Dolls Johnny Thunders and Jerry Nolan and ex-Demons guitarist Walter Lure in the Heartbreakers. Television was a stronger unit, better equipped for the exploratory improvising with their new bassist, Fred Smith. And when Hell left the Heartbreakers in late 1975 to finally front his own band, the wailing, incendiary Voidoids, the new Heartbreakers, with bassist Billy Rath, rapidly locked in, becoming the definitive punk rhythm section in short order.

Talking Heads seemed an unlikely choice as touring partners for the Ramones, but both groups exemplified a kind of minimalism with a frequently wry sense of humor.

1976

Jamaican producer Lee Perry writes, records, and releases a running commentary on the apocalyptic mood hanging over this "Year of Punk," presenting to the world

outside Jamaica "short, sharp shocks" like Junior Murvin's "Police and Thieves" and Max Romeo's "War In A Babylon."

1977

Reggae group Culture predicts an unruly summer for the year when "Two Sevens Clash"; on 7/7/77, Jamaicans stay home from work in droves.

When it came to down-and-dirty punk rock, the Heartbreakers were the real deal; L to R, drummer Jerry Nolan, bassist Billy Rath, guitarist Walter Lure, and rock and roll outlaw Johnny Thunders.

Social conditions in the U.K., where a generation of unemployed young people could see no future beyond a half-life on the dole, proved considerably more susceptible to punk's endearing charms than the still-flush U.S. of A. ("Now that *America's* economy is going down the toilet and things are beginning to crumble and fall apart, they're turning a definite eye toward punk," says former Sex Pistols front man John Lydon, a.k.a. Johnny Rotten. "*Now* they get it. I suppose it's not really music for the overprivileged.") In 1973, King's Road clothing-shop owner and silver-tongued hustler Malcolm McLaren had been inspired by the New York Dolls' London visit. In early 1975 he briefly lived in New York City and managed them, but he seemed more intrigued by Richard Hell, who had concocted a distinctive look to go with his music—spiky, cropped hair, torn T-shirts and jeans that might well be held together with safety pins, and a glazed, "pretty vacant" mien that spelled either "youth apocalypse" or "heroin," depending on who was deciphering it. Of all the songwriters in all the CBGB bands, Hell was the one with the generational anthems and big ideas. "I belong to the blank generation," he sang, to a tune he'd basically ripped off from the old Rod McKuen novelty record "Beat Generation," "and I can take it or leave it each time." What he *meant* was "I belong to the _____ generation," as in "fill in the blanks"—a generation that hadn't been labeled and was therefore free to create itself, just as Richard Meyers had created "Richard Hell." But perhaps the average rock fan could be forgiven for taking one look at Hell's zoned-and-stoned visage on the cover of his 1977 *Blank Generation* album and figuring he meant "blank" as in "absent," as in "void"—after all, he did call his band the Voidoids. Richard was sending mixed signals: Meyers may have written the songs, but the guy on the record jacket looked like Hell.

Malcolm McLaren attempted to lure Hell and Television to England,

1977

Television, Talking Heads, Richard Hell and the Voidoids, the Dead Boys, the Heartbreakers, the Saints, the Clash, the Sex Pistols, the Vibrators, and other bands release debut albums, making '77 the Year of Punk.

but there were no takers. Soon the bondage-trousers-and-T-shirts magnate returned to London alone, determined to put together his own "punk-rock" band from the somewhat unpromising materials at hand. There was a young, amateurish, larcenously inclined guitarist named Steve Jones hanging out at McLaren's clothing shop, Sex. He was slamming out Faces covers with a bassist (Glenn Matlock, soon to be sacked for his love of the Beatles and his preference for chords more sophisticated than the major triad) and a drummer, Paul Cook. They were a rowdy, drunken lot, but Jones and Cook really clicked and were soon kicking up a massive, hard-driving wall of sound, with or without a bass player. Individually their chops may have been rudimentary; together they *rocked.* Another plus was their first-rate equipment, pilfered from rich rock stars with ample insurance policies and lax security.

When McLaren introduced his recruits to "their" new lead singer, Steve Jones, for one, was appalled. There stood Johnny Rotten in his "I Hate Pink Floyd" T-shirt, with a sneer that was a dental disaster, eclectic musical tastes, zero musical experience, and a "singing" voice that would make Bob Dylan sound mellifluous. In short, he was the ideal front man for a band promising nothing less than the end of rock and roll. "It's as old as I am, rock and roll," Rotten noted in 1980, "so it's no good to me, is it? From my point of view, the Sex Pistols were a piss-take on rock and roll, just a good laugh. After that band, there can never, ever be a rock and roll band again. It's finished now, it's over, it's done its good stuff and had its day." It was good copy for the journalists, and guaranteed to outrage anyone who fervently believed in "the music that will set you free."

The Ramones, who'd signed with Sire Records and recorded their first album, *Ramones,* played in London in July 1976. "Everywhere we went, we met kids that said they were starting a band that week," remembers

New York's iconic punk poet Richard Hell wails with his Voidoids, including slash-and-burn guitarist Robert Quine, right.

273

1977

The Sex Pistols headline
a summer "Anarchy in
the U.K." tour with the
Damned, the Clash,
and one of British punk's

prime musical inspirations,
Johnny Thunders's
Heartbreakers.

**Anarchy in the U.K. in the
dread guise of the Sex
Pistols; L to R, bassist Sid
Vicious, vocalist Johnny
Rotten, guitarist Steve
Jones; drummer Paul Cook
is unseen but not unheard.**

Johnny Ramone, "and some of them turned out to be the Damned, the
Clash. I guess the Sex Pistols had started a few months prior to that. We
were hoping, at that point in our career, that kids would be seeing us and
starting bands that were in some way like us. We wanted to see a movement
come out of this." They got their wish. The Ramones, too, had started with
little in the way of instrumental prowess. "I had bought my first guitar just
prior to starting the Ramones," says Johnny. "Me and Dee Dee started and
then we got Joey. It was all very new; we put records on, but we couldn't
figure out how to play the songs, so we decided to start writing songs that
were within our capabilities. They turned out to be long songs played
quickly, and we just fell into our style as we went along, without any really
conscious effort."

The Ramones said they'd been influenced by "everything that went
down in rock and roll from the first time we saw Elvis." The Sex Pistols
claimed to have little interest in the music that preceded them, and Rotten,
at least, hoped nobody would come after them. But the Pistols and the
Ramones were alike in one important respect: At a time when much of rock
was getting so "progressive" that it was becoming little more than loud easy-
listening fodder, they were taking the music back to basics: three chords,
drive, excitement, attitude—and *youth*. Rock stars were sixties hippie-dips,
"dinosaurs," insulated from their public by drugs, lackeys, mansion walls,
and blacked-out limo windows. Across the U.K., disaffected kids were ready
for some music they could call their own. It was the fifties all over again.

The year 1976 was the British monarchy's Silver Jubilee, and Punk
Year One. Into the feel-good media frenzy over the royals' lavish celebrations, the Sex Pistols dropped "God Save the Queen," a record as welcome
as a letter bomb, packaged in an attractive Jamie Reed picture sleeve with
ransom-note lettering and a portrait of the queen with a safety pin through

1977

Bob Marley and the Wailers and producer Lee Perry celebrate the punk/reggae crossover phenomenon in their single "Punky Reggae Party."

1978

"Ever get the feeling you've been cheated?" Johnny Rotten asks the San Francisco audience at the Sex Pistols' final performance.

her nose. "God save the queen! The fascist regime!" shrieked Rotten like a harpy from hell. "There's NO FUTURE FOR YOU!" It was one of those sublime rock and roll moments.

By the summer of '77, with Jamaica's Rastafarians anticipating "blood and botheration" when "the two sevens clash," the Pistols were singing about "Anarchy in the U.K." and headlining an "Anarchy" tour with the Clash, the Damned, and, from New York, the Heartbreakers. Like the Ramones a year earlier, the Heartbreakers gave the "little London boys" a crash course in punk-rock musicianship; as players they were considerably more accomplished than the Ramones, and thus had more to teach. Setting tempos just rapid enough to maximize the music's kinetic volatility, slower than the Ramones but with more force and drive, the Heartbreakers left a lasting impression on British punk-rockers who were interested in honing their craft and their feel. The album they recorded in London that year, *L.A.M.F.* (the New York street-gang acronym for Like A Mother Fucker), sounded like a bottomless sludge pit. Remixed by Johnny Thunders and some capable English cronies in 1984, *L.A.M.F. Revisited* is a punk-rock classic, deserving of shelf space next to the Sex Pistols' *Never Mind the Bollocks, Ramones,* Patti Smith's *Horses,* Hell's *Blank Generation,* the Buzzcocks' *Singles Going Steady,* Wire's *Pink Flag,* and perhaps best of all (if it isn't too musicianly for this company), Television's masterpiece *Marquee Moon.* If more bands had followed the Buzzcocks' example and assembled the best of their 1976–78 singles on an LP, there would be more albums on the list. Singles were the ideal format for punk's hit-git-and-split methodology, and trying to hear all the good ones is a worthy but daunting task.

Speaking of singles, Bob Marley and the Wailers' "Punky Reggae Party," a 1977 single not on any authorized Wailers album, served notice of mutual affinities between punk and Jamaica's mystical, insurgent, highly

Manchester's Buzzcocks inaugurated punk's Do It Yourself ethos in the U.K. with their self-produced debut EP *Spiral Scratch.*

1978

Punk begins to chafe
against its self-imposed
musical boundaries; fresh
directions are charted
by LPs as disparate as
No New York (Producer

Brian Eno's documentation
of NYC's no wave/noise
scene); Alex Chilton's *Big
Star 3rd;* and ex–Pink Fairy
Mick Farren's *Vampires
Stole My Lunch Money.*

politicized reggae idiom. On the punk side, this affinity took several forms. Some rockers emerged mesmerized and spiritually fortified from their contacts with reggae. Clash bassist Paul Simonon, for example, grew up in London's racially mixed Brixton area and danced and listened to reggae's immediate precursors, ska and rock steady, throughout his adolescence. "A lot of white people would say, 'Oh, reggae's really boring, the bass is always the same,'" he avers. "But when you're actually in one of those clubs, you understand why the bass is as it is. Because it's something to move to; it's your footsteps, it's the feel, and that's an aspect that you can only really find out by being in a club, because that's where the music was meant to be played."

Simonon remembers an early lyric by Clash vocalist Joe Strummer: "Dig some reggae but don't play any." The group's original songs, some of them inspired by reggae culture or by the experience of being caught up in London's first major race riots during the annual Notting Hill Carnival, were some of the most powerful statements to come out of early British punk. Unfortunately, their first album also included an ill-advised mangling of one of the period's most gorgeous and relevant reggae singles, Junior Murvin's "Police and Thieves." Although the record's producer, Lee Perry, later worked with the Clash briefly, and the band's cover version must have generated some royalties, their "Police and Thieves" did not meet with his approval. "A lot of people say, 'Oh, it's nothing like reggae,' our particular version," says Simonon. "Well, it wasn't meant to be. It was supposed to be a punk-rock version. I did hear years later that Lee Perry said we'd ruined it, but he's from a different cultural background, so I can understand his opinion." This from a man who had taught himself bass by playing along with reggae records.

"There were a lot of bands around that time doing very, very duff

1979

Punk's musical diversifica-
tion proceeds with
landmark albums such
as Joy Division's *Unknown
Pleasures,* the Buzzcocks'
Singles Going Steady,

Public Image Ltd.'s
Metal Box (a.k.a. *Second
Edition*); XTC's *Drums
and Wires;* and the Fall's
Live at the Witch Trials.

versions of reggae," says John Lydon. "I hated those bands, couldn't stand the Police with their 'Roxanne' and all that kind of stuff. It was very cynical, you know, and *evil.* You've got to come from your own roots first and foremost, and if you don't have any, then you're in the wrong business." All very noble, but what about Lydon's post–Sex Pistols band (*not* a rock and roll band, he insisted), Public Image Limited? ("It's what most people seem to buy, the public image rather than the fucking music.") P.I.L.'s second album, *Metal Box,* is an innovative and often riveting record, a postpunk milestone, but rhythmically and sonically it owes more than a little to the spacey, recombinant reggae idiom known as dub. It's fine, but it's not exactly Lee Perry.

Ah, but what is? Lee Perry, that is. Also known as Scratch, a.k.a. the Upsetter, Perry was shocking proper Jamaicans in the mid-sixties when he sang and chanted his way through "rude" ska hits like "Doctor Dick." A few years later, it was Perry who shepherded the music out of its slow-and-raunchy rock-steady groove and dropped it in the reggae pocket with "People Funny Boy," and Perry who developed the mystical, deeply Rastafarian roots reggae sound with his late-sixties Upsetters lineup. Perry produced the 1969–70 Bob Marley and the Wailers recordings most aficionados still consider Marley's best. Again, singles: "Duppy Conqueror," "Small Axe," "Lively Up Yourself," "Trench Town Rock," not to be confused with the later Island remakes. When Marley moved on to international stardom, he plucked bassist Aston "Family Man" Barrett and drummer Carlton Barrett out of Perry's studio band and took them along as full-fledged Wailers. Under the Upsetter's guidance they had developed into one of the most acute and incisive rhythm sections anywhere. Rock and roll (if we can call it that) doesn't come any better than the music of Bob Marley and the Wailers, Lee Perry, and their visionary Rasta brethren. And since it

**Lee Perry, producer and
mystic *auteur,* pioneered
dub psychedelia and
reggae rhythms.**

Punk shades into post-punk as innovative bands gleefully shred genre distinctions: Black Flag's *Damaged;* X's *Wild Gift;* the Birthday Party's

Prayers on Fire; the Gun Club's *Fire of Love*; the Flesheaters' *A Minute to Pray A Second to Die;* and the Fall's *Slates* EP.

Bob Marley, Iron Lion of Zion, Rasta visionary, as gifted a songwriter and as mesmerizing a performer as rock and roll has seen.

originated largely as Jamaica's response to New Orleans r&b in the late fifties, and derives from the same rhythmic traditions, I think we can legitimately (if not exclusively) consider it rock and roll Jamaican style. Personally, I wouldn't be caught dead on that proverbial desert island without my Marley/Perry and rock-steady singles tapes. Alas, there isn't room in the present work for the more detailed discussion this music merits.

Punk rock—our original point of departure—was neither designed nor intended to endure. Most of the original bands seemed to come with their own built-in self-destruct mechanisms. Of the CBGB bands, only the Ramones and Blondie sustained careers well into the eighties. Except for Television, who called it quits in 1978 but regrouped in 1991 for an excellent eponymous album and a brief club tour, only the Ramones have lasted into the nineties. The Sex Pistols themselves self-destructed in 1978. "Ever get the feeling you've been cheated?" Johnny Rotten asked the audience at the final Pistols show in San Francisco. "That wasn't directed at the audience," he now says. "It was directed at us onstage, because we had been cheated, and we cheated ourselves."

But if the individual *bands* haven't lasted, the punk flame has continued to burn brightly. Before it can gutter out in one locale (as in New York and London in the late seventies), it's sparking a conflagration somewhere else. At the beginning of the eighties the hot spots included Los Angeles (where X, Fear, Black Flag, the Flesheaters, the Circle Jerks, the Germs, and the Blasters ruled), San Francisco (with the Dead Kennedys and Flipper), and Washington, D.C. (where Minor Threat set a musicianly standard for intelligent hard core and subsequently mutated into Fugazi, reigning gurus of 1990s D.I.Y.).

Finally, in 1991, a mere decade and a half after Punk Year One, American punk (with varying admixtures of seventies hard rock and metal)

1982

A year of new bands with fresh directions and powerful statements from punk icons: Flipper's *Generic Flipper;* Fear's *Fear: The Record;* the Birthday Party's *Junkyard;* Richard Hell's *Destiny Street;* and Lou Reed's post-Velvets masterpiece *The Blue Mask.*

reached critical mass. Once Seattle's punky power trio, Nirvana, sold millions of records for Geffen, it was only a matter of time until some lucky D.I.Y. indie label released an album with comparable appeal. In 1994–95, the Epitaph label, founded by the Orange County hardcore band Bad Religion, sold more than four million copies of the Offspring's aptly titled *Smash.* Offspring vocalist Dexter Holland, a former high school valedictorian, was roughly one dissertation away from a Ph.D. in molecular biology. And there he was, shouting "You stupid dumb-shit goddamn motherfucker" live on national television's "1994 *Billboard* Music Awards." Holland is a far cry from Joey Ramone or Johnny Rotten—or maybe it isn't such a far cry after all.

Run DMC, purveyors of hard rhymes and hard beats, whose collaboration with hard rockers Aerosmith on "Walk This Way" introduced rap to suburbia; L to R, DJ Run, Jam Master Jay, and D.M.C.

Rock

Planet

New York City's South Bronx was a forbidding urban moonscape in the mid-seventies. Overcrowded tenements sat side by side with buildings that had been burned, gutted, and abandoned; whole neighborhoods had the look of a defeated enemy capital after aerial bombardment. Into this environment of desolation, further fractured by gang warfare and drug trafficking, came a Jamaican immigrant who called himself DJ Kool Herc. In Jamaica, the disc jockeys who spun records at outdoor sound-system dances and "toasted," or rhymed, over the grooves had long been cultural heroes; the biggest and best of them were as much stars as any singer or instrumentalist.

Kool Herc brought this culture of the toasting/rapping DJ to the Bronx, and the impromptu Jamaican-style street dances he presided over became wildly popular. He'd set up his speakers outside a public housing project or in a park, help himself to the electric grid by splicing into the base of a street-lamp pole, and chant his own rhythmic commentary into a microphone over the discs he spun. His dances attracted homegrown aspirants who begged for a chance to "get on the mike" and "rock the house," and an athletic new breed of "break" dancers who cut jerky, robotlike movements in with more fluid steps, then flipped over and stood on their heads, spinning and whiplashing to the rhythms. Once again, a deprived and neglected community was creating a new kind of rock and roll culture

1974

Kraftwerk's Moog synthe-
sizer stylings, first used on
their *Autobahn* LP, inspire
later electro funk/hip-hop.

1979

The Sugar Hill Gang score
the first rap hit, "Rapper's
Delight." The direction to
"hip-hop, don't stop"
clearly announces that
the future has arrived.

that would inevitably find its way into the homes of almost every teenager in America—and the world.

The terms "hip-hop" and "rap" are often used interchangeably to describe this culture. But strictly speaking, rap is the verbal art of rhythmic rhyming. Hip-hop refers to rap's immediate cultural surround: the DJ's manipulation of records and turntables to create fresh musical collages and percussive "scratching" effects, the break dancing, the graffiti art, the piecing together of individual sartorial styles by "collaging" various items of brand-name apparel. Taking their cues from the organization of the teenage gangs endemic to areas like the South Bronx, hip-hoppers banded together in "posses," providing the template for a new kind of pop group. There were rappers, working the crowd from the front of the stage. Behind them, where one was used to seeing guitars, drums, and keyboards, were the DJ's, creating a recombinant mix-and-match of beats, breaks, and sonic shards through the virtuosic manipulation of vinyl records and turntables. L.L. Kool J and other rappers toured with two DJ's, playing lead and rhythm turntables. Other members of the posse might dance or leave graffiti "tags," work the crowd, or act as stage security or bodyguards.

At first, rap and hip-hop didn't seem to offer established performers any serious long-term competition. Surely the rap format was so limited and reductive that it couldn't possibly last. (Of course, "they" had said the same thing about rock and roll.) Like much of the period's best and most innovative rock, hip-hop and rap received little or no airplay outside a few inner-city areas; radio formats were more restrictive and exclusionary than ever in the late seventies and early eighties. But the new music proved remarkably self-sustaining. In tried-and-true rock and roll fashion, hip-hop absorbed elements from the musics around it and creatively recycled elements of its own past.

MTV begins broadcasting
pop music videos around
the clock, kicking off with
the otherwise forgotten
novelty hit "Video Killed
the Radio Star."

Afrika Bambaataa's
"Planet Rock" and
Grandmaster Flash's
"The Message" take
hip-hop a giant step
toward musical maturity.

In 1982, two seminal singles pointed the way ahead. DJ Afrika Bambaataa and his rap crew, Soul Sonic Force, combined their raw South Bronx vocal attack with Kraftwerk-style synthesizers and sequencers, collaborating with producers Arthur Baker and John Robie to create a new electronic dance music on "Planet Rock" (and on its follow-up, "Looking for the Perfect Beat"). And at New Jersey's Sugar Hill Records, which was run by Sylvia Robinson of Mickey and Sylvia/"Love Is Strange" fame, the pioneering Bronx DJ Grandmaster Flash and his rap crew, the Furious Five, recorded "The Message." This was one of the biggest of the early rap hits, and the first to show that rap could be a vehicle for trenchant social protest, as well as for the boasting and come-ons that were holdovers from earlier street-corner r&b. Bambaataa's use of studio technology became hip-hop's dominant musical direction for a while; Flash's records bridged hip-hop and funk, backing the DJ's innovative turntable manipulations and his crew's taut rapping with an outstanding band, later known as Fats Comet and/or Tackhead. This Sugar Hill house band went on to become perhaps the definitive funk rhythm section of the eighties, collaborating with British reggae/dub producer Adrian Sherwood on a series of innovative dance singles and albums and backing a powerful vinyl collaboration between James Brown and Afrika Bambaataa. The group's bassist, mighty Doug Wimbish, joined black hard-rock band Living Colour in the early nineties.

But rap's full-scale commercial breakthrough, when it finally came, was a product of neither the Bambaataa/Baker nor the Flash/Sugar Hill camp. Run DMC, two rappers and a DJ from Queens, New York, had been making records for the Def Jam production company of Rick Rubin and Russell Simmons that were rap at its most stripped-down, all hard-edged voices and thunderous drum-machine rhythms: no band, no melody, just the Word and the Beat. On their 1986 album *Raising Hell,* the Run DMC

"Looking for the Perfect Beat": DJ Afrika Bambaataa, of the Bronx, New York's Zulu Nation, pioneered electro-hip-hop with his "Planet Rock."

1982

Michael Jackson's "Beat It," with guest guitarist Eddie Van Halen, opens up MTV to Michael Jackson and other black artists.

1983

Run DMC reject flashy stage outfits, appearing in the Adidas-and-sweats semi-suburban street style of their Queens neighborhood.

team tried something new: They covered a heavy-metal/hard-rock tune, Aerosmith's "Walk This Way," with Aerosmith vocalist Steven Tyler and guitarist Joe Perry as guests. Rick Rubin (whose credit on Run DMC albums read "reducer" rather than "producer") was a thrash-metal fan who produced Slayer and Danzig as well as rap records. But this was not simply a producer/reducer's innovation. Hip-hop DJ's and audiences had frequently included metal records by the likes of Aerosmith and AC/DC in their musical mix, and younger musicians in hip-hop and metal were increasingly forming mutual-admiration societies. Propelled by hard drum-machine beats and Joe Perry's sheet-iron guitar riffs, marketed with the help of an upscale, MTV-ready video, "Walk This Way" established hip-hop, formerly an inner-city phenomenon with more club than radio play, as a fixture in suburban rec rooms across America. Inevitably, it was a white rap group, former punk-rock joke band the Beastie Boys, who took hip-hop to the top of the album charts. Their debut, *Licensed to Ill,* sold four million copies right off the bat, making it the fastest-selling debut album in CBS Records history. English rockers New Order, born out of the ashes of the outstanding postpunk band Joy Division after the intensely emotive lead vocalist, Ian Curtis, hung himself, also turned to hip-hop. Their "Blue Monday," produced by "Planet Rock" mastermind Arthur Baker in New York, became the best-selling 12-inch single ever.

Rappers were not the only black artists reaping commercial benefits from the rap/metal crossover. Michael Jackson and his producer, Quincy Jones (a former jazz trumpeter and arranger whose early pop productions had included the white-bread hits of Lesley Gore) had contracted the influential metal guitarist Eddie Van Halen to play on "Beat It," a single from Jackson's *Thriller* album. Videos helped *Thriller* become the best-selling album in pop-music history, and it was the video for "Beat It," with Eddie

1983

"Blue Monday," a dance single by Joy Division survivors New Order, spotlights the producing and mixing expertise of Afrika Bambaataa's co-producer

Arthur Baker; it is the U.K.'s best-selling 12-inch single ever.

NEW ORDER

Van Halen's guitar prominently featured, that broke the ice for black-music videos on the increasingly crucial MTV. (The cable pop-music channel had begun with a hodgepodge of corporate "new wave" videos, but as its de facto monopoly gave it unprecedented influence on record sales, its playlist had become as restrictive as any commercial radio format.) Contrary to the initial expectations of MTV programming execs, white teenagers proved highly receptive to rap. The addition of crunching heavy-metal guitar riffs may have helped the new idiom get over initially, but it was soon standing tall on its own terms; "Yo! MTV Raps" became the channel's most popular show in the early nineties, with hardly a guitar in sight.

In fact, as early as the beginning of the 1980s, guitar-based rock and roll had seemed in imminent danger of creative exhaustion. While dance-pop superstars such as Michael Jackson, Madonna, and Prince dominated the sales charts and the airwaves, teenagers flocked to hear "progressive" and heavy-metal bands whose guitar vocabularies were still locked into the blues-derived riffing and classical/kitsch virtuosity of the late sixties and early seventies. There were various alternatives, even in the rarefied heights of the pop charts. Bruce Springsteen wrote songs for and about the casualties of America's postindustrial recession and cynical feed-the-rich social programs; with his steamroller E Street Band he revamped the Phil Spector wall of sound and early sixties Brill Building pop/r&b stylings. U2 achieved worldwide megastardom with their minimalist take on the sonic trance/drone legacy of the Velvet Underground, Television, and Joy Division, aided enormously by vocalist Bono's evident sincerity and empathetic communication with concert audiences. Tom Petty and the Heartbreakers (not to be confused with Johnny Thunders's mid-seventies crew) and Athens, Georgia's REM revived the jangly 12-string guitar textures and folksy fingerpicking of the mid-sixties Byrds for audiences too

U2's Bono, with bassist Adam Clayton at right, brought the "rattle and hum" of droning, post-Velvets rock into the arenas in the eighties.

1983

Metallica's *Kill 'Em All* brings the concise aggression and post-Ramones speedcar tempos of punk to the heavy-metal idiom; original lead guitarist Dave

Mustaine, accused of having a "bad attitude" (!) leaves to form his own thrash-metal band, Megadeth.

Dave Mustaine (top) created an influential punk/metal guitar style with Metallica before starting his own adventurous band, Megadeth. Vocalist Henry Rollins of Black Flag (bottom) dared to slow hard-core punk down to a sludgy, sub–Black Sabbath crawl.

young to remember the original. Peter Gabriel, former front man for the British progressive band Genesis, composed atmospheric, musicianly techno-rock soundscapes that increasingly incorporated influences and musicians from various Asian and African traditions.

Amid the ups and downs of chart action and trend hopping, heavy metal changed more slowly, offering the same sort of continuity represented by the vocal-group sound in black pop. Above all, metal was the cult of the white male adolescent, providing a rite of passage for each new generation. But even within this (relatively) conservative musical idiom, change was in the air.

Throughout the eighties, metal was slowly being revitalized by the legacy of punk. For the new generation of fans, the punk/metal antipathies of the late seventies were already ancient history. The populist strain of punk epitomized by the Ramones had evolved into hard core, a brutally intense, meat-and-potatoes idiom that was often aurally similar to the more energetic sort of heavy metal known as "thrash." When kids who grew up with hard-core punk and the early thrash of British bands like Mötörhead began starting groups of their own, the result was a fresh, sturdy, fast and furious hybrid that combined the velocity and aggression of hard core with the more flamboyant fretboard virtuosity traditional to metal. Metallica, Megadeth, Slayer, Exodus, Anthrax, and Danzig were among the most inventive of these bands.

Meanwhile, some of the more adventurous punk and hard-core musicians were growing restive within the severe stylistic limitations of "loud fast rules." Two bands in particular led the way in radically slowing the music down without sacrificing an iota of its abrasive edge. Black Flag, in Los Angeles, and Flipper, in San Francisco, adapted the sludgy tempos and brooding minor-key drone of early-seventies metal bands such as Black

1984

Madonna Louise Ciccone drops her middle and last names and records the first of a series of dance-pop hits that draw on the beats, style, and turntable expertise she encounters at NYC dance clubs such as the Fun House and the Roxy.

1985

The Live Aid charity concert trots out rock's sixties royalty but cuts off Run DMC before their first number can get properly under way.

Sabbath to the in-your-face imperatives of early-eighties punk. A new school emerged, drawing on the legacies of metal, thrash, punk, hard core, and seventies hard rock in varying degrees and rapidly diversifying into subgenres, among them grindcore and grunge. The latter found a home under the gray, rainy skies of the Pacific Northwest . . . and Flipper inspired the Melvins, who begat Nirvana, led by former Melvins roadie Kurt Cobain. After Nirvana's commercial breakthrough with their 1991 album *Nevermind,* fellow Seattle bands such as Soundgarden, Pearl Jam, and Alice in Chains were soon storming the pop charts—and disavowing the grunge label due to massive media overkill.

In the early eighties, several New York art-punk bands had anticipated Flipper and Black Flag, perfecting their own version of the slowing-to-a-crawl maneuver. Teenage Jesus and the Jerks, the Contortions, Mars, DNA, and future guitar-symphony composer Glenn Branca's Theoretical Girls (among others), christened with the tongue-in-cheek rubric "no wave," made some of the slowest, noisiest, most deliberately *excruciating* rock and roll ever heard—before or since. Most of these bands were antimelody, anti-entertainment, anticharisma, anti-anti-anti. In general, their careers were as brief as their performances. ("We can't stand to hear *ourselves* play for longer than fifteen minutes," said Teenage Jesus singer-guitarist Lydia Lunch.) But in rock and roll, yesterday's horrible noise has a way of becoming today's hot commodity. Building on both no wave and the New York–centered sonic-illuminist tradition of the Velvet Underground and Television, Sonic Youth emerged from the city's Lower East Side in the mid-eighties. Their skills were formidable, their stylistic and sonic range and their grasp of the music's history encyclopedic. But their most valuable contribution to the continuing evolution of rock and roll was their guitar tunings.

The Melvins' (top) abrasive edge, screwy humor, and slower-than-slow trudge riffing inspired Kurt Cobain. James Chance (bottom) of the Contortions, whose manic punk/funk riffing and in-your-hair performance confrontations predated the likes of the Red Hot Chili Peppers by almost a decade.

287

1986

They said it couldn't be done, but here it is: Metallica's *Master of Puppets,* a thrash-metal "concept" album

1987

The Beastie Boys' *Licensed to Ill* sells four-million copies, the fastest-selling debut album in CBS Records' history.

Pearl Jam's lead singer Eddie Vedder goes audience surfing in his Butthole Surfers T-shirt.

If guitar-band rock and roll had seemed to be growing moribund, it was perhaps because rock's restricted vocabulary of harmonies, melodies, and song forms could only be recombined into a finite number of configurations. Whatever you played, it was highly likely that someone had played it before. Sonic Youth tackled this problem head-on: Each song was written for specific guitars (often pawn-shop atrocities), and each guitar in Sonic Youth's extensive arsenal was tuned to intervals deliberately incompatible with conventional chords and harmonic cadences. This approach opened up an apparently infinite field of fresh melodic and harmonic options. Several U.K.-based guitar bands had already been forging their own post-punk, post-no-wave synthesis when Sonic Youth appeared on the scene. There was the Fall, an abrasive, ratchety-sounding agitprop outfit who had first recorded in 1979 and continued to define the leading edge of postpunk rock through much of the eighties; the original lineup of Public Image Limited, with vocalist John Lydon (formerly Johnny Rotten) and the resourceful guitarist Keith Levene; the Australian-bred Birthday Party, with Nick Cave on vocals and the instantly recognizable barbed-wire guitar sound of Rowland S. Howard; and the Jesus and Mary Chain, who sometimes sounded like an unlikely hybrid of the Velvet Underground and the Beach Boys. Sonic Youth's arrival inspired another, younger wave of British guitar bands—My Bloody Valentine, the Wedding Present, Swervedriver—and encouraged them to explore alternate tunings.

America's rock underground finally emerged from the hermetic world of local clubs, fanzines, D.I.Y. record labels, and touring-by-van as a result of Nirvana's 1991 success story—after having been ignored by the corporate record business since the original punk explosion of the late seventies. Sonic Youth was among the immediate beneficiaries, though they had already been signed by the corporate Geffen company after years on

1987

Ireland's U2, having begun as "new wave" primitives with the heavily Joy Division–influenced debut album *Boy,* reach the rarefied plateau of super-stardom with their #1 album *The Joshua Tree.*

indie labels. Even straight-up punk made its long-delayed debut on the pop charts. Veteran punkers like Fugazi and Bad Religion rejected offers from the majors and sold substantially on their own D.I.Y. labels. (Bad Religion's label, Epitaph, proudly boasted "the finest in punk since 1982.") Younger bands like Green Day said they'd rather practice and tour than try to run a record company and gleefully helped themselves to the corporate bucks.

Despite the significant originality of Sonic Youth and other contemporary guitar bands, all these groups are essentially working in a format that dates back to the Beatles. Rock and roll has always been a recombinant art form; each of its major exponents has had to investigate the music's rich and varied heritage, constructing a "new" style and sense of identity from a distinctive, carefully chosen, highly personal array of influences. But rock's more thoughtful musicians and critics have generally put a premium on innovation, and this emphasis is not entirely misplaced. While we like to feel that the music we are most drawn to will last, we tend to listen in the present tense; the best rock and roll speaks to us urgently in the language of the moment, even as it's helping us define that language and that moment.

Besides, nobody really knows which of today's sounds will prove of lasting value—*nobody.* Could anyone have suspected, back in the mid-seventies, that two of the most influential bands of the period would turn out to be the New York Dolls and Aerosmith? At the time, both bands seemed to be little more than low-rent Rolling Stones rip-offs, with the Dolls' David Johansen and Johnny Thunders and Aerosmith's Steven Tyler and Joe Perry mugging through their variously tacky Mick-and-Keith routines. As things turned out, the particular way in which the Dolls presented their Stones rips—fast, loud, sloppy, spirited, cross-dressing, and crazed—was a fundamental inspiration for the entire New York punk movement. Aerosmith's Stones rips were more hard-rock/metal-oriented

1987

Guns 'N' Roses' *Appetite for Destruction* rocks more convincingly than the entire recorded legacy of its most evident inspiration, Aerosmith.

1988

New York City's Sonic Youth deliver their double-LP masterpiece *Daydream Nation*—their last indie album before signing with David Geffen's DGC label.

than glam-punk. As such, they were even easier to emulate, and ever since the platinum-selling Guns and Roses acknowledged that they'd got their start doing just that, hair-band hopefuls have been name-dropping Aerosmith to every record company A&R man who crosses their path. Nor could anyone have predicted in the mid-seventies that black hip-hop DJ's would soon be intercutting snatches of Aerosmith and Kraftwerk with their funk, or that Tyler and Perry would help Run-DMC "break" rap in the suburbs and on the pop charts. I rest my case.

As of the mid-nineties, the rap/hip-hop/dance-music culture is itself more than fifteen years old. Disco has come and gone and come again, this time in the guise of house, techno, trance, and ambient dance-music and the British subculture of the all-night rave. Rap's founding fathers have come and gone and come again, this time as "old school" elder statesmen making guest appearances on "new school" discs.

But compared to the guitar band scene, hip-hop and house and the rest are still young, and their vitality is beyond question. In some ways, hip-hop's growth echoes the early days of rock: Parents and authority figures blame it for everything from delinquency to murder to teenage pregnancy; municipalities and venues accuse its performers of stirring up riots or transgressing against public morality, and attempt to ban live shows and/or recordings. The competition and attrition rate within the field (and on the streets) is so fierce that this year's big deal is almost certain to become next year's has-been. First albums generally prove to be best albums; a hit album is usually the prelude to a commercial and critical flop. Still, a number of artists have managed to accumulate a consistently impressive *body* of work. Among them are Grandmaster Flash and the Furious Five (whose body of work is their string of exceptional singles); Run DMC; Public Enemy, significant both for the ideas and principles embodied in their rhyming

Taking cues from seventies funk icons such as James Brown, P-Funk, and the Isley Brothers, committed hip-hop artists continue to address urgent issues and "fight the power"; L to R, P-Funk's George Clinton with Public Enemy's Flava Flav (top) and Chuck D.

1988

Megadeth's richly varied album *so far, so good . . . so what!* suggests today's thrash-metal head-bangers are tomorrow's progressive rockers.

1988

Hip-hop wholeheartedly embraces social relevance and Stagger Lee attitude with the release of Public Enemy's *It Takes A Nation of Millions to*

Hold Us Back, Boogie Down Productions' *By All Means Necessary,* and Niggas With Attitude's debut album *N.W.A. and the Posse.*

and for the complexity and richness of the layered samples and rhythms crafted by their producers, the Bomb Squad; and the members of NWA (Niggers With Attitude), as a group and later as solo artists—especially the definitive "gangsta" rap productions of Dr. Dre (hip-hop's Phil Spector?) and his protégés. Of course, by the time you read this list it's likely to be substantially out of date. And that's why we've spent so much of this book talking about beginnings, origins, roots—the stuff of history. The best way, maybe the *only* way, to understand what rock and roll is and how it works is to learn as much as we can about where the music came from and how it got here from there. You won't learn much about today's rock and roll, let alone tomorrow's, from any book; the music changes much too fast, and too unpredictably, for that. If you're curious about the state of rock and roll, present tense, you should be *listening to the music.* If you haven't been keeping up with your listening, why are you reading this?

Of course, the urge to prognosticate can be irresistible, so before I go, I'll offer one cautious prediction: Whatever transpires next in the world of rock and roll, whatever events deflect it from its present course and propel it helter-skelter on a new and unexpected tangent, are likely to be stirring right now, PROBABLY NOT IN THE CONTINENTAL UNITED SNAKES.

Some background: During the sixties and seventies, media pundits everywhere decried American pop music's global outreach. Surely, with the developed world's mass media pumping up the volume, rock in particular would drive indigenous musical cultures underground, or destroy them altogether. . . . *but no.* Instead, the Jamaican model has prevailed. Reggae showed that a developing culture could actively resist media imperialism by creating its own rock and roll from its own roots on its own terms.

In the eighties and nineties, Caribbean islands, African nations, European and Asian ethnic groups, have all contributed distinctive, traditionally

1991

Nirvana's *Nevermind* LP and its hit single "Smells Like Teen Spirit" represent the American indie rock underground's long-awaited breakthrough.

1992

Nirvana's commercial success ushers in a new Golden Age of Northwest rock with Pearl Jam, Soundgarden, the Melvins, Mudhoney, L7, Hole, Tad, and others, making the world safe for flannel shirts, ripped jeans, wah-wah pedals, and amp distortion by the bucketful.

rooted strains of electric dance music to the world's ever-quickening musical dialogue. There's *zouk* from Guadeloupe, *mbalax* from Senegal, *mbaqanga* from the South African townships, *soca* from Trinidad, *compas* from Haiti—the list goes on, and on. At the same time, young musicians in many of these cultures have been selectively making specific American rock idioms their own. Brazil and Cuba are producing world-class thrash-metal bands. West Africa threatens to overtake Jamaica as the world's leading producer of roots reggae. Indigenous hip-hop scenes flourish as far afield as Zimbabwe and Northern Ireland. Eastern Europe has its Zappa-esque progressive rock, its own punk, and even death-metal (said to be particularly popular in Poland). Already, these outsider musics are utilizing recording and video technology to win audiences outside their own cultures. In international urban centers from Paris to Abidjan, savvy producers are working with handpicked studio musicians from a dozen different African countries and Caribbean islands, playing mix-and-match with disparate local idioms in a conscious, determined effort to create the synthesis that will set the world on its ear. The outsiders want to be insiders; they *insist*. One of them might be the next Bob Marley, perhaps the next Elvis. Stay tuned.

The Unruly Top Tens

Making top ten lists and voting in year-end polls has always bothered me. Some records come on like gangbusters but don't hold up; others have more subtle virtues that become apparent only after some time has elapsed. Then there's the comparing-apples-and-oranges problem. Which is better, a classic Little Richard single or the first Velvet Underground album? What does "better" *mean* when each item in the comparison is arguably *the best of its kind*? Our solution is a typically unruly one: more top tens. And it's still highly likely that something essential has been left out. Records are listed in no particular order.

RP

Roots of Rock Top Ten

1 *Slave Shout Songs from the Coast of Georgia,* The McIntosh County Shouters (Folkways, LP)

2 *Sounds of the South,* Alan Lomax field recordings (Atlantic, 4 CD's)

3 *Masters of the Delta Blues,* various artists (Yazoo, CD)

4 *The Complete Recordings,* Robert Johnson (Columbia, 2 CD's)

5 *Texas Music Vol. 2: Western Swing & Honky Tonk,* various artists (Rhino, CD)

6 *The Immortal Hank Williams* (Polydor, CD)

7 *The Great 1955 Shrine Concert,* various gospel artists (Specialty, CD)

8 *The Chess Box,* Muddy Waters (Chess, 3 CD's)

9 *The Chess Box,* Howling Wolf (Chess, 3 CD's)

10 *Tougher Than Tough: The Story of Jamaican Music* (Island, 4 CD's)

Classical R&B Top Ten

1 *The R&B Box: 30 Years of Rhythm and Blues,* various artists (Rhino, 6 CD's)

2 *The Doo Wop Box,* various artists (Rhino, 4 CD's)

3 *The Birth of Soul: The Complete Atlantic Rhythm & Blues Recordings 1952–1959,* Ray Charles (Atlantic, 3 CD's)

4 *The Cobra Records Story,* various artists (Capricorn, 2 CD's)

5 *Shame, Shame, Shame,* Smiley Lewis (Bear Family, 4 CD's)

6 *I Like Ike! The Best of Ike Turner* (Rhino, CD)

7 *Sam Cooke's SAR Records Story,* various artists (abkco, 2 CD's)

8 *Fess: The Professor Longhair Anthology* (Rhino, 2 CD's)

9 *T-Bone Walker: The Complete Recordings 1940–1954* (Mosaic, 6 CD's)

10 *Good Rocking Tonight,* Roy Brown (Rhino, CD)

Classic Rock and Roll Top Ten

1 *The Specialty Sessions,* Little Richard (Specialty, 3 CD's)
2 *The Complete Sun Sessions,* Elvis Presley (RCA, CD)
3 *The Sun Records Collection,* various artists (Rhino, 3 CD's)
4 *Out of New Orleans,* Fats Domino (Bear Family, 8 CD's)
5 *The Chess Box,* Bo Diddley (Chess, 2 CD's)
6 *The Chess Box,* Chuck Berry (Chess, 3 CD's)
7 *The Jerry Lee Lewis Anthology* (Rhino, 2 CD's)
8 *The Crickets,* Buddy Holly and the Crickets (MCA, CD)
9 *The Coasters: 50 Coastin' Classics* (Rhino, 2 CD's)
10 *Monkey Hips and Rice: The "5" Royales Anthology* (Rhino, 2 CD's)

Modern Rock Top Ten

1 *The Velvet Underground & Nico* (Polygram, CD)
2 *Let It Bleed,* The Rolling Stones (abkco, CD)
3 *Revolver,* The Beatles (Capitol, CD)
4 *Roger the Engineer,* The Yardbirds (Epic, LP)
5 *The Ultimate Experience,* Jimi Hendrix (MCA, 5 CD's)
6 *Highway 61 Revisited,* Bob Dylan (Columbia, CD) (Note: Even better is the 1966 "Royal Albert Hall" concert bootleg, scheduled for its long-awaited "official" CD release as this is written.)
7 *Led Zeppelin* (Swan Song/Atlantic, 4 CD's)
8 *John Lennon/Plastic Ono Band* (Capitol, CD)
9 *The Band* (Capitol, CD)
10 *Layla,* Derek and the Dominos (Polygram, CD)

The Funkiest Top Ten

1 *Star Time,* James Brown (Polydor, 4 CD's)
2 *Curtis Mayfield and the Impressions: The Anthology 1961–1977* (MCA, 2 CD's)
3 *What's Going On,* Marvin Gaye (Motown, CD)
4 *Sam Cooke: The Man and His Music* (RCA/abkco, CD)
5 *Dictionary of Soul,* Otis Redding (Atlantic, CD)
6 *Queen of Soul,* Aretha Franklin (Atlantic, 4 CD's)
7 *Hitsville USA: The Motown Singles Collection 1959–1971* (Motown, 4 CD's)
8 *The Complete Stax/Volt Singles, 1959–1968* (Atlantic, 9 CD's)
9 *Tear the Roof Off (1974–1980),* Parliament (Mercury, 2 CD's)
10 *There's a Riot Goin' On,* Sly and the Family Stone (Epic, CD)

The Punk Rock Top Ten

1 *Marquee Moon,* Television (Elektra, CD)
2 *Never Mind the Bollocks, Here's the Sex Pistols* (Warner Bros., CD)
3 *Blank Generation,* Richard Hell and the Voidoids (Sire, CD)
4 *L.A.M.F. Revisited,* Johnny Thunders and the Heartbreakers (Receiver UK, CD)
5 *Ramones,* The Ramones (Sire, CD)
6 *The Modern Dance,* Pere Ubu (Blank/Mercury, LP)
7 *Unknown Pleasures,* Joy Division (Qwest, CD)
8 *Fun House,* The Stooges (Elektra, CD)
9 *Los Angeles/Wild Gift,* X (Slash, CD)
10 *Hits,* The Birthday Party (4 A.D., CD)

Postmodern Top Ten

1 *The Best of Grandmaster Flash* (Rhino, CD)
2 *Daydream Nation,* Sonic Youth (Geffen, CD)
3 *Metal Box* (a.k.a. *Second Edition*),
   Public Image Ltd. (Virgin, CD)
4 *King Tubby Meets Rockers Uptown,*
   Augustus Pablo (Rockers, CD)
5 *Remain in Light,* Talking Heads (Sire, CD)
6 *Entertainment!,* Gang of Four (Warner Bros., LP)
7 *Fly,* Yoko Ono (Apple/Capitol LP; or, the
   first disc in Ryko's 6-CD Yoko Ono box,
   "London Jam")
8 *so far, so good . . . so what!,* Megadeth
   (Capitol, CD)
9 *Big Star 3rd/Sister Lovers,* Alex Chilton
   (Ryko, CD)
10 *It Takes a Nation of Millions to Hold Us Back,*
   Public Enemy (Def Jam/Columbia, CD)

Planet Rock Top Ten

1 *Songs of Freedom,* Bob Marley (Island, 4 CD's)
2 *Zombie,* Fela Anikulapo Kuti (Mercury, CD)
3 *Zulu Jive,* various artists (Earthworks, CD)
4 *The Harder They Come,* various artists
   (Mango, CD)
5 *The Chimurenga Singles 1976–1980,*
   Thomas Mapfumo (Shanachie, CD)
6 *Go Go Crankin': Paint the White House Black,*
   various artists (Island/4th & Broadway, LP)
7 *The Wild Magnolias* (Polydor, CD)
8 *Club de Esquina,* Milton Nascimento and
   Lo Borges (Polydor, CD)
9 *Innervisions,* Stevie Wonder (Motown, CD)
10 *Live Live Juju,* King Sunny Ade and His
   African Beats (Ryko, CD)

Your Own Top Ten

1 _____

2 _____

3 _____

4 _____

5 _____

6 _____

7 _____

8 _____

9 _____

10 _____

Bibliography

Bangs, Lester. *Psychotic Reactions and Carburetor Dung.* Edited by Greil Marcus. New York: Knopf, 1987.

Berry, Chuck. *Chuck Berry: The Autobiography.* New York: Harmony, 1987.

Berry, Jason, Jonathan Foose, and Tad Jones. *Up from the Cradle: New Orleans Music Since World War II.* Athens, Ga.: University of Georgia Press, 1986.

Bockris, Victor. *Uptight: The Velvet Underground Story.* London: Omnibus Press, 1983.

Boggs, Vernon W. *Salsiology: Afro-Cuban Music and the Evolution of Salsa in New York City.* New York: Excelsior Music Publishing Co., 1992.

Booth, Stanley. *The True Adventures of the Rolling Stones.* London: Sphere Books–Macdonald and Co., 1989.

Clarke, Donald, ed. *The Penguin Encyclopedia of Popular Music.* New York: Viking-Penguin, 1989.

Corbett, John. *Extended Play: Sounding Off from John Cage to Dr. Funkenstein.* Durham, N.C.: Duke University Press, 1994.

Cott, Jonathan, and Christine Doudna, eds. *The Ballad of John and Yoko.* New York: Rolling Stone Press–Doubleday, 1982.

The Country Music Foundation. *Country Music and the Musicians.* New York: Abbeville, 1988.

Dance, Helen Oakley. *Stormy Monday: The T-Bone Walker Story.* Baton Rouge, La.: Louisiana State University Press, 1987.

Davis, Stephen. *Hammer of the Gods: The Led Zeppelin Saga.* New York: William Morrow, 1985.

DeCurtis, Anthony, ed. *Present Tense: Rock and Roll and Culture.* Durham, N.C.: Duke University Press, 1992.

_____ , and James Henke, eds., with Holly George-Warren. *The Rolling Stone Illustrated History of Rock and Roll.* New York: Random House, 1992.

Escott, Colin, and Martin Hawkins. *Sun Records: The Brief History of the Legendary Record Label.* New York: Quick Fox–Division of Music Sales Corp., 1980.

Ferris, William, and Mary L. Hart, eds. *Folk Music and Modern Sound.* Jackson, Miss.: University Press of Mississippi, 1982.

Friedman, Robert A. "Making an Abstract World Concrete: Knowledge, Competence, and Structural Dimensions of Performance Among Bata Drummers in Santeria." Ph.D. dissertation, Indiana University, 1982.

George, Nelson. *The Death of Rhythm and Blues.* New York: Plume-Penguin, 1988.

_____ . *Where Did Our Love Go?: The Rise and*

Fall of the Motown Sound. New York: St. Martin's, 1985.

Gillespie, Dizzy, with Al Fraser. *To Be or Not to Bop: Memoirs—Dizzy Gillespie.* New York: Doubleday, 1979.

Gillett, Charlie. *The Sound of the City: The Rise of Rock and Roll.* New York: Pantheon, 1983.

Gordon, Robert. *It Came from Memphis.* Boston: Faber and Faber, 1994.

Guralnick, Peter. *Sweet Soul Music: Rhythm and Blues and the Southern Dream of Freedom.* New York: Harper and Row, 1986.

Hannusch, Jeff. *I Hear You Knockin': The Sound of New Orleans Rhythm and Blues.* Ville Platte, La.: Swallow Publications, 1985.

Hebdige, Dick. *Subculture: The Meaning of Style.* London: Methuen and Co., 1979.

Heylin, Clinton. *From the Velvets to the Voidoids: A Pre-Punk History for a Post-Punk World.* New York: Penguin, 1993.

Hirshey, Gerri. *Nowhere to Run: The Story of Soul Music.* New York: Times Books, 1984.

Hoskyns, Barney. *Across the Great Divide: The Band and America.* New York: Hyperion, 1993.

Johnson, Marc. *An Ideal for Living: An History of Joy Division.* London: Proteus Books, 1984.

Keil, Charles, and Steven Feld. *Music Grooves.* Chicago: University of Chicago Press, 1994.

Kienzle, Rich. *Great Guitarists.* N.p.: Facts on File, 1985.

Kozak, Roman. *This Ain't No Disco: The Story of CBGB.* Boston: Faber and Faber, 1988.

Litweiler, John. *Ornette Coleman: A Harmolodic Life.* New York: Scholarly Press, 1994.

Lomax, Alan. *Folk Song Style and Culture.* New Brunswick, N.J.: Transaction Books, 1978; reprint, no. 88 of the Publications of the American Association for the Advancement of Science, Washington, D.C., 1968.

_____ . *The Land Where the Blues Began.* New York: Pantheon, 1993.

Lornell, Kip. *"Happy in the Service of the Lord": Afro-American Gospel Quartets in Memphis.* Chicago: University of Illinois Press, 1988.

Martin, Linda, and Kerry Segrave. *Anti-Rock: The Opposition to Rock 'n' Roll.* New York: Da Capo Press, 1993.

Oliver, Paul. *Songs and Saints: Vocal Traditions on Race Records.* Cambridge: Cambridge University Press, 1984.

Osterberg, James (Iggy Pop), with Anne Wehrer. *Iggy Pop: I Need More.* New York: Karz-Cohl Publishing, 1982.

Palmer, Robert. *Jerry Lee Lewis Rocks!* New York: Delilah–G. P. Putnam's, 1981.

_____ . *Baby That Was Rock and Roll: The Legendary Leiber and Stoller.* New York: Harvest–Harcourt Brace Jovanovich, 1978.

_____ . *The Rolling Stones.* London: Sphere Books, 1984; reprint, New York: Rolling Stone Press–Doubleday, 1983.

_____ . "Sam Phillips: The Sun King; A Revised History of the Roots of Rock and Roll." Memphis, vol. III, no. 9 (1978).

Pareles, Jon, and Patricia Romanowski, eds. *The Rolling Stone Encyclopedia of Rock and Roll.* New York: Rolling Stone Press–Summit, 1983.

Pavlow, Big Al. *The R and B Book: A Disc-History of Rhythm and Blues.* Providence, R.I.: Music House Publishing, 1983.

Pruter, Robert. *Chicago Soul.* Chicago: University of Illinois Press, 1991.

Rebennack, Mac (Dr. John), with Jack Rummel. *Under a Hoodoo Moon.* New York: St. Martin's, 1994.

Reeves, Martha, and Mark Bego. *Dancing in the Street: Confessions of a Motown Diva.* New York: Hyperion, 1994.

Robbins, Ira A. *The Trouser Press Guide to New Wave Records.* New York: Charles Scribner's, 1983.

Rollins, Henry. *Get in the Van.* Los Angeles: 2.13.61 Publications, 1994.

Rosenthal, David H. *Hard Bop: Jazz and Black Music, 1955–1965.* New York: Oxford University Press, 1992.

Savage, Jon. *England's Dreaming: Anarchy, Sex Pistols, Punk Rock and Beyond.* New York: St. Martin's, 1991.

Schaffner, Nicholas. *Saucerful of Secrets: The Pink Floyd Odyssey.* New York: Harmony, 1991.

Shannon, Bob, and John Javna. *Behind the Hits: Inside Stories of Classic Pop and Rock and Roll.* New York: Warner, 1986.

Shapiro, Harry. *Waiting for the Man: The Story of Drugs and Popular Music.* London: Quartet Books, 1988.

Silvester, Peter J. *A Left Hand Like God: A History of Boogie-Woogie Piano.* New York: Da Capo Press, 1988.

Stearns, Marshall W. *The Story of Jazz.* New York: Oxford University Press, 1956; reprint, 1973.

Strickland, Edward. *Minimalism: Origins.* Bloomington, Ill.: Indiana University Press, 1993.

Taylor, Arthur. *Notes and Tones: Musician-to-Musician Interviews.* Europe: privately printed, 1977; reprint, New York: Perigee Books, 1982.

Thompson, Dave. *Space Daze: The History and Mystery of Electronic Ambient Space Rock.* Los Angeles: Cleopatra, 1994.

Thompson, Robert Farris. *Flash of the Spirit: African and Afro-American Art and Philosophy.* New York: Random House, 1983.

_____ . *African Art in Motion.* Los Angeles: University of California Press, 1974.

Walser, Robert. *Running with the Devil: Power, Gender, and Madness in Heavy Metal Music.* Hanover, Mass.: Wesleyan University Press/University Press of New England, 1993.

Wexler, Jerry, and David Ritz. *Rhythm and Blues: A Life in American Music.* New York: Knopf, 1993.

White, Charles. *The Life and Times of Little Richard: The Queen of Rock and Roll.* New York: Harmony, 1984.

Wiener, Jon. *Come Together: John Lennon in His Time.* New York: Random House, 1984.

Wolff, Daniel, with S. R. Crain, Clifton White, and G. David Tenenbaum. *You Send Me: The Life and Times of Sam Cooke.* New York: William Morrow, 1995.

Young, James. *Nico: The End.* Woodstock, N.Y.: The Overlook Press, 1992.

Index

Country and western, 2, 17, 21, 31, 49, 73. *See also* Rockabilly
"Country Boy," 60
County, Wayne, 186
Crawford, Hank, *56*
"Crazy Country Hop," 76
"Crazy Man Crazy," 25
Cream, 121–22, *121*, 123, 229
Cropper, Steve, 90, 91, *91*, 97, 218, *219*, 220, 221
Crosby, David, 105, 109, 166
Crosby, Stills, and Nash, 171
Crudup, Arthur "Big Boy," 26
Crystals, 37, 40, 41, 42
"Cry to Me," 118
Cuban music, 53, 57–65, 69, 77, 88
Culture (group), 272
Curtis, Ian, 284
Curtis, King, 36, 38, 95
Curtom publishing, 85

D
Dade label, 241
Dale, Dick, 39, 41, 227
Damned, 274, 275
Dances:
African traditional, 53, 67–69, *70*, 72
break dancers, 281, 282
crazes, 36, 61, 69, 91–92, 241
See also specific dances
Dando, Evan, 148
Dandrel, Louis, 192
Danielou, Alain, 130, 149
Danko, Rick, 106, *106*
Danzig (group), 193, 286
Davenport, F. M., 66
Davis, Gary, 224
Davis, Jimmie, 81
Davis, Michael, *185*
Davis, Miles, 229

Daydream Nation, 290
Dead Boys, 260, 265
Dead Kennedys, 278
Dean, James, 21
"Dedicated to the One I Love," 220–21
Def Jam (production company), 283
Delmore Brothers, 17
Delta Cats, 199
DelTones, 41
Densmore, John, *183*
Detroit, 95, 182, 183–84, 185, 248–49. *See also* Motown
Diamond Dogs, 187–88
Diddley, Bo, 15, 28, 29, 30, 31, *44*, 46, 59, 62, 69, 72–76. *See also* Bo Diddley beat
Dionysus: Myth and Cult (Otto), 148, 149–50
Di Perna, Alan, 260
"Dirty Work at the Crossroads," 205
Disc jockeys:
cult of personality, 135
payola, 33, 137–39
programming by, 6, 146
rap, 56, 281, 282, 283, 284, 290
rhythm and blues, 18–21
See also specific names
Disco, 290
"Disco Inferno," 255, 256
Disraeli Gears, 123
D.I.Y. ethos (Do It Yourself), 9, 41, 264, 265, 275, 278, 289
D.M.C., *280*
DNA (group), 287
"Dock of the Bay," 96
Dodds, E. R., 148
Dodds, Johnny, 29
Do It Yourself ethos. *See* D.I.Y. ethos
Domino, Fats (Antoine), 20, *21*, 22, 23, 29, 31, 60, 65, 82, 139, 199, 232

Dominoes, 23, 216–17
Don and Dewey, 32
"Don't Let the Joneses Get You Down," 246
Doors, 179, 182, 183, *183*, 185, 186
"(Do the) Mashed Potatoes," 241, 242
Dot Records, 19
"Double Trouble," 214
Downing, Big Al, 225
"Down on the Farm," 225
"Down on the Street," 185
"Do You Love Me," 36, 87, 242
Dozier, Lamont. *See* Holland-Dozier-Holland
Dr. Dre, 291
Dream Syndicate. *See* Theater of Eternal Music
Dreja, Chris, *119*
Dr. Funkenstein. *See* Clinton, George
Drifters, 29, 35, 37, 39
Dr. John, 220
Drone (sound), 233, 285
"Dr. Robert," 110
Dr. Ross, 147
Drugs, 160–62. *See also* LSD; Marijuana
Dub (reggae idiom), 277
Dunn, Bob, 197, 198
Dunn, Donald "Duck," 90, 91, *91*, 94, 97
Durham, Eddie, *191*, 192, 196, 197
Dylan, Bob, 96, *98*, 99–108, 109, 110, 114, 117, 162–63, *163*, 171, 182

E
Eagles, 171
Earth, Wind and Fire, 89, 238, 253
East-West, 182
Ebenezer Baptist Church (Chicago), 72
Ed Sullivan Show (TV program), 101–2
Edwards, Bob, 226

307

Credits

Chapter 10

280 © Ebet Roberts

283 Dorothy Low

285 © Ann Summa/Onyx

286 top: © Michael Uhil/Ebet Roberts
    bottom: © Ezra Maurer/Ebet Roberts

287 top: © Jay Blakesberg/Retna
    bottom: © Ebet Roberts

288 © Jeff Mayer/STAR FILE

290 © Aaron Rapoport/Onyx

293 Walter DeVenne

299 Archive Photos

325 © Real London, photo by Neil Menneer

• Our thanks to all those who helped with timeline memorabilia, including Colin Escott, Skippy White's, Stereo Jack's, Newbury Comics, Nostalgia Factory, Cheapo Records, Wex Rex, Tower Records, Picture Paradise, Walter DeVenne, the Rock & Roll Hall of Fame, Susan Washington, Karen Johnson, Hilary Finkel, Kelly Tyler, Tom Strong, Jennifer Parrish, Jenna Novic, and Susan Teta.

• Grateful acknowledgment is made to the following for permission to reprint copyrighted material: From "Do You Love Me," by Berry Gordy, Jobete Music Co., Inc., © 1962 • From "The Tears of a Clown," by Stevie Wonder/William Robinson Jr./Henry Cosby, Jobete Music Co., Inc./Black Bull Music, © 1967 • From "Say Man," by Ellas McDaniel, © 1959 (Renewed), Arc Music Corporation. All rights reserved. Used by permission • From "Let's Do the Slop," by Joe Cook, © 1957, Renewed 1985, EMI BLACKWOOD MUSIC INC. (BMI). All rights reserved. Used by permission • From "Tutti Frutti," by Richard Penniman and Dorothy La Bostrie, © 1955, 1956, Renewed 1983, 1984 VENICE MUSIC, INC., license from ATV MUSIC (VENICE). All rights reserved. Used by permission • From "Purple Haze," by Jimi Hendrix, © 1967 Bella Godiva Music, Inc. All rights reserved. Used by permission • From "The Slummer the Slum," by Lowman Pauling and Obediah Carter, ©1958, Fort Knox Music, Inc., and Trio Music Co., Inc. All rights reserved. Used by permission • From *I Hear You Knockin'* by Jeff Hannusch, Swallow Publications, Inc., 1985. Used by permission • From "Cold Sweat," by James Brown and Alfred Ellis, © 1967 Dynatone Publishing. All rights administered by Unichappell Music, Inc. All rights reserved. Used by permission, WARNER BROS. PUBLICATIONS, INC., Miami, FL 33014 • From "God Save the Queen," by Glen Matlock, John Lydon, Paul Cook, and Steve Jones, © 1977 Glitterbest Ltd. and WB Music Inc. All rights administered by CAREERS–BMG MUSIC PUBLISHING, INC. (BMI). All rights reserved. Used by permission, WARNER BROS. PUBLICATIONS, INC., Miami, FL 33014.

Thanks also to Allen Ginsberg for permission to print from his interview, © Allen Ginsberg.

About the Author

ROBERT PALMER was the *New York Times*'s first full-time rock writer and chief pop critic (1976–88) and has been a contributing editor at *Rolling Stone* since the early seventies. He has taught courses in American music at Yale, Carnegie-Mellon, Bowdoin, the University of Mississippi, and Brooklyn College, where he was the first Senior Research Fellow of the Institute for Studies in American Music to teach and write a musicological monograph on rock and roll. He is the author of *Deep Blues* and other books and served as writer and music director for two award-winning documentary films, *The World According to John Coltrane* and *Deep Blues*. Since producing the latter film's sound track CD for Atlantic Records, he has produced a number of raw juke joint blues CD's for the Fat Possum label, winning a number of polls and awards. He is the chief advisor for the ten-part WGBH/BBC series.

The text of this book is set in Minion, a contemporary digital type family created by designer Robert Slimbach. It is inspired by classic old style typefaces of the late Renaissance. Named after one of the type sizes used in the early days of typefounding, Minion means "a beloved servant," which reflects the type's useful and unobtrusive qualities.

Display type is set in Franklin Gothic Heavy, designed by Morris F. Benton in 1903.

Design by Gaye Korbet, Elles Gianocostas, and Polly Lockman of WGBH Design.